Hungary

Hungary

The Rise and Fall of Feasible Socialism

NIGEL SWAIN

VERSO

London · New York

First published by Verso 1992
© Nigel Swain 1992
All rights reserved

Verso
UK: 6 Meard Street, London W1V 3HR
USA: 29 West 35th Street, New York, NY 10001-2291

Verso is the imprint of New Left Books

ISBN 0-86091-357-0
ISBN 0-86091-569-7 (pbk)

British Library Cataloguing in Publication Data
A catalogue record for this book is available from the British Library

Library of Congress Cataloging-in-Publication Data
A catalogue record for this book is available from the Library of Congress

Typeset by Leaper & Gard Ltd, Bristol
Printed in Great Britain by Biddles Ltd, Guildford

This book is dedicated to the memory of
JANE KENRICK (1944–1988),
who offered unfailing encouragement in the
early stages of the project.

Contents

Introduction

This book started out as something rather different. Its original intention was to attempt to convince those in the West who were attracted by or interested in socialism that there was something to be learned from Hungarian market socialism. It was not intended as an apologia for Hungary, but it took the view that successive economic reforms in that country, especially since the New Economic Mechanism of 1968, represented a serious attempt to create market socialism, with which the West should be better acquainted. The Western debate on market socialism which was stimulated by the publication of Alec Nove's *The Economics of a Feasible Socialism* required, in this author's opinion, the complement of a concrete case history – Hungary.

With this in mind, the book was to have suggested, first, that Hungary's economic experience was not as alien to that of Western Europe as it might seem; and, second, more problematically for many on the radical left, that there was much, in the economic sphere particularly, that was socialist about the policies introduced by the regime that came to power in Hungary in 1945. To this end, it constructed the notion of a 'socialist project' and sought to indicate how, whatever the nature of the social formation that was finally created in Eastern Europe, the economic aims and intentions of those involved in the political events that created it were similar to those of socialists today. This done, the book's intention was to have been to explain both theoretically, and with historical example, how the model of central planning adopted by those pursuing Hungary's 'socialist project' did not, and could not, work. On the other hand, the book was to have argued, Hungary's application of market socialism over some twenty years demonstrated that, while market socialism was not problem-free, it was an incomparably superior model to that of the centrally planned

1

command economy, all the more so when associated, as Hungary's had been since the late 1970s, with an encouragement of petty commodity production in all sectors of the economy. Socialists in both East and West, the argument was to have run, would benefit from engaging directly and concretely in the continuing Hungarian debates over how to resolve the problems present in this market socialist model.

These two fundamental ambitions (insisting that Hungary embarked on a 'socialist project' in 1945, and demonstrating market socialism's superiority over the command economy) remain. But a third intention has been forced on the author by the events of 1989: documenting why Hungary's '1968 paradigm' of market socialism must be seen as ultimately flawed. The New Economic Mechanism certainly preserved Hungary from the economic collapse that Poland has suffered; but it failed to provide an environment in which enterprises could produce goods of the quality and technological sophistication required by world markets; and by failing to export successfully, Hungary failed to generate sufficient funds to keep socialist-inspired welfare systems in effective operation. Even the creators of market socialism in Hungary came to believe that their earlier views had been 'naive'. History has turned its back on an attractive and plausible real-world option. The choice for those on the left in politics now lies between a world-scale centrally planned utopia, and a competitive market economy with mixed forms of ownership, which is susceptible to control by social democratic or social market regulation. On the left, there is no 'third way' of market socialism. And since a world-scale centrally planned economy, if it worked at all, would be technologically stagnant, for reasons to be discussed in Chapter 3, and could not be democratic, socialists are obliged to work within the social democratic perspective.

Readers will have heard such arguments before from the right, and it is depressing to have to present them from the left. For those who remain unconvinced, the book will at least present an informed account of why it was that socialists and radicals in Hungary – the dissidents that sections of the Western left supported over many years – came to believe so wholeheartedly that socialism had failed. And an understanding of this process is of no minor historical interest. It was, after all, the Hungarian decision to let East Germans emigrate via Austria in the late summer of 1989 that triggered the fall of the Honecker regime, and initiated the collapse of all other Eastern European regimes with the exception of Poland.

The book's first chapter presents the decline of the old regime: the growing consensus that property reform was inevitable, and the collapse of the political structure when the leadership was changed and civil society gave the Party the very gentlest of pushes. Chapters 2 and 3 seek to establish the extent to which the policies Hungary pursued in the 1940s and 1950s corresponded to the requirements of a 'socialist project' as understood in the West. Chapter 2 focuses on the establishment of the socialist economy, Chapter 3 on central planning and Marxist economics. Chapters 4 and 5 shift the focus to problems with the socialist economic model: attempts to readjust the balance after 1956, final recognition that something more radical was required by the mid 1960s, and the recurring weaknesses of market socialism in the 1970s and 1980s. Chapters 6 and 7 consider people and relationships rather than economic abstractions, addressing respectively the problems associated with workplace democracy and the labour market on the production side of the economy, and successes and failures in stimulating greater social equality and an adequate system of public welfare in the fields of distribution and consumption in the context of the economy's three defining characteristics: bureaucratic control, shortage, and 'second economy'. The inability of the economy to support a framework of socialist institutions in relation to production and social consumption was a crucial factor in the decline of social morale which precipitated Hungary's peaceful revolution.

The most widely published chronicler of Hungary's economic decline and its underlying causes in 'plan bargaining', 'regulation bargaining' and 'soft budget constraints' is János Kornai. While his earlier works on the operation of centrally planned economies are universally admired, his concept of 'soft budget constraints' has been accused of lacking rigour, and his recent unabashed acceptance of radical laissez faire economics for the transition to capitalism[1] has been viewed with dismay. Whilst agreeing up to a point with this assessment of Kornai's earlier works, and distancing itself very clearly from his prescriptions for post-socialist economic policy, this book nevertheless constitutes a defence of the notion of 'soft budget constraints' – but it interprets the concept in a much broader sense than that in which it is usually understood.

In the final chapter of his book on the economics of shortage,[2] Kornai considers very briefly social relations and state paternalism towards enterprises. It is the purpose of Chapters 6 and 7 of this book to push further than Kornai had the space or the inclination to do this aspect of 'soft budget constraints'. The 'soft budget constraint' is much more than an economic abstraction. It is a social relationship, and one that determines control over the means of production. It is not (or rather not only) a propensity for the government to have weak credit or monetary policies. It is rather managers of large state enterprises and collective farms consistently exporting second-rate produce to the Soviet market because this is the easiest way of being successful, of keeping their jobs and retaining the material rewards that accompany them. It is managers permanently lobbying the political decision-makers via their friends in the industrial ministries in order to maintain their situation of privilege. It is managers, immune from significant criticism 'from above', and protected by the political system from independent trade unions or functioning workplace democracy 'from below', pursuing their self-interest in second-rate sales to the Soviet market rather than taking on technologically more demanding Western markets. It is state revenues usurped by managers in the form of subsidies for their enterprises being denied to the health, welfare or educational systems. 'Soft budget constraints' lacks rigour as a purely economic concept, but it refers to a real and powerful social relationship around the control of the means of production, an intrinsic concomitant of bureaucratic control.

One of the most original contributors to the analysis of the mechanisms of social inequality in a non-market ('soft budget constrained') context is Iván Szelényi who, working together with György Konrád, has produced, over the past two decades and more, a succession of stimulating theoretical concepts. On the basis of sociological work on housing inequalities written at the end of the 1960s,[3] they first developed the notion of 'centralized redistribution',[4] a concept which neatly pinpoints certain characteristics of social inequalities under socialism, and which will be used extensively, although not uncritically, in Chapter 7 to structure the discussion of socialist inequalities in the sphere of distribution.

The next stage in the Konrád/Szelényi intellectual biography is insightful, but more fanciful. 'Centralized redistribution' becomes 'rational redistribution', and those with the necessary 'transcontextual' knowledge to perform 'rational redistribution' (the intellectuals) become the new class *in statu nascendi* of 'actually existing socialism' – on the road to class power. Socialist society is seen as being divided into (increasingly rational) redistributors and a working class which does not participate in redistribution.[5] That is to say, the discovery that, under the process of centralized redistribution, the intellectuals benefit disproportionately in the distribution of the socially produced surplus product, is developed into a claim that, by virtue of a common commitment to the rational ordering of things, in the particular context of actually existing socialism, intellectuals share a similar class position with regard to redistribution of the social surplus product. All subsections of the intelligentsia – the cadres, the technocrats and the critical intelligentsia – act, it is claimed, as teleological redistributors maximizing the share of the national income available for redistribution in the interests of a conception of the needs of society as a whole.[6] This theoretical development is less convincing. It is not clear that intellectuals share

4

similar material interests, nor is it made explicit how they act in concert to realize them. As Kornai demonstrated as early as 1956, enterprise managers (a subset of the intellectuals) act rationally in pursuance of their own, private, short-term interest in meeting those economic targets which affect their bonus payments, and these have nothing to do with the macro-economic good, nor the share of national income redistributed.[7]

Although the view of intellectuals as a unified class is questionable, and the mechanisms by which class power is exercised remain obscure, Konrád and Szelényi's analysis of the intellectuals posits an interesting process whereby the purely technocratic intelligentsia ally with the ideological dissident intellectuals to take on and defeat the equally ideological cadre intelligentsia, so creating a unified, fully rationalized political bureaucracy – the final victory of the socialist intelligentsia.[8] What happened in Hungary between 1988 and 1990 was more complex than this. In order to overcome the political bureaucracy (the cadre intelligentsia), the economic bureaucracy too had to be broken and deprived of its rationality, being replaced by private, competing, no longer nationally coordinated and, in this sense, no longer rational ownership. Capitalism was restored; no unified intelligentsia took power; and society ceased to be socialist. Nevertheless, the processes that Konrád and Szelényi identify (the increasing unity of interest of technical and opposition intellectuals, and the demise of the cadre intelligentsia) were crucial factors in the decline of the old regime, in pushing social crisis to legitimation crisis, and finally to political crisis – as Chapter 1 will make clear.

1

The Collapse of the Socialist Economy

Consensus on Property Reform

It is difficult to isolate a single date in the history of Hungary's socialist experiment that might be taken to symbolize the collapse of the Party (in Hungary's case the Hungarian Socialist Workers' Party) and the country's return to capitalism. Political reform was more or less continuous from 1988 onwards, although a Rubicon of sorts was crossed somewhere between the spring and early summer of 1989. In the Hungarian case the transition to a Western-style multi-party democracy and the restoration of capitalist relations of production was not the consequence of a sudden political crisis. It was the end result of a decade-long economic crisis, of gradual acceptance by politicians and economists alike that production relations simply could not go on in the old way, and that market reform should be extended to property reform if efficiency were to increase to the point where exports were technologically acceptable to world markets and the productive sector generated sufficient wealth to fund adequate health and social welfare systems. Why, after Hungary's forty-year experiment with a socialist economy, this view had become such common currency, held by people who in the West would be considered radical or alternative as much as by the nascent petty entrepreneur, is the subject of the bulk of this book. For the purposes of this chapter it is necessary to indicate that public opinion had indeed abandoned socialism, and how, in the absence of any commitment to the economic cornerstones of the old regime, its political structures melted away with scarcely a need to be pushed.

In December 1988, a consultative committee established by the government to consider further economic reform published its pre-liminary report. Its contents revealed much in common with the economic reform proposals then being put forward by the recently established Alliance of Free Democrats, as well as those advanced later by the Hungarian Democratic Forum; and these proposals all shared much in common with the proposals of concerned radical economists published in 1987 in a document entitled *Turnabout and Reform* (see below). And these again resembled many of the suggestions put forward during the 'holding company' reform discussions of the early 1980s (considered more fully in Chapter 5). In one sense, this is hardly surprising. Many of the people involved in the early 1980s discussion were also involved in *Turnabout and Reform*; and a cursory glance at the latter's list of contributors reveals an authorship consisting of an old guard of economists fairly evenly divided between the reformist wing of the Hungarian Socialist Workers' Party and the future Alliance of Free Democrats, and a younger guard who eventually found a home in the Hungarian Democratic Forum.

But there was more to this than the fact that the same economists were advising all shades of political opinion. The need for property reform within the Hungarian economy as a mechanism for extending market relations from simple reproduction into expanded reproduction, for encouraging flexibility and dynamism in the institutional structure of the economic system, was an idea whose time had come. As the 1980 reformers propounded the need for property reform, the older guard of the '1968 paradigm' market socialists (discussed more fully in Chapter 5) admitted the 'naivety' of their earlier positions.[1]

The case for property reform is inextricably linked with the problem of imposing 'hard budget constraints' on public sector enterprises (which will be a recurrent theme in Chapter 5). 'Soft budget constraints' can, in a sense, be seen as inherently socialist, and a good thing in areas which impinge on social policy. But when they are an all-pervasive character-istic of an economic system their result is two-fold. In terms of the present, they result in a waste of resources that could be used for additional economic and, more tellingly, social expenditure elsewhere. In relation to the future, they reduce both incentives to innovate and the ability to invest quickly enough (as Bauer's characterization of invest-ment cycles presented in Chapter 5 will suggest) to keep up with world technological development; this means that exports do not meet world standards, so initiating a cycle of increasing debt.

Hungary's reform economists from the early and mid 1980s addressed two issues: how to impose 'hard budget constraints' on Hungary's large enterprises, and how to wrest control from enterprise management and introduce effective social control over its activities.[2] Their solution was to reinvent property and, more important, a market in property. The former would introduce greater identification; the latter increased anonymity. That is to say, property in itself would enhance commitment and incentives generally, on the grounds that people have a greater interest in assets that they own than in those they merely administer for a third party, the state. A property market, on the other hand, would allow the development of two things: 'external ownership', and the creation of the necessary conditions for ending monopolies. The ownership of shares in enterprises by 'external' parties was seen as a means of wresting ultimate control of the enterprise from all individuals directly involved in its operation, especially from enterprise management with its close ties to the economic administration. Ownership would thus become sufficiently anonymous to impose the necessary 'hard budget constraints' on enterprises. 'External owners', it was argued, would be interested primarily in maximizing their own long- or short-term benefit, not in the fate of any particular enterprise in which they happened to have shares. The existence of a market in enterprise shares would further facilitate the creation of new companies prepared to compete in any sector where profitable production was likely and so reduce the incidence of monopoly.

In the 1980s discussions, three scenarios evolved for creating these new ownership relations. The first envisaged 'cross ownership', by which state enterprises would be obliged to become public limited companies and buy shares in each other, while banks would be encouraged to extend their holdings in non-banking sectors. The second 'self-management' scenario envisaged extending the Enterprise Council developments of 1985 (see Chapter 5) by giving workers shares in their own enterprises. And the third was a scenario in which all bodies formerly funded from the state budget, such as local authorities, educational institutions, hospitals, and cultural institutions, would become self-governing. Rather than receive a cash grant from the government, the necessary credit mechanisms would be created for them to establish a foundation from which they would maintain a portfolio of shares. These self-governing holders of community property would then enter the market, via a newly developed network of broking institutions, and become significant 'external' shareholders in the nation's assets.

By the late 1980s, most of the major political actors had rejected an exclusively 'self-management' solution, partly because it was seen to have failed in 1985. Initial analysis of the Enterprise Council democracy revealed it to exist in form but not content. But it was also rejected because, following the standard arguments against self-managed economic units, they were seen as inherently conservative and therefore not to be encouraged as the predominant form of production unit in the economy. The 'cross ownership' scenario has also been accused of being potentially conservative in that the market would not be sufficiently diverse to encourage the flow of foreign capital into new, rather than joint, ventures. More fundamental is the question of just how 'external' such 'cross ownership' shareholders could be. Under such a scenario, a situation could easily develop in which 'the management elite 'would be the final owners'.

By mid 1988 the new guard leadership of the Hungarian Socialist Workers' Party gave in to two decades of pressure and took steps which both initiated property reform and in a fundamental sense reintroduced capitalist relations. For Hungarian citizens, 1988 is best remembered for the introduction of the radical, and very unpopular, tax reform which imposed two new taxes on individuals (the Personal Income Tax and the General Turnover Tax, or Value Added Tax) and a new Entrepreneurs' Profits Tax. Tax reform further extended to socialist sector enterprises, where many special purpose taxes such as the wages tax, the accumulation tax and the tax on assets were all abolished and replaced by a single flat rate profits tax at a rate of 50 per cent. At the national level, however, the most significant developments were the liberalization plan, accepted by the Central Committee in July 1988, which resulted in a 32–35 billion forint reduction in subsidies, the ending of controls on 67–68 per cent of consumer prices and 35–40 per cent of convertible currency imports, together with the passing of the company and investment laws at the end of the year for implementation in 1989. Other measures introduced in 1988 continued the 'semi-monetarized' reforms to be discussed in Chapter 5: in March 1988 the government introduced Treasury Bills as a mechanism for funding government debt and regulating the money supply, and, in September, banks and financial institutions were permitted to issue Bills of Deposit as a means of saving.

The change that the company and foreign investment laws brought about was fundamental, although they might have been applied with less enthusiasm if political events in 1989 had not taken the course they did. The company law, in a fundamental sense, can be seen as having reintroduced capitalist – certainly embryonic capitalist – relations into Hungary in two ways. First, it conceded the principle that natural and legal persons could own, buy and sell shares in the means of production, distribution and exchange. Second, less abstractly, it was the legislation that was actually used throughout 1989 and 1990 for both piecemeal, spontaneous and state-initiated privatization. If the company law permitted the development of domestic capitalism, the law on foreign investments permitted foreign capitalists to repatriate their profits, and do so on very generous terms. Section 1 of the law guaranteed full and immediate compensation in the currency of the investment if a foreign investor's company should be nationalized. Section 32 guaranteed the free transfer of that proportion of the profit due to the foreign investor

10

(determined in the initial joint venture agreement) in the currency of the original investment. Sections 15 to 17 dealt with a range of tax incentives foreign investors could enjoy, beginning with a 20 per cent tax reduction for investments of as little as five million forints (approximately £55,000 in 1990), and ending with a five-year complete tax holiday for ventures valued at over twenty-five million forints where the foreign investment was 30 per cent of the total and the project was in an area considered by the government to be particularly important to the economy. In addition, top foreign managers were permitted to repatriate 50 per cent of their post-tax income.[3]

If by the end of 1988 the governing party had accepted the principle of property reform, the programmes of all the major political actors by the end of the 1980s included calls for all three of the types of property reform discussed above in differing degrees, together with the encouragement of direct foreign investment. The purchase of shares by self-governing bodies scenario declined in importance somewhat in the Free Democrats' propaganda during the first year of its operation, and was taken over by the Democratic Forum, who also placed a propaganda emphasis on employee share-ownership schemes. What all sides, with the exception of the old regime government, opposed was the piecemeal version of the 'cross ownership' scenario which occurred in 1989 and 1990 after the passing of the Company Act. Objections to this piecemeal 'spontaneous privatization' were based on the fact that the state received nothing for the sale of its assets, and there was no adequate supervision of the process. Enterprise management itself determined who was to be the new owner, without reference to the state, shareholders (because there were none) or the workforce. Questions were raised in the press and in parliament about numerous privatizations of this ilk, such as that of the stationery shop chain ÁPISZ, the Ajka Glass Factory, the Hungar Hotels chain, the sale of many regional newspapers to the German Springer group, and the sale of the building housing the famous Gerbeaud coffee house to a West German property company. In fact, many of the more forward-looking state enterprises such as Videoton (the television and computer manufacturer) anticipated the new Company Act and, making use of 1875 legislation, restructured themselves as wholly state-owned holding companies, with numerous subsidiaries which took the form of limited liability companies and in which the holding company held the majority (often the vast majority) of the shares.

The economic history of the second half of the 1980s suggested that a nominally self-managed economy of near monopoly producers in the context of the 'semi-monetarized' controls of the Hungarian economy of the 1980s offered no solution to the problems which Chapter 5 will christen the '1968 paradigm'. By the end of the decade, all shades of economic opinion in Hungary had come to believe in the need for property reform and had actually implemented it. But economic discourse did not take place in a vacuum. The reason why enterprise managers, economic administrators and the political apparatus finally accepted the arguments that had been presented to them for the previous decade and more was partly the size of the foreign debt (see Chapter 5), but, more significantly, it was the populace's loss of faith in the system and the Party's loss of faith in its own legitimacy to rule.

Crisis of Legitimacy

By the end of 1988, the notion that one of the central pillars of socialist economies – state property – would have to be removed had come to be accepted by large sections of intellectual opinion. The period from 1985 onwards also witnessed several signs that the legitimacy of the regime was coming increasingly into question. As Chapters 5 to 7 will demonstrate, from the mid 1970s, and more clearly from the early 1980s, the twin characteristics of Hungary's economic situation were stagnation in the socialist sector and an increasingly encouraged 'institutionalized dualism' between the 'first' and 'second' economies to counter the first economy's worst effects. The consequences of this were two-fold: a decline in social morale, and the gradual birth of extensive if not mass opposition. After more than a decade of the government obliging Hungarians to lead a double life, forcing them to take on a second job simply to survive, and tacitly encouraging them, via the institution of Enterprise Economic Work Partnerships (see Chapters 5 and 6), to adopt one set of values when working for themselves in a partnership, and another, much more instrumentalist set when working for the state, it is not surprising that observers began to notice a decline in both altruism and a sense of social solidarity.

From the late 1970s to the late 1980s, Elemér Hankiss produced a series of articles documenting, in an ever more precise fashion, the social pathology of Hungary's failure to create new community values. Having successfully destroyed all institutions of the old world's 'civil society', Hungary's socialism failed to create new ones, a telling failure in a society dominated by shortage, where petty corruption became inevitable.[4] Hankiss's vast output, which moves from noting an imbalance between economic growth and the value system to discovering a 'second society' to mirror the 'second economy', is based on rather little empirical evidence. Its significance is two-fold, however. First, he provides some concrete evidence for a decline in social morale over the socialist period. This is reflected in the results of an international survey on social values to which he refers on a number of occasions. This survey shows, for example, that:

> To the question ... 'Is there anything you could sacrifice yourself for, outside your family?' 50 to 60 percent of the Englishmen, Frenchmen, Germans, Spaniards and Italians answered: 'No, I would not sacrifice myself for anything outside my family.' In Hungary, the corresponding figure is 85 percent. To the question 'Would you raise your children to have respect for other people?' the European average of 'Yes' answers was between 40 and 60 percent, while the Hungarian figure was 31 percent.[5]

The second significance of Hankiss's work is simply the popularity it achieved. His models of first and second society work in skeletal, over-simplistic dichotomies: first society is homogeneous, diffuse, atomized, second society is differentiated and integrated; first society is organized vertically, second society is organized horizontally; first society is dominated by politics, second society by social and economic concerns; first society is strongly ideological, second society is non-ideological or allows many ideologies. His statement that 'the evolution of the second society was the most significant movement of the 1960s and 1970s in Hungary'[6] hardly takes our understanding of the period beyond the standard account of Kádárism, namely that it was characterized by a 'social compact' between economic opportunity and political obedience, and by the slogan 'he who is not against us is with us'. The popularity of Hankiss's work has to be explained rather by the idea of 'second society' itself, by the fact that in their daily lives people were experiencing the schizophrenia of the institutionalized dualism of first and second economy. The idea of 'second society' struck a chord with everyday social experience.

Public opinion poll findings over the period also reveal a dramatic decline in the population's faith in the government's ability to solve the economy's problems and achieve socialist targets. An analysis of the responses to public opinion surveys carried out by the Hungarian Public Opinion Research Institute over the ten years or so preceding 1988 found a significant change in attitude in 1982 and again in 1986. In 1982, unspecified 'dissatisfaction' became focused on the economy and day-to-day economic problems. In 1986, the public seemed to lose faith in the leadership's ability, and felt not only that they were worse off than before, but also that the economy in general was in decline. The Institute constructed two indices, one reflecting evaluations of the national economic situation, and the other evaluations of individuals' personal economic situation, both indices ranging from +100 to −100. In 1982,

the personal index fell from −38.0 to −63.0, and the national index from
+26.25 to +3.0. Both then recovered marginally until 1986, when a
very marked decline took place. The personal index fell from −57.5 at
the beginning of 1986 to −74.66 at the end of 1987. The fall in the
national index was even more marked, from +17.0 in early 1986 to −
39.75 at the end of 1987.[7]

This decline in the population's faith in the ability of the government
to solve the economic crisis is mirrored by a general feeling that the
government is failing to meet what might be considered socialist
objectives. Table 1.1. shows responses to the question 'In what ways is
Hungary better than the West?' and reveals a catastrophic decline in
belief in the regime's ability to provide the basic welfare measures that
had previously constituted the superiority of Eastern European countries for commentators from East and West alike. Belief that Hungary's
education system was better at providing a satisfactory education for its
children fell from 98 per cent in 1981 to 87 per cent in 1986, and then
plummeted to 46 per cent on a national basis, and only 27 per cent
amongst intellectuals, in 1988. Belief in Hungary's superiority in
providing material well-being fell equally dramatically, from 46 per cent
to 29 per cent to 10 per cent, with only 1 per cent of intellectuals by
1988 believing that material well-being was better in Hungary than in
the West.

This loss of faith in the regime's ability to guarantee basic socialist
values was complemented, in 1988, by a high degree of cynicism (or

Table 1.1 What is better in Hungary when compared with the West?
(% of respondents)

	1981	1986	1988	1988 Party	1988 Intelligentsia
Possibility of bringing children up satisfactorily	98	87	42	46	27
Right to work	96	93	80	88	80
Level of health supply	90	66	47	45	23
Level of social morality	88	81	50	59	38
Balanced family life	86	73	36	40	24
Material welfare	46	29	10	9	1
Equal opportunities	78	69	38	49	29
Freedom to express views	74	67	43	50	29
Money keeps its value	66	41	6	6	2
Chances of getting a flat	63	39	16	19	5
Amount of free time	58	46	27	26	17

Source: G.L. Nagy, 'A kettészakadt társadalom', *Jelkép*, vol. X, no. 4 (1989), p. 55.

realism) concerning the motives of the Party. As Table 1.2 indicates, even Party members believed that the Party represented the interests of its own upper leadership, its apparatchiks, or enterprise management before that of the workers.

Nevertheless, there remained a high national commitment to welfare principles, reflected partly in the fact that all Hungary's new political parties consider the state should have a role in guaranteeing minimum standards in health care, even if all also call for the development of private, insurance-based schemes. The high welfare expectations of the population can be seen in the results of an international survey on attitudes to inequality and welfare.[8] Public support for welfare was highest in Hungary in a survey which also covered Italy, West Germany, Britain and the Netherlands in Europe, together with Australia and the USA. Some 78 per cent of Hungarians strongly agreed that the state should provide everyone with a guaranteed basic income, compared with 67 per cent in Italy, 51 per cent in West Germany and 20 per cent in the USA.[9]

This national commitment should be tempered by findings presented in Table 1.3, however, which indicate social difference in this commitment. In 1988, the population as a whole was more concerned with jobs for all and ending poverty than were Party members or intellectuals; while the latter two strata considered democracy considerably more important than did the population as a whole. For all, free medical provision was a universally low priority, although it was considerably lower for intellectuals than the populations as a whole.

On balance, public opinion polls reveal a commitment to socialist

Table 1.2 Whose interests does the party represent? (ranking of answers)

	Population as a whole	Party members	Intellectuals
Top party leadership	1	1	1
Workers in party apparatus	2	2	2
Enterprise managers	3	3	3
Party members	4	5	4
Intellectuals	5	6	7
Workers	6	4	5
The young	7	8	8
Peasants	8	7	6
The old	9	10–11	11
Small entrepreneurs	10–11	10–11	9
Non-party members	10–11	9	10

Source: Nagy, p. 56.

Table 1.3 What would your ideal society be like? (ranking of responses)

	Population as a whole	Party members	Intellectuals
Incomes reflecting performance	1	1	1
Human rights	2	5	3
Jobs for all	3	10	12
Ending poverty	4–5	11	10
Constant economic growth	4–5	4	4–5
Social justice	6–7	3	4–5
No inflation	6–7	6	7
Democracy	8	2	2
Free medical system	10	12	15
Religious freedom	13	14	13

Note: not all rankings listed.

Source: Nagy, p. 61.

values of public welfare, but a growing belief that Hungary's socialist economy was failing to produce the wealth necessary to support it.

The Emerging Political Crisis

This decline in the legitimacy of the regime was accompanied by growing political activity. The first political event of significance in the history of the downfall of Hungary's socialist project was the two-and-a-half-day political gathering held at Monor in June 1985. Organized by Ferenc Donáth, a veteran of 1956 and active communist organizer during the war, this meeting was significant not simply because it took place at all, but because it was the first attempt to bridge the divide between 'urbanized' (democratic opposition) and 'populist' (critical creative writer) opposition groups. The next issue of significance was the *Turnabout and Reform* affair which dominated most of 1986 and early 1987. By April 1986, the pro-reform economists László Antal, László Lengyel and Márton Tardos decided that the economic crisis was becoming so grave that they should put together some sort of document spelling out their case for renewed economic reform. They were supported in this endeavour by key Party figures, namely Imre Pozsgay, head of the Patriotic People's Front, and Rezső Nyers, father of the 1968 New Economic Mechanism. In the autumn of 1986 the document they produced, entitled *Turnabout and Reform*, was debated by various academic bodies; and at the end of October it was handed over to the Patriotic People's Front, who in turn passed it on to the Central

Committee. But here an impasse was reached. In the Central Committee's view, it was the Party's job to draw up programmes for the country, not the Patriotic People's Front's; and the document was ignored.

However, the rapid deterioration of the economic situation and the mushrooming debt did not go unnoticed by the Party, and in November 1986 it issued a decree calling for an end to the negative trends of 1985–86. In early 1987, as the authors of *Turnabout and Reform* were considering presenting a version of the document to a debate of the Social Policy Committee of the Patriotic People's Front in May 1987, they were suddenly called upon to have a version ready by the end of March for discussion by a group working alongside the Central Committee. This group debated the document on 13 April 1987, and a version of this variant was published in *Economic Review* in June and July;[10] in July 1987, the Central Committee issued a statement calling for a stabilization plan to reimpose control over the economy. A political footnote to the saga concerns the fate of the Finance Research Institute of the Ministry of Finance, where many of the economists involved in the document worked. The institute was closed 'for reasons of economy'. Undaunted, the institute's economists capitalized on measures introduced in 1986 to encourage market entry (discussed in Chapter 5) to form a new, independent Finance Research plc.

The remainder of 1987 saw the publication of another significant document, and another, more significant political gathering, at which Pozsgay's influence was discernible once more. The document was the special June issue of the samizdat *Beszélő* entitled 'The Social Contract'. It analysed the current situation, asserted that a crisis could not be avoided and called for political pluralism, an autonomous parliament and freedom for the press. Although it came out in favour of a multi-party system in principle, it did not think it was appropriate in the current situation. The gathering took place on 27 September, at the house of Sándor Lezsák in the village of Lakitelek, and marked the foundation of the Hungarian Democratic Forum as a movement. Some 160 people attended to hear speeches calling for political and social reform by Pozsgay, representatives of the populist opposition such as Gyula Fekete and István Csurka, and Mihály Bihari, author of a much-discussed book on democracy and reform.[11] The statement produced at the gathering was not made public until Pozsgay, to the horror of the Party faithful, included most of its contents in an interview with *Magyar Nemzet* in November.

In December 1987, the decision was taken to hold a special Party Conference between 20 and 22 May 1988. During the ensuing six months, the Kádár wing of the Party appeared to be incapable of appreciating the significance of the new social mood. It lashed out unthinkingly to suppress dissent, while reform-minded individuals went ahead and created alternative institutions and mobilized opposition support. In December, Kádár made the first of a series of speeches and television appearances denying the existence of a crisis; meanwhile Nyers and others inside and outside the Party began talking about forming the New March Front, an umbrella group for unifying the nation. More significantly, on 30 January 1988 the Democratic Forum held the first of a series of public meetings at Jurta Theatre on the subject of the role of parliament. An estimated five hundred people attended, although Hungarian Socialist Workers' Party members were instructed not to attend on threat of expulsion. Similar meetings followed in March and May.

On 17 March, Kádár addressed the country on television stating again 'there is no question of any sort of crisis ... everyone has to do their work as before, only better and more diligently'. Yet on the same day, the Network of Free Initiatives came into being. This umbrella group, initiated by the Democratic Opposition, had hoped to cover all opposition groups, but the central core of the Democratic Forum rejected the idea. Most, although not all, under the umbrella transformed themselves into the Alliance of Free Democrats some months later. Meanwhile, in a final desperate move to restore Party discipline, which only strengthened the reformers' hands, on 9 April the Party expelled four prominent reformers: Mihály Bihari, political scientist and active in the New March Front, Zoltán Bíró, literary historian and a founder member of the Democratic Forum, Zoltán Király, member of parliament, journalist and active in the New March Front, and László Lengyel, economist, active in the New March Front, and one of the organizers of *Turnabout and Reform.*

By the time of the special Party Conference of May 1988, ten years of stagnating living standards (see Chapter 5) combined with the inability of social policy to meet socialist expectations in the workplace (see Chapter 6) or in relation to social equality and social policy (see Chapter 7) resulted not only in a decline of social morale but also in the beginnings of a political legitimation crisis.

The HSWP: In Power, in Crisis, and not in Control[12]

The sudden acceleration of political change following the removal of Kádár, and his appointment to the new, and entirely honorary, role of Party president, can only be understood in the context of the change of guard in the political leadership that took place at the same time. The

May 1988 Party Conference and the Central Committee session that followed it was 'the most radical and most peaceful change of guard in a communist party leadership that has ever happened under normal conditions'.[13] Thirty-seven new members joined the 108-member Central Committee. Two-thirds of these had been members only since 1985, and only thirteen had been in the Committee since 1966. In short, not only Kádár, but the whole of the narrowly defined Kádár group fell from power. The new leadership was no longer of the generation whose vision of a socialist project had built Hungary's socialism; it was a generation for whom an imperfect socialism and institutionalized dualism were increasingly a fact of life.

After the Party Conference of May 1988 the Hungarian Socialist Workers' Party (HSWP) remained the party in power, in that it was the governing party with a clear majority of parliamentary seats. However, as summer turned to winter, and winter to spring, it became clear that Party discipline was wearing exceedingly thin. The reformist wing became more vocal in its demands for change. At the same time, the Party leadership was obliged to accommodate itself to an unfamiliar form of politics in which, although it held the trump cards, the political agenda was increasingly being set by political forces and political organizations outside its control.

The period from May 1988 to the elections fell into neat seasonal sections. The summer of 1988 was characterized by uncertainty. Despite the extent of the change of guard within the HSWP leadership, it was not immediately apparent that May's Party Conference was more than a palace revolution. The signs were ambiguous. On the pro-reform side, the Party adopted in July the more radical of two proposed economic programmes, and both Pozsgay and Grósz made speeches suggesting that a multi-party system was not inconceivable. On the anti-reform side, in June a demonstration commemorating Nagy's death was broken up. Meanwhile, the opposition continued the tactic of large public gatherings. Between 25 and 31 August one such was held at the Balatonszemes Express camp near Szárszó, the place where, in 1943, the 'populists' had discussed their conception of postwar society.

It was only in the autumn of 1988 that the die was cast firmly in favour of reform. On 5 September, at Lakitelek once more, the Hungarian Democratic Forum held a second meeting at which it transformed itself from a movement to an organization with a membership (but still not a party), capable of running candidates at forthcoming elections. The Central Committee declared itself ready, on the 27th, to talk to the New March Front and Hungarian Democratic Forum.

As autumn turned to winter, the spectre of a multi-party system began to haunt the HSWP. Pozsgay now was of the persuasion that 'classical experience shows that the simplest technology in this respect (pluralism) is the multi-party system'. Some days later, the Alliance of Free Democrats was formally constituted. Even worse for the HSWP, its old rival, the Smallholders' Party, was re-founded in Szentendre on 12 November, and the Social Democrats joined the fray in January 1989.

On 14 January the New March Front made the first attempt to establish dialogue between the HSWP and the new parties, suggesting the formation of a countrywide national committee, comprising opposition and government parties alike, which would be vested with the power to pass legislation until such time as elections were held. The idea was stillborn because of Democratic Forum objections. Nevertheless, the HSWP Central Committee meeting of 11 February formally accepted the prospect of a multi-party future. The next step was the creation of the Opposition Round Table on 22 March 1989 in response to a suggestion by the Forum of Independent Lawyers. Its more modest aim was to unify the opposition around a negotiating strategy, and it included eight of the new opposition groupings: the Bajcsy-Zsilinszky Fraternal Society; the Alliance of Young Democrats; the Smallholders' Party; the League of Democratic Trade Unions; the Hungarian Democratic Forum; the Hungarian People's Party; the Social Democrats; and the Alliance of Free Democrats.

The Hungarian Socialist Workers' Party and the Opposition Round Table had very different views about how negotiations should take place, and this delayed the commencement of negotiations until June. The Opposition Round Table proposed that all its members should be invited to the talks, that the negotiations should be bilateral and each side should express its opinion alternately, that the chair should rotate, that there should be a joint communiqué, and that there should be a concrete agenda which should include the subject of elections and a number of other important issues. The HSWP wanted the non-specific agenda of solving the crisis, and a round-table meeting in the traditional sense, with all shades of opinion represented, including the Ferenc Münnich Society, the Patriotic People's Front and other groups that are generally considered Party 'fronts'. Finally, on 29 May the HWSP offered greatly revised terms to the Opposition Round Table which were not rejected out of hand. In return for the HSWP's acceptance that the meetings should produce binding agreements, and its willingness to join the other parties in signing a document renouncing the exclusive right to issue orders to the armed forces, the Opposition Round Table gave way on the issue of there being a third party to the talks made up of 'front' organizations. On 10 June the commencement of talks was announced.

Meanwhile, reform within the Party gathered pace. In February, the first meeting of a Reform Circle within the HSWP took place in

Csongrad county, with approximately one hundred participants. Hard-liners Lukács and Berecz lost their positions on the Political Committee in April. The month also witnessed a statement from the Political Committee permitting horizontal links between Reform Circles (that is to say, factions) within the Party, and a Reform Workshop took place at Kecskemét, with eighty representatives from thirty groups listening to speeches demanding a Party Congress in the autumn, and the resigna-tion of Kádár as Party president. Kádár's resignation duly followed in May, a year after his defeat at the special Party Conference. In May too, the Party resolved to relinquish control of its private militia, the Workers' Guard, and have it integrated into the army; and, having initially proposed a Party Conference only for the autumn, following the first National Council of Reform Circles at Szeged on 20 May, the Central Committee committed itself to a full Party Congress.

Before taking political events on to the election of 1990 which ended 'socialist' rule in Hungary, it is worth taking stock of the political actors that had emerged by the summer of 1989. A distinction can be made between the new political organizations which, under one guise or another, were responsible for creating the conditions which allowed the emergence of multi-party politics, and the 'nostalgia' or 'continuation' parties which joined in once the process was under way.

The biggest of the new political actors was the Hungarian Democratic Forum. By May, its membership had increased to 15,000, while 750 delegates attended its first National Convention in March. It still declined to call itself a party, preferring the phrase 'independent intellectual–political movement'. Its origins lay in the 'populist' tradition of Hungarian thought, as represented by a group of critical writers in the 1930s, some of whom formed the National Peasant Party after the war. As with other political movements in this tradition, it was greatly influenced by the idea of the unique Hungarian 'Third Way' discussed in Chapter 2, and by the writings of István Bibó.[14] Although it claimed not to be a movement of writers, five of its nine founding members were writers or poets, and there was a literary bias to its policies. It was stronger on emotive issues, such as freedom, democracy and nation-hood, than on concrete economic programmes, which were tinged with populism. Its enthusiasm for the Hungarian nation, and concern at the declining birth rate, made it strongly pro-family and some of its members took a firm anti-abortion stance. Others extended national-ism to anti-semitism.

The second major new political organization was the Alliance of Free Democrats. Although it was often presented as a continuation of the 'urbanized' as opposed to 'populist' tradition in Hungarian thought, it is more appropriate to stress the modernity of the movement. It was a child of the socialist world; its links were with the Democratic Opposition of the 1970s, with the producers of samizdat, with Marxism, and with practical attempts to reform social inequality such as the Poor Support Fund.[15] Its leading figures are lapsed Marxists, with a firm commitment to political and economic reform, and a strong social and environmental conscience. By May, it had by far the most elaborated programme of the opposition groups, which is not surprising given the high proportion of economists, sociologists and lawyers in its membership. It was conscious of this intellectual bias and did not expect to become a mass party; and it was somewhat surprised when it did.

The remaining new groups were less significant. The Alliance of Young Democrats did not consider itself a party, but thought it might run candidates in forthcoming elections. It saw itself as an independent youth group committed to reform. Rather than evolve a full national programme, it engaged in issue-based politics, extending to ecology and minority rights in addition to issues that specifically concerned the young. It had played a prominent role in organizing demonstrations and petitions, and was in favour of a market economy and liberal politics. Its Alice Madzsár Women's Group was the nearest thing to a women's movement on the political scene, and had organized the women's demonstration against the Bős-Nagymaros dam in September 1988.

The Endre Bajcsy-Zsilinszky Fraternal Society existed to further the values of the person whose name it bears. Bajcsy-Zsilinszky was a member of the pre-war Smallholders' Party (see below) and resistance organizer who was executed in the last weeks of the war. This wide brief allowed the society to take a stand in support of a host of reform issues and organize a variety of political events. The Left-wing Alternative Association came from a very different political tradition. It saw itself as left wing in the Western, rather than Eastern European, sense, opposing both capitalist restoration and Stalinism. Its ultimate goal was the classic Marxist notion of the association of free producers. The Ferenc Münnich Society, on the other hand, was the only political actor of any stature then committed unambiguously to restoring the political system prior to May 1988.

In May 1989, only three 'nostalgia' or 'continuation' parties were of significance. Hungary's Social Democratic Party (the Social Democrats) claimed in February 1989 to be operating in eighteen Budapest districts and eighty places in the provinces. Its programme was that of a welfare state based on a parliamentary democracy and the rule of law, with free, strong trade unions and a mixed economy. Despite being courted by the social democratic parties of Western Europe, the party could not be considered a serious force, being hopelessly split between an old guard and young pretenders. The Independent Smallholder, Land Labourer and Citizen's Party (Smallholders' Party) suffered from similar problems of schism. Its programme was essentially a continuation of what it had proposed in the 1930s: free elections, a multi-party system, freedom of the press, a market economy with special emphasis on small industrialists and traders, and support for the family. The only other 'nostalgia' party of any significance at this time was the Hungarian People's Party, a continuation of the postwar National Peasant Party, which functioned briefly as the Petőfi Party in 1956. It was formed in February 1989 out of the Péter Veres Society, which was itself founded in November 1988 with the intention of working in cooperation with the Patriotic People's Front.[16] It claimed a membership of 15,000–17,000 and boasted an organization in every county. Its policy focused very much on agricultural and rural issues such as local government reform and a new land law, although not necessarily a new cooperative law. Its critics viewed the party with suspicion: it was too closely tied to the Patriotic People's Front where many National Peasant Party politicians found careers after their party had ceased to function. Others saw it as the party of the collective farm presidents.

Other former political parties which had declared themselves by May 1989 but could not yet be considered serious forces were: the Independent Hungarian Democratic Party, the Christian Democratic People's Party, the Hungarian National Christian Democratic Labour Party, and the Hungarian Independence Party. A vast range of independent trade unions and other social groups had also emerged which, although important in extending Hungary's 'civil society', were not important political actors.

Pozsgay's Reform Communist Gamble in the Ascendency

In the summer and early autumn of 1989, it looked as if Pozsgay might pull it off. The reform wing of the Hungarian Socialist Workers' Party grew from strength to strength, culminating in the creation of the new Hungarian Socialist Party at the emergency Congress of 7–10 October 1989, and a deal was struck with the Opposition Round Table on 18 September with which, until the very last minute, all parties appeared to be satisfied.

June and July 1989 were dominated by funerals, by the ceremonial reburial of Imre Nagy on 16 June, and by the death of Kádár on 6 July. Both occasions brought large crowds on to the streets, although the Nagy reburial was a much larger media event, attracting Hungarian emigrés from all over the world, as well as the new opposition leaders. Some of the speeches made at the Heroes' Square ceremony and by the graveside were extremely critical of the old regime and of Soviet influence – perhaps the first time that such views were voiced publicly on television for a mass audience. Kádár's funeral was less stage-managed; indeed the authorities seem to have been surprised at how many people came to pay their last respects to the man who had dominated Hungarian politics for over thirty years. Long queues developed outside the HSWP headquarters where he was lying in state, and the building was kept open long into the evening to cope with demand.

Between these two funerals, two significant political developments took place. First, the reformist wing of the Party strengthened its position by effectively squeezing Grósz out of power, a development many had not expected to take place before the October Congress. On 24 June it was announced that the Party would be led by a four-person praesidium comprising Nyers, Németh and Pozsgay alongside Grósz, who was now in a minority of one in the company of three eminent reformers. Second, the Hungarian Democratic Forum finally took the decision, which many within its membership had resisted since its formation, to become a political party. This did not end discussion of the topic however, and in early July it set up a committee to explain to the membership how the Forum could act both as an intellectual political movement and as a political party. As part of its strategy to transform itself into a party, the Democratic Forum set about equipping itself with a set of policies, especially economic policies, and quietly abandoned the poets' dream of the 'Third Way'. A further indication that politics was changing towards a more conventional party structure was the fate of an initiative by self-styled 'leading intellectuals' in August. A group of intellectuals, including Hankiss, called for the holding in October of another conference to discuss the fate of the nation along the lines of the earlier Monor and Szárszó conferences. The call was not heeded. The era of intellectual movements and politics dominated by intellectuals seemed to have come to an end.

Negotiations with the Opposition Round Table continued throughout the summer, almost stalling on a number of occasions, especially during the period when Pozsgay was on holiday. Consistent themes in the discussions, which were never fully resolved, were the issues of Pozsgay's candidacy for the new post of president, and the issue of the Hungarian Socialist Workers' Party withdrawal from workplaces. The deal on offer from the Party was that it would agree to withdraw from workplaces if the Round Table agreed to support Pozsgay as candidate for president. Other issues that spiced political debate before the conclusion of negotiations in mid September were the questions of whether or not to allow East German tourists to leave for the West, and the scandal of the Party setting up private limited liability companies to which it transferred such assets as rest homes and sports facilities in advance of responding to opposition demands to give a full account of its wealth. The latter became known as the Next 2000 affair, after the name of one front company of this type. The most dramatic event concerning the former question, before the government finally decided to let the East Germans leave officially (so precipitating the downfall of the Honecker regime), was the 'pan-European picnic' at Sopron organized by the Democratic Forum, when numerous participants symbolically walked to the West across a border, where no barbed wire had existed since the previous May.

The agreement between the Opposition Round Table and the Party announced on 18 September was in many ways a victory for Pozsgay. He had strengthened his position within his own party by successfully concluding negotiations before the Congress. He had not conceded the right of the Party to organize in workplaces, nor had he committed the Party to winding up the workers' militia entirely, and the issue of reporting on the Party's wealth was left rather unclear. Furthermore, Pozsgay's personal prospects of becoming a strong president, even if the future government were a Democratic Forum one, or some form of coalition between the Forum and the Party, looked secure. The Round Table discussions had agreed on the election of a president by popular ballot before holding parliamentary elections. Pozsgay would almost certainly win the presidential election and thus would enhance the chances of his party in the later parliamentary elections. The only cloud on the horizon was the totally unexpected announcement by the Free Democrats on the day that the agreement was signed that they would not add their signatures to the document, although neither would they exercise their right to veto it. In their view, the constitutional arrangements they had come to were too important to lose; but they could not put their names to a document that conceded to Pozsgay the four advantages listed above.

In the build-up to the brought-forward XIVth Party Congress in October, this appeared to be no more that an irritation, and even the announcement by the Free Democrats and Young Democrats that they were going to start collecting signatures to force the country to have a referendum on the four issues hardly posed a threat, since they were unlikely to collect the necessary signatures. Furthermore, as it emerged from later discussions in the Democratic Forum when the Forum's own candidate for the presidency was proposed, Pozsgay at this time enjoyed the support of the Forum's leadership in his presidential bid. The XIVth Congress also went more or less Pozsgay's way, although a rump of hard-liners did not agree with the Party's change of name and, with

Grósz and Berecz as leading luminaries, formed (or in their view continued) the Hungarian Socialist Workers' Party. The Hungarian Socialist Party committed itself to democratic socialism, a multi-party system, a market economy, the withdrawal of Soviet troops, and later applied to join the Socialist International. Nyers was elected Party president, and the Party's official presidential candidate was Pozsgay. Creating this new reform-oriented Party was no small achievement. The few Reform Circles of the spring of 1989 had mushroomed by the Congress to eight different 'platforms' within the Party, and the final formation of the Hungarian Socialist Party was made possible, after much behind-the-scenes negotiating, only when the Popular Democratic Platform came to an agreement with the Reform Alliance group.

The Reform Communist Dream Falls along with the Regimes of Eastern Europe

Pozsgay's reform communist ambitions were not to be. They were destroyed by three developments of the autumn and early winter of 1989, and by the spring of 1990 it was clear that the former Communist Party would only be a minor actor in future Hungarian politics. The first of these changes, although the hardest to assess, is the demise of socialist regimes in all Hungary's neighbours. The process that reform communists such as Pozsgay and Horn had started by agreeing to let East Germans emigrate via Austria now backfired. When socialist regimes were disappearing from Europe, there was little advantage to be gained from being a reform communist, however genuine the commitment to reform might be. In the popular imagination, Pozsgay, Németh, Nyers and Horn were easily tarred with the same brush as Honecker and Jakes.

   The remaining two changes concerned the nature of the opposition. Between the summer and its second congress, which eventually took place on 21 October 1989, the Democratic Forum more or less completely remoulded itself as a right-of-centre political party, and sought to distance itself from both the populist romantics and reform communists such as Pozsgay who had been active in the early days of Lakitelep. The party accepted the resignation of Zoltán Bíró, one of the four excluded from the Hungarian Socialist Workers' Party in the spring of 1988, as interim leader, and elected a new president, József Antall, whose father had been a member of the Smallholders' party and Minister for Reconstruction in the postwar coalition government. Antall himself had been briefly active in the reformed Smallholders' Party before joining the Forum. Similarly, all mention of the 'Third Way' now disappeared from its party literature. The Forum also felt obliged to put forward its own presidential candidate, rather than support Pozsgay for the post, although in choosing the relatively unknown Lajos Für it was accused of hoping he would lose. At this Congress, the party presented its full programme, which was much more comprehensive than any previous policy statement, and included a lengthy section on economic policy, formerly its weak point, written by its young guard of economic experts from the Planning Office who had contributed to *Turnabout and Reform*.

But most significant of all perhaps, and eclipsing for a time the Democratic Forum, was the rise of the Free Democrats as a mass political movement. While the Socialist Party and the Democratic Forum were conducting their congresses and planning for the presidential elections, the Free Democrats and the Young Democrats were collecting signatures for their referendum. By 17 October 1989, they already had the necessary 100,000 signatures to make a referendum mandatory on the government, but they went forward and collected a further 100,000 for good measure. Meanwhile the government passed legislation disbanding the workers' militia, obliging the Socialist Party to give an account of its property and withdraw from workplaces, so the only matter in dispute was when and how the president should be elected.

The date chosen for the referendum was 26 November, and despite what the Free Democrats interpreted as illegal moves by parliament to amend the wording and order of the questions, and calls by the Democratic Forum to boycott the referendum, the Free Democrats, who were now supported by the Social Democratic Party and the Smallholders' Party as well as the Young Democrats, won. By 4 p.m. on the day of the referendum the necessary 50 per cent turnout had been passed, and the Free Democrat supported answers gained very marginally, a matter of some six thousand votes, over 50 per cent of the vote.

This victory boosted the support of the Free Democrats enormously, and temporarily clouded the reputation of the Democratic Forum. The boycott call did not come well from a party supposedly committed to democracy, and led to suspicions that the Forum had only called for a boycott because it expected the 50 per cent turnout would not be reached and would then be able to claim political apathy as positive political support. The prestige of the Free Democrats was further raised by their exposure of the 'Danube-gate' scandal. At the beginning of January 1990, a former secret service officer provided the Free Democrats with evidence that the service was still tapping the phones of opposition politicians. The Free Democrats milked the opportunities this provided for proving their total opposition to an irredeemably undemocratic regime, and finally obliged the Minister of the Interior to resign and the government to set up a committee to investigate the activities of the secret service.

The radical effects of these three political developments can be seen from Table 1.4, which gives the results of a series of voting intention surveys taken over the first fifteen months of multi-party politics in Hungary. Until October–November 1989, the Hungarian Socialist Party (as it was re-christened) still commanded the largest share of the vote, and would have been a major force in any coalition government, especially if Pozsgay held the presidency. After November 1989, support for the Socialists fell dramatically, while, in December, after the referendum, support for the Free Democrats increased substantially, and went on increasing as the electoral campaign progressed.

The winter of 1989 and early spring of 1990 were devoted to electioneering. On 21 December it was announced that Németh had resigned from his post in the Socialist Party leadership so that he could stand as an independent candidate, and the following day, after much press speculation, it was announced that parliament would dissolve on 16 March 1990 with elections on 25 March. By this time some eighty-four parties had been formed in Hungary, sixty-four of which had registered formally as such, and forty-eight of which declared an intention to run in the election. In the event, however, only ten parties registered sufficient candidate nominations to be included on the National List and stand a chance of significant power. They were joined

Table 1.4 Percentage support for major parties 1989–90*

	Date of survey												
	Jan	*Mar*	*May*	*Jun*	*Jul*	*Aug*	*Sep*	*Oct*	*O–N*	*Nov*	*Dec*	*Jan*	*Mar*
HDF	11	17	13	13	14	18	24	20	27	22	23	21	21
AFD	7	12	6	5	3	6	6	7	9	8	14	18	20
ISP	10	10	12	6	11	9	7	6	5	9	12	16	16
HSP	–	–	–	–	–	–	–	35	25	16	16	11	10
HSWP	23	34	32	29	37	32	23	–	6	7	5	4	–
AYD	11	9	16	9	7	7	11	10	8	13	8	7	7
CDPP	–	–	–	5	2	4	4	3	5	4	3	3	5
HSDP	6	11	12	12	10	8	8	6	4	8	6	5	6
HPP**	1	8	5	5	4	3	3	4	2	3	4	2	–

*% of those who stated which party they would vote for, not of those asked.
**Péter Veres Association in January 1989.

Source: HangSúly, vol. 1, no. 1, p. 19; no. 4, p. 19; no. 5, p. 18; no. 6–7, p. 35; no. 8–9, p. 35; no. 10, p. 20; *Magyar Nemzet*, 22 November 1989, 17 February 1990, 14 March 1990.

on the list by two essentially non-party organizations: the Agrarian Alliance and the Patriotic Election Coalition, a party formed by the Patriotic People's Front to allow independent candidates to stand.

Between May 1989 and March 1990, all parties had consolidated their political programmes and had become organizationally and financially much more secure. The Hungarian People's Party suffered a decline though, as political thought moved away from 'Third Way' scenarios and the Agrarian Alliance took away some of its collective farm constituency. The Socialists aside, two broad camps emerged. On the one hand there was the liberal cum social democratic wing which included the Free and Young Democrats, and the much less significant Social Democrats, who still suffered from schism, despite the appointment in the summer of a younger generation woman president who had supposedly created party unity. They supported rather quicker economic privatization, civic values and individual rights. The other camp – consisting of the Democratic Forum, the Christian Democratic People's Party (which since May had built itself into a small but serious Christian Democratic Party) and the Smallholders' Party – was of a national–Christian persuasion. They tended to be slightly more cautious on the speed of privatization, although they were equally condemnatory of spontaneous piecemeal privatization. What characterized their right-of-centre politics was not so much economics as their nationalism and their patriarchy. In addition to their policies to promote Hungary as a Christian nation, all expressed profound belief in the virtues of the family and motherhood. The Democratic Forum made a point of rejecting Western-style women's movements in its party programme. It also allowed itself, via radio broadcasts by István Csurka and the Csurka-edited *Hungarian Forum*, to play on the undoubted anti-semitism of some of its members and supporters in order to gain votes, although party policy continued to condemn explicitly all racism. The Smallholders also developed an elaborated agricultural policy which marked them off from all other parties. They want to reverse forty years of history and return landownership to the situation of 1947, that is, after the land reform but before the first attempts at collectivization. The old men of the party seemed determined, at the expense of anachronistically reintroducing peasant agriculture, to fight old battles to the last, although a younger generation of spokespersons insisted that 1947 was just a starting point for restructuring landownership and they did not expect a return to small-scale farming.

One of the last acts of the old regime was to establish a State Property Agency to handle privatization and bring to an end the spontaneous privatizations which by the spring of 1990 had been condemned in parliament and criticized exhaustively in the economic press. In order to obtain the expertise necessary for the task, the administration signed consultancy agreements with Barclays Zoed Wedd, Price Waterhouse, and Baker and McKenzie to write their operational handbook. The Agency claimed in its first month to have already insisted on a better price being obtained for IBUSZ, the Hungarian Travel Company.

The results of the two rounds of the elections are given in Tables 1.5 and 1.6. The former Socialist Party fared considerably worse than the Communists' 16.9 per cent showing forty-five years earlier.[17] The Democratic Forum, on the other hand, in a sense matched the Smallholders' 1945 victory. In the second round, the Forum and its future government allies, the Smallholders and the Christian Democratic People's Party, jointly gained 58 per cent of the vote, compared with the Smallholders' 1945 result of 57 per cent.

Antall took his time forming his administration, which was finally announced on 16 May 1990. It was made up of eight members of the Hungarian Democratic Forum, four members of the Smallholders, three independents and one member of the Christian Democratic People's Party. The new Minister of Agriculture was a member of the Smallholders' Party; the new Minister for Popular Welfare was a member of the Christian Democratic People's Party; and the new Ministry for Industry and Commerce was one of new guard critical economists of the *Turnabout and Reform*, Planning Office school. In its first year in power the Democratic Forum-led coalition government demonstrated above all else a propensity to procrastinate and defer firm decisions of all kinds, but especially those with potentially unpleasant electoral consequences.

Table 1.5 Parliamentary seats, March–April 1990

	Regional list	Individual constituencies		National list	Number of seats
		round 1	round 2		
HDF	40	3	111	10	164
Free Democrats	34	0	35	23	92
Smallholders	16	0	11	17	44
HSP	14	0	1	18	33
Young Democrats	8	0	1	12	21
CDPP	8	0	3	10	21
Agrarian Alliance	–	0	1	–	1
Independent	–	2	4	–	6
Multi-party	–	0	4	–	4
Total	120	5	171	90	386

Source: Heti Világgazdaság, 14 April 1990, p. 5.

Table 1.6 Percentage of vote March–April 1990

	Round one: regional list	Round two: constituencies
Hungarian Democratic Forum (HDF)	24.73	42
Alliance of Free Democrats (AFD)	21.39	24
Independent Smallholders (ISP)	11.73	11
Hungarian Socialist Party (HSP)	10.89	9
Alliance of Young Democrats (AYD)	8.95	5
Christian Democratic People's Party (CDPP)	6.46	5
Hungarian Socialist Workers Party (HSWP)	3.68	
Hungary's Social Democratic Party (HSDP)	3.55	
Agrarian Alliance	3.13	
Entrepreneurs' Party	1.89	
Patriotic Electoral Coalition	1.87	
Hungarian People's Party (HPP)	0.75	
Hungary's Green Party	0.36	
National Smallholders' Party	0.20	
Somogy Christian Coalition	0.12	
Hungary's Cooperative and Agrarian Party	0.10	
Independent Hungarian Democratic Party	0.06	
Freedom Party	0.06	
Hungarian Independence Party	0.04	

Source: Heti Világgazdaság, 14 April 1990, p. 5; *Magyar Nemzet,* 10 April 1990, p. 4.

It was accused of being authoritarian, as illustrated by the fact that it brought the State Property Agency under state rather than government control; but it failed even to push through its initial predilection for enforcing compulsory religious education in schools. It lost much of its support during a summer of procrastination, and was roundly defeated in the local elections in September–October. The real victor of these elections was the Alliance of Young Democrats, who increased their vote considerably, while the Free Democrats lost some ground. The Small-holders lost even more ground, but remained a force because their major issue – land reform – was a popular one, and because some party members had extended it to encompass 'reprivatization' (the return of assets to their pre-socialist owners) in other areas of the economy besides agriculture. The new democratic political structures survived a three-day taxi and lorry driver blockade in October 1990, but a year after the elections key legislation necessary for further economic transformation, and promised for the first few months of the govern-ment, had not been passed by parliament.

The reintroduction of capitalist economic relations in Hungary is assured, indeed in crucial respects it has already taken place; and the upshot of the account presented in this book is that this was probably inevitable. The reinforcement of nationalism and patriarchy, however, was not inevitable, but must be understood in the light of the old regime's persistent failure to pursue a self-conscious social policy (see Chapter 7), so leaving the field open for more traditional ideologies. The nationalist and patriarchal versus individualist and liberal divide in Hungarian politics should be stressed. No political party of electoral consequence in Hungary today is in favour of national, even social, ownership of the means of production. If the Democratic Forum appears to favour a more gradualist approach to privatization it is for ideological reasons of preserving Hungarian property against the tide of foreign ownership, not from any commitment to national ownership itself. In post-socialist Hungarian politics the commitment to a social democracy–social market economic structure is not at issue; the question is whether it comes associated with national, Christian and patriarchal or individualist and liberal values.

The Demise of Popular Front Policies in Postwar Hungary

Hungary prior to Socialist Industrialization

Hungary falls within that eastern part of Europe which underwent the 'second serfdom'. While, in western Europe, the manorial system slowly disappeared between the twelfth and sixteenth centuries, in Europe east of the Elbe, from about the fifteenth century, a process of increasing serfdom set in as landowners sought to maximize their agricultural surplus for sale to the western urban markets. Meanwhile, the death of Hungary's Louis II at the battle of Mohács in 1526 resulted in Habsburg claims to the Hungarian throne which, after the liberation of Buda from the Turks in 1686, the Habsburgs pursued unopposed and the Diet of 1687 established Hungary legally as one of the hereditary provinces of the Habsburgs. By the end of the seventeenth century, then, the stage was set for Hungary's future role as an agricultural exporter within the Habsburg empire. Two factors impeded the development of industrial activity in Hungary. First, the western lands were already more advanced industrially and enjoyed comparative advantage. Second, and more significant, the strongest political force in Hungary – the nobility, which had gained from Maria Theresa confirmation of their exemption from direct taxation in return for their support during the War of Austrian Succession – had a vested interest in maintaining the status quo.

Despite Hungary's revolution in 1848 – which failed to achieve independence from Austria but succeeded in abolishing the institution of serfdom (first by the revolutionaries on 18 March 1848, and then by the Austrian reaction in 1853) – underlying economic relations remained unchanged. The abolition of serfdom did not change the agricultural orientation of the economy, nor its role within the larger imperial economy. By the last third of the nineteenth century, following the Compromise of 1867, Hungary was constitutionally an equal partner in the Austro-Hungarian Dual Monarchy which ruled an extensive empire in central and eastern Europe. But, economically, it remained very much the junior partner, with an economic structure not dissimilar from that of the lands over which it ruled. Political equality did little to transform its economic structure; and when significant industrial development did take place in the Monarchy as a whole, from the 1870s onwards, it was characterized, in Hungary as in Austria, by concentration, cartelization, and protectionism. Nevertheless, there is evidence to suggest, as Berend has argued, that Hungary, by developing agriculture-related industries, had been on the point of industrial take-off when the First World War intervened.

> Hungary was practically the only European country to be able to transform part of her grain export into the export of food products. Hungary's milling industry became an exporter on a world scale, second only to Minneapolis, because of the Hungarian invention of the roller mill.[1]

Hungary's potential industrial take-off was ended abruptly by the First World War and its aftermath. The short-lived Soviet Republic of 1919 was suppressed by foreign military might, and an ordinance of 7 August 1919 restored to its previous owners all private industrial and commercial property that had become communal property only months earlier on 21 March 1919. The Trianon Treaty of June 1920 (the Eastern European equivalent of the Treaty of Versailles) deprived the former Hungarian part of the empire of 67.3 per cent of its land and 58.4 per cent of its population. Hungary became suddenly a small nation, dependent on trade for survival. Its economy did not respond well to this new challenge, and relative economic stagnation ended only when Hungary's economy became increasingly integrated into the Third Reich and the pre-war boom induced by munitions production. The only exception to this was the period between 1924 and 1929 when there were signs that an independent Hungary with a new National Bank was achieving a degree of economic success; although evidence also suggests that much foreign investment was not put to effective use. An economy dominated by a few families with extensive industrial investments and close ties to the landed aristocracy could not develop a coherent industrial strategy for breaking out of its inherited position of supplier of agricultural products to the more developed world; and agriculture remained dependent on high levels of input from an economically tied labour force.

The Second World War devastated much of the Hungarian economy, although the productive capacity of manufacturing industry was actually greater even immediately after the war than in 1938 because of the 40 per cent increase in capacity during the war itself.[2] Hungary lost 90 per cent of its railway bridges, 69 per cent of its locomotives, and 86 per cent of its railway trucks. The total level of damage was estimated by Hungaria Lloyds at five times the annual income in pre-war years, or 40 per cent of 1944 national income.[3] Some 20 per cent of this damage was inflicted by German and Arrow Cross destruction of capacity as the Germans retreated.[4] The worst destruction was in agriculture (16.8 per cent), transport (16.8 per cent) and private houses (23.9 per cent). However, the majority of the damage was to products and materials rather than machinery, tools and plant, and this meant that reconstruction could be quite rapid. As a German ally, despite its attempts to negotiate a separate peace, Hungary was obliged to pay reparations, predominantly to the Soviet Union. Under its ceasefire agreement with the latter, Hungary's reparations obligations to the Soviet Union over six years totalled 200 million dollars, those to Czechoslovakia 30 million dollars, and those to Yugoslavia 70 million dollars. In addition to this, the Potsdam agreement ceded all German property in Hungary to the Soviet Union.

Government policies in Hungary as elsewhere in liberated Eastern Europe were based around the 1930s strategy of the Popular Front. Socialist patterns of ownership, except for the commanding heights of the economy, were seen as a long-term goal. The emphasis was on control. The months immediately following liberation from the Germans in 1945 were ones of chaos. The provisional government struggled to assert its authority over spontaneous popular forces for reform and democratic control both in the fields of land reform and the control of factories. While the government was struggling to establish itself and move its seat from Debrecen to Budapest, popular forces were at work in the countryside and in the factories of liberated areas. Workers' councils, helped by Soviet troops, took over the running of many factories and ad hoc committees took over local administration.[5] The provisional government was quick to limit the powers of these spontaneously formed committees. In February 1945 it gave the works councils a supervisory and suggestion-making role only, and returned powers of decision-making and of disposal to enterprise owners. Of more lasting significance, 'land claimants' committees' set about organizing a land reform.[6] By the time the provisional government passed its land reform legislation on 15 March 1945, in many areas this was recognition of a *fait accompli*:[7] the peasants had already seized the land. The reform affected some 9.3 million hectares, 35 per cent of Hungary's total land area. Although the inequalities of the past centuries were removed at a stroke, the average area of distributed land was only 2.9 hectares, and the plots of the former 'dwarf-holders' increased on average from only 0.8 to 1.1 hectares, still too small to provide a livelihood, let alone the basis for efficient agricultural production. Elections followed on 4 November 1945 with the following results: the Smallholders' Party, with a slogan of 'God, the Homeland and Private Property', won 57 per cent of the votes, the Social Democrats won 17.4 per cent, and the Communist Party won 17 per cent, the National Peasant Party 6.8 per cent, and the Bourgeois Democratic Party 1.7 per cent.[8] Despite the clear victory for the Smallholders it was agreed that the new coalition government should include all the parties which had made up the provisional government.

Throughout 1946 and 1947, although government control over the economy was extended by degrees and communist histories make analogies with the period of 'dual power' in the Soviet Union, policy-making was very much in the Popular Front mould. Only the mines (in 1946) and the banks (in 1947) were nationalized for ideological reasons. Other large enterprises were brought under state control because of bankruptcy and their important role in meeting reparations obligations. Price controls were somewhat more extensive than the Popular Front paradigm might require, but they have to be seen in the context of the highest inflation in world history.

Following the nationalization of the mines – which extended only to the mines themselves, not to the conglomorate companies which owned them together with much wider economic interests – the Communist Party gained control of the Supreme Economic Council and thus effective control of all economic decision-making. On 1 August 1946 Hungary introduced a new currency, the forint, which, combined with the strict wage and price controls introduced at the same time, solved the inflationary spiral at a stroke; but it also increasingly isolated the economy from the world price system. By the end of July, inflation had reached dizzying heights. One dollar was equal to five quintillion (10^{30}) pengős,[9] and the price index, taking 26 August 1939 as one, had increased to 0.4×10 to the power of thirty.[10] On 1 December 1946 the Manfred Weiss works, the Ganz works, the Rimaurány Iron Works and the Magyar Vagon és Gépgyár at Győr were effectively nationalized to ensure they met their reparations obligations. All the companies were heavily in debt and could not produce profitably because of price controls; yet they were under an obligation to supply 60 per cent of their product for reparations.

In 1947 attention switched to planning; and the effects of the Cold War began to be felt. Both the Communist Party and the Social Democrats (with the help of Nicholas Kaldor, then lecturer at the LSE) drew up indicative plans calling for, in the finally accepted version, 10 per cent of national income to go to investment, of which 30 per cent was to be in agriculture, and 80 per cent on an increase in living standards.[11] The plans differed on two fundamental issues: the raising of foreign loans and the nationalization of the banks. The Social Democratic plan was premissed on foreign loans and did not see a need for bank nationalization. The Communist Party plan made no assumption about foreign loans and advocated bank nationalization. Following Hungary's (Moscow-inspired) rejection of the Marshall Plan, the Communist Party variant won by default. Foreign loans were simply not forthcoming, and, in the ever tenser political climate, the Social Democrats did not want to be seen as defenders of big capital by opposing bank nationalization, which followed in November 1947. This time nationalization was extended to subsidiary companies controlled by the banks, a further ninety-one companies, so bringing 78 per cent of pre-war financial institutions and 58 per cent of workers in manufacturing industry into the state sector. However, there was no change in the spheres of activity of the banks.[12]

If the Truman Doctrine and the Marshall Plan were to split Europe into two camps, the prospect of a peace treaty between Hungary and the Allies gave the Soviet Union, exercising its influence via the Allied Control Commission and its Communist Party allies, only until September to ensure that Hungary was irrevocably committed to the Soviet camp. Rákosi's strategy to achieve this end was two-fold: to employ what he later termed 'salami tactics' to both weaken the political opposition and prevent a centre-left alliance between the right wing of the Social Democrats and the left wing of the Smallholders' Party, and to engineer the election of a clearly pro-Soviet government before the peace treaty came into effect. A central moment in both strategies was the discovery of the right-wing 'Hungarian Community Conspiracy' which was used as a pretext to discredit the Smallholder prime minister and effectively destroy the party itself. In the following elections the Communist Party emerged, thanks to well-documented extensive double voting,[13] as the largest party in parliament; although, with only 22.3 per cent of the vote, compared with 16.4 per cent for the Democratic People's Party (not part of the coalition), 15.4 per cent for the Smallholders' Party, 14.9 per cent for the Social Democrats, 13.4 per cent for the National Independence Party (not part of the coalition) and 8.4 per cent for the National Peasant Party, it held by no means the majority.[14]

With the exception of the economic weight within the national economy of those major companies forced by (partly politically induced) bankruptcy into the state sector, nationalizations up to the end of 1947 were no more radical than those carried out in postwar France;

and the three-year plan as originally adopted was scarcely more interventionist then France's Monnet Plan.[15] In the political sphere, although the Communist Party had always enjoyed a privileged position because of its ties with the Soviet forces, it was only in the heightened tension of the early Cold War that the Party began openly to disregard constitutional niceties.

The 1948 Great Change: From Popular Front to Soviet Communism

Histories of Hungary describe 1948 as the year of the 'great change'. Internationally it was the year of the Berlin Crisis, the Prague Revolution, and the final stage in the Stalin–Tito rupture. In Hungary, it was the year in which nationalization was effectively completed, when the final stage of Rákosi's salami tactics was completed and the Communist Party fused with the Social Democrats to form the Hungarian Workers' Party, when a system of bilateral trade agreements with the Soviet Union was established, when the notion of a national road to socialism was irrevocably rejected, when agricultural collectivization suddenly appeared on the political agenda, and, most important, when a Soviet-type mechanism for economic planning was introduced into the economy.

In February, the government nationalized bauxite mines and such aluminium production as was not under Soviet control.[16] It also reorganized the electrical works, nationalized as part of the nationalization of the mines, into a separate state company.[17] Further significant nationalization took place on 25 March when all plants employing one hundred or more people were taken into state hands; this affected some 594 companies employing 160,000 workers, and extended the socialist sector to cover three-quarters of the workforce.[18] State ownership in industrial sectors was as follows: mining and smelting 100 per cent; iron, steel and machine tool 91 per cent; electrical energy production 98 per cent; construction 92 per cent; printing and publishing 92 per cent; light industry 75 per cent; leather industry 87 per cent; rubber industry 93.5 per cent; paper industry 54 per cent; food supply 55 per cent.[19] Meanwhile trade was orientated increasingly towards the Soviet Union (see Table 2.1), as the Soviet Union set up a series of bilateral trade deals with its satellites and blocked attempts to create other forms of trading networks in the area. The measures taken in 1947 to stimulate industrial collaboration between Hungary and Czechoslovakia in aluminium production and Poland and Hungary in coal were abruptly ended after an editorial in *Pravda* on 28 January 1948 attacked the

Table 2.1 Hungary's foreign trade with the Soviet Union
and major groups of countries

		Soviet Union	CMEA	Other
1938	import	0.11	18.73	81.27
	export	0.09	10.43	89.57
1947	import	11.40	29.73	70.27
	export	15.03	36.31	63.69
1948	import	14.72	33.78	66.22
	export	17.27	34.90	65.10
1949	import	21.44	43.92	56.08
	export	24.91	49.03	50.97

Source: I. Pető and S. Szakács, *A Hazai Gazdaság Négy Évtizedének Története 1945–1985. Az Újjáépítés és a Tervutasításos Irányítás Időszaka 1945–1968*, Budapest 1985, p. 94.

Balkan Federation project.[20] In February, Hungary signed a Cooperation and Mutual Aid Treaty with the Soviet Union; and in mid 1948, when it was firmly in the Soviet camp, Hungary was absolved from repaying half of its outstanding reparations obligations.[21]

On the political front, the employers' association (GYOSZ) was dissolved on 4 April. Following the nationalizations, it had no role to play. More significantly, pressure grew in the Communist and Social Democrats parties for merger. The left-wing Social Democratic interpretation of political events was that, after the defeat of the Smallholders' Party, the forces of reaction were turning their attention to the right wing of the Social Democrats, and these could be stopped only by a strong, unified workers' party.[22] For the Communist Party, union with the Social Democrats was necessary in order to ensure a parliamentary majority. On 12 June the IVth Congress of the Communist Party and the 37th Congress of the Social Democratic Party voted in favour of fusion, and the first congress of the new Hungarian Workers' Party took place over the following two days. In the late summer and autumn, the political situation became more acute. Rajk was demoted from Minister of the Interior to Minister for Foreign Affairs, a preliminary to his arrest and show trial as a Titoist. On 27 November, in the light of worsening relations between Yugoslavia and the Soviet Union, the Hungarian Workers' Party formally adopted a line rejecting the notion of a separate national road to socialism.[23] In December Cardinal Mindszenty was arrested after the discovery of his alleged conspiracy against the state. The Hungarian assets of Western companies were also nationalized at this time after their management had been accused of anti-government activities. Following the Nitrokémia show trial of the spring, for example, which was supposed to 'expose' the treachery of capitalists and the right wing of the Social Democrats,[24] the management of MAORT, the American-owned oil company, was arrested in August and accused of sabotage because its production levels were not considered high enough. The company was subsequently taken into state hands.[25] A similar device, this time with the accusation of spying, was used against the English Hutter and Lewer chemical company in October.[26]

But more important than events in high politics was the silent revolution which was being carried through in the sphere of economic organization. Following the February Prague coup in Czechoslovakia, on 3 March 1948, in secret and in defiance of Social Democratic opposition which rejected closer ties between the administration and the economy,[27] the Communist Party's Political Committee took the decision to elaborate plans for the branch administration of industrial plants, and called on all Party cells and Party trade union members to draw up lists of trustworthy cadres.[28] The Communist Party had gained control of the Ministry of Industry in February 1948 when Antal Bán, the Social Democratic Minister, was forced into exile and was replaced by the Communist Imre Karczag. On 20 March 1948 the ministry was reorganized on a sectoral branch structure.[29] In April, industrial directorates were established in each branch of industry, although they nominally operated independently of the branch ministry. On 7 May, the government issued an ordinance defining the roles of the directorates and fitting them into the institutional system. It became their duty to prepare plans for their industries in the light of the decrees of the National Planning Office.[30] The directorates effectively received all property rights over the enterprises, including the right to appoint management. The newly nationalized enterprises thus lost all autonomy and were effectively run administratively from the state budget.[31] At the same time, the bodies running existing nationalized enterprises in the fields of heavy industry, electrical industry and the mines were given, in addition to their economic duties, administrative powers similar to those enjoyed by the directorates.[32] Similar moves took place in the nationalized banking sector, where Soviet-style single account banking was now introduced. The Hungarian National Bank became cash department and bookkeeper for the whole of state industry. The Credit Bank became the Investment Bank, administering funds provided by the Hungarian National Bank for projects approved by the National Planning Office. The Pest Hungarian Commercial Bank became the Foreign Trade Bank, and the Discount Bank and Savings Banks became the basis for the National Savings Bank.[33]

On 1 June 1948 the Materials and Prices Office was abolished. Its materials supply functions were taken over by the National Planning Office, and its price regulating functions by the Supreme Economic Council.[34] This paved the way for planning by means of material balances, although this technique was not adopted until the first five-year plan of 1950. During the course of 1948 the role of the National Planning Office was steadily transformed from that of advice-giver and coordinator to that of overall supervisor of the entire economic system. It performed this task on an essentially ad hoc basis, however: no law was passed clarifying its role until 1972.[35]

In addition to this total transformation of the system of economic management, a number of important policy decisions were taken throughout the course of 1948 which broke with the spirit of the three-year plan and the Popular Front strategy of the provisional government. First, it was decided to adjust the weights of various components in the plan in favour of industry. Industry, heavy industry especially, was to receive more investment (up from 26.5 to 35 per cent), agriculture was to receive less (down from 30.4 to 18 per cent), and the projected increase in living standards was reduced from 80 to 10–20 per cent.[36] Second, 'rationalization' was encouraged within the state sector: 'branch foreign' activities (such as the commercial or service units of industrial enterprises) were closed down, and plant specialization was increased. The total number of plants fell; horizontal cooperation between enterprises was discouraged in favour of vertical links within the administrative hierarchy.[37] Third, in October the trade unions were reorganized. The previous fifty-strong craft structure was transformed and slimmed-down to a nineteen-strong industry structure, adopting the principle of one plant one union.[38]

Finally, 1948 also saw a significant change in agricultural policy. The Communist Party had kept collectivization very much on the back burner throughout the postwar years, and had given only lukewarm encouragement at the time of the land reform to radical sections of the peasantry who had wanted to set up cooperatives immediately.[39] This was partly out of loyalty to the programme of the provisional government, and partly because overhasty collectivization was assumed to have been a reason for the failure of Hungary's 1919 Republic of Soviets.[40] In September 1947 Cominform delegates had suggested the need for rapid collectivization and Imre Nagy had rejected the policy at a Political Committee meeting in December 1947. His influence thereafter waned as Gerő took on unofficial responsibility for agriculture in addition to his official responsibilities for industry and transport, so making an opening for András Hegedűs as his agricultural advisor. Nagy was finally relieved of his Party responsibility for cooperative policy in 1949.[41]

But in 1947 no further moves toward collectivization had been taken.

At Cominform's meeting on 27 June 1948, however, one of the criticisms levelled at Yugoslavia was its failure to pursue collectivization. The meeting reaffirmed the view that capitalism is not fully abolished until collectivization has been achieved. On 30 June 1948, the central leadership of the Hungarian Workers' Party accepted this line, and on 20 August, in a speech in the provincial town of Kecskemét, Rákosi suddenly put the creation of collective – that is, producer cooperative – farms back on the national agenda,[42] despite the fact that a week prior to this speech the government had passed an ordinance regulating the activities of the land cultivators' cooperatives as general village rather than producer cooperatives.[43] A week after Rákosi's speech, regulations were passed sanctioning the takeover of rented land in the hands of larger peasant – kulak – holdings. Of the 80,655 hectares taken over under these regulations, 60 per cent went to newly formed cooperatives and 40 per cent to private peasants. By November, not only had the idea of a separate 'national road' to socialism been abandoned, but there was talk of full collectivization within three to four years;[44] and in December the government issued an ordinance presenting in detail the Basic Laws of three types of producer cooperative group that could be formed within the land cultivators' cooperatives.[45] (It was only in 1950 that legislation was passed concerning Type III producer cooperatives which operated independently of the land cultivator cooperatives.[46])

After such a momentous year, 1949 saw the tying up of loose ends. On 1 January 1949 Hungary became a founding member of the Council for Mutual Economic Assistance (CMEA); in February, show trials continued with the Cardinal Mindszenty case, followed in June by that of Rajk, former Minister of the Interior and now branded a Titoist and spy. In February too, the Hungarian Independent People's Front replaced the National Independence Front in order to establish a joint list for the elections.[47] By the time of its congress in March, it had become clear that the Front was to act as a vehicle for destroying the remaining parties rather than bringing them together – many right wingers from the other parties had already been forced to resign in the summer of 1948.[48] Also in March, the remaining functions of works councils were taken over by the trade unions.[49] On 15 May elections were held again, at which the Hungarian Independent People's Front received 96 per cent of the vote. In this nominally coalition government, the Smallholders' Party received the Ministries of Trade and Religion and Education, and the National Peasant Party received Agriculture and Construction.[50] After the election, the local committees of the National Independence Front dissolved themselves, and with them the local organs of the National Peasant and Independent Smallholder Parties. However, no law or ordinance was ever passed abolishing the parties.[51]

Between September 1948 and March 1949, the Hungarian Workers' Party undertook a membership survey, and in the process purged its membership by 300,000. Many considered this purge necessary because of the significant numbers who had joined the Party during the coalition period for reasons of self-advancement. However, the membership survey was used primarily to expel from the Party many former Social Democrats.[52]

In economic life, the final touches of the Soviet model were added. The Supreme Economic Council was wound up in mid 1949; a child of the postwar coalition period, it was now superfluous. Its First Secretary, Zoltán Vas, was transferred to become president of the National Planning Office, where real economic power now lay.[53] In mid 1949 the Ministry of Industry was split into ministries for Heavy Industry and Light Industry.[54] In August 1949 a new, socialist constitution was passed, and in October the remaining large commercial companies were nationalized. On 28 December nationalization was concluded when all foreign-owned firms, all domestic companies employing more than ten people, and all printing and electrical plants of any size were taken into state hands.[55] The year also witnessed the beginnings of such Stalinist stalwarts as Stakhanovite labour competition,[56] the 'kulak list', which contained 71,600 families in that year,[57] compulsory deliveries for agricultural products at below-cost prices[58] and 'voluntary' peace loans, which raised over 750 million forints in 1949.[59] And the economic show trials continued. In November managers of the Standard Electrical Company (a subsidiary of IT&T) were arrested and charged with economic sabotage and espionage. The resulting sentencing, in the following year, of a US and a UK citizen to fifteen years' imprisonment led to a dramatic worsening of US–Hungarian relations.[60]

Popular Front Policies and Socialism

These, then, were the key events in the turbulent period during which the Hungarian Communist Party, with the support of considerable sections of the Hungarian working class and the Soviet Union, succeeded in both achieving power and laying the foundations of one particular variant of a socialist economy. This book is about economic and social models for socialism, and as such it requires the drawing of some general lessons from these particular events. Yet the period under consideration constituted a very specific historical conjuncture with few parallels, and, when viewed with the benefit of hindsight, few apparent choices for those concerned. What can be learned about the feasibility of Popular Front political strategies and democratic routes to socialism, or even about a possible 'Third Way' from an historical epoch in which so few alternatives apparently existed and whose outcome was known from the start?

The remaining section of this chapter will endeavour to make the following four points. First, in this specific conjuncture of Soviet domination and the intensifying Cold War, Popular Front policies and notions such as the 'Third Way' were non-starters. The only realistic outcome was the Stalinist version of Soviet communism which in fact prevailed. Nevertheless, all was not preordained. Hungarian communists and their allies had to work hard to achieve their results, for which they enjoyed widespread, although not majority, support. Second, 'Third Way' theories, which were popular at the time and widely canvassed again by the Hungarian Democratic Forum and other new parties in the spring and summer of 1989, exhibited more optimism than political realism. Third, the Social Democratic version of Popular Front policies, although by no means unrealistic, could only have been achieved in the context of a 'mixed economy', with French-style economic planning which many on the radical left today would not consider to be socialist. Fourth, and complementary to the previous point, although the Hungarian Communist Party greatly exaggerated 'conspiracy' and 'sabotage' by the political right in order to achieve its immediate political goals, there might be some lessons to be learned from the Hungarian case about how socialist governments should handle non-cooperation on the part of the population at large. If, in the seemingly unlikely conjuncture of a socialist regime coming to power in the West with the forces of law and order and security on its side (for this is what Communist Party domination of the Ministry of the Interior and the presence of Soviet troops achieved), what guarantees are there that it too would not slip into non-democratic solutions?

How much autonomy did communists and socialists in Hungary have? Were they in charge of events at all, or were they merely puppets acting out a carefully planned Soviet scenario? Soviet intentions towards Eastern Europe until approximately the middle of 1946 were uncertain. On the one hand, as Fejtő notes, from the very first offer of US aid during the war, Stalin was more interested in the postwar settlement than the pursuit of the war[61] and leaders of the emigré communist parties in Moscow were instructed to prepare Popular Front type policies for their countries well before the war ended. On the other hand, there was a clear ambiguity in Soviet policies in that, as Pethybridge among others has noted, Stalin had little reason to impose reparations and ransack Eastern Europe, as was done in the early postwar years, if Soviet domination of the area were already envisaged.[62] Seton-Watson identifies three stages in Eastern European postwar revolutions: genuine coalition (with a common short-term programme, pursuit of fascists, fairly radical social reforms and relative freedom of speech, except for the taboo of criticizing the Soviet Union); bogus coalition (with Communist Party dominated coalitions, bourgeois parties driven into opposition, restrictions on distributing opposition newspapers when Communist Party controlled unions 'refused to print calumnies against the people's authorities', and opposition meetings broken up while the police 'objectively' looked on); and monolithic regimes (when well-purged social democratic parties were fused into the Communist Party and all open opposition was suppressed).[63]

The Hungarian case follows this periodization closely. During the phase of genuine coalition, that is to say until mid 1946, the Soviet Union and the Hungarian Communist Party probably believed in the Popular Front strategy, and saw Soviet-style socialism as only a long-term goal. All that was inevitable at this stage was that the Communist Party would play an important role in whatever polity emerged. Writing in 1945 István Bibó, member of the National Peasant Party and proponent of the 'Third Way', did not consider the 'dictatorship of the proletariat' as a realistic possibility. He saw the fear of it, and the policies such a fear elicited, as a real danger.[64] Similarly, Lukács, in his criticism of Bibó in 1945, argued with great conviction that the 'dictatorship of the proletariat' was not on the cards.

Nevertheless the Communist Party's political authority belied its electoral support, and this can only be attributed to its privileged links with the occupying forces. In the immediate postwar chaos, the Communist Party had Soviet transport at its disposal, while the other parties struggled to find vehicles.[65] As the situation stabilized, the Communist Party took over the Ministry of Transport in May 1945, placing Gerő at its head.[66] The Communist Party also managed to establish dominance of the trade union movement, despite the unions' traditional ties with the Social Democratic Party. The Social Democrats were disadvantaged because many of their leaders were in camps and because they lacked the Communist Party's discipline.[67] The political manoeuvrings of 1947 might be explicable in terms of the Soviet Union's desire for simply a friendly government in Hungary rather than a socialist ally, but by 1948, after the creation of Cominform, the policy of going forward to the 'dictatorship of the proletariat' and Seton-Watson's 'monolithic regime' was clearly in place. By 1949, the choice of economic model was beyond doubt, with Soviet advisors present in every ministry.[68]

On the other hand, even allowing for Soviet intentions and the advantage that alliance with the Soviet Union gave the Communist Party over its political opponents, the Communist Party did have a job to do in

1947–48. Rákosi's 'salami tactics' required political skill and judgement, and the job would have been considerably more difficult without left-wing Social Democrats who, despite doubts about the Communist Party, believed in working-class unity and the reality of threats from the political right. Even during Seton-Watson's 'bogus coalition' there were political choices to be made, and choices based on an analysis of the state of international politics, not just the fear of imprisonment. A key figure in this process was György Marosán, a left-wing Social Democrat. To the Social Democratic wing of the labour movement he is seen as a traitor, if not a secret lifelong communist.[69] Yet many on the left of the Labour Party (and further left) would sympathize with his reluctance to be won over by Denis Healey (then a young worker in Labour's International Office) to an anti-Soviet, anti-communist, anti-Marxist version of socialism;[70] many would understand the desire to create a united labour movement in the face of the machinations of international capital, with its secret plots on the one hand and its economic aid with strings attached on the other; and few would predict that the reward one might receive for toiling ceaselessly to achieve the political goal of party unity would be imprisonment.[71] Nor could the merger of the parties and the takeover of power have been achieved without substantial grassroots support. Many, especially the young, were impressed by the activity of the Communist Party, the fact that it got on and implemented its policies, compared with what was seen as constant political bickering within and between the other parties. There was widespread popular opposition to the old order. Despite fears concerning the 'dictatorship of the proletariat', the Communist Party was the least compromised by the old regime, and was seen to be the party doing most to prevent its return.[72]

If there were moments, at least, when postwar Eastern Europe was not acting out a Soviet foreign policy scenario and when genuine political choices could be made, how did the Popular Front policies fare, and what alternatives were offered by the other parties? The Small-holders' Party stood for private property and economic democracy and the introduction of progressive income tax rather than existing consumption taxes. In conception it was a party of peasants and a section of the bourgeoisie, although forces further to the right gathered around it because of the Allied Control Commission's restrictions on party formation. It was a party in favour of Anglo-Saxon economic and political structures, but with a Dutch or Danish model for agriculture. The provisional government's policies were seen as the basis for government, rather than the first step in a longer-term process.[73] In the inflationary period, it had not supported intervention.[74] In March 1947 the party announced that its three-year reconstruction plan was in preparation and would appear in book form. But when parliament debated the plan proposals in the spring of 1947, it turned out that the Smallholders' Party had no elaborated plan, and party representatives admitted that they did not deal separately with questions of production and finance.[75] Yet this is not surprising. The Smallholders' Party, as a right-of-centre party, believed in the market rather than planning. Its programme entailed creating conditions, political and economic, in which it was advantageous to invest in Hungary and then 'leaving it up to the market'. As a party spokesman expressed it on another occasion, 'private capital has to be stroked and coaxed to get the desire to invest going in the country'.[76]

The policies of the National Peasant Party were restricted, in terms of concrete proposals, to issues directly concerning the peasantry. On the other hand, much of the discussion about the 'Third Way' has to be seen in the context of an internal National Peasant Party debate in 1945 concerning the degree of support to be given to the Communist and Smallholders' parties. The 'populist' politicians in this debate, such as Illyes, forwarded 'Third Way' policies;[77] but the left wing won the day. The National Peasant Party agreed not to distance itself from the Communist Party and, from then on, supported such issues as the nationalization of the banks. Nevertheless, it retained an independent agricultural policy and supported small-scale private property.[78]

The 'received wisdom' of the later Party establishment was that the 'Third Way' thesis was just an ideology of peasant romanticism propounded by Hungary's populist writers of the 1930s. It was rather more than that, but it was certainly more successful in expressing a political ideal than proposing an elaborated economic strategy. István Bibó, not a member of the Party's leadership, is the best known proponent of the thesis in the postwar context:

> those who want to make Hungary a Soviet client state are traitors, those who want to restore the Habsburgs in Hungary are traitors, those who try to place before Hungary that false alternative that the choice is only between these two are doubly traitors because between the two there is a third way, the only correct way, the possibility of a democratic independent free Hungary following a policy of internally balanced but radical reform.[79]

What this entailed in terms of day-to-day politics, when stripped of the lengthy bemoaning of the repeated injustices fate had directed towards the nationalist aspirations of the Hungarian people, was a purge of the extremists of right and left and a strengthening of links between the Social Democrats and the National Peasant Party, rather than the proposed alliances with the Communist and Smallholders' parties respectively. What it meant economically was the initial adoption of capitalist policies to start reconstruction, attract foreign loans and stimulate entrepreneurial spirit and the willingness to invest, which would then be followed by a policy supporting the formation of cooperatives and similar self-governing bodies.[80] The only concrete proposal with economic implications in Bibó's writings at this time is the suggestion that Hungary adopt Erdei's ideas about developing, as a model for regional reform, the 'Agrarian Towns'[81] of the Great Plain, with their close ties between town life and the agricultural hinterland.[82]

The Social Democrats had the most elaborated strategy, in the form of their three-year plan proposal in 1947. The party had from the start favoured an economy with a strong private sector, but where the state played an important role. It did not propose nationalization of the banks, but was in favour of strongly progressive taxation and state control of credit and foreign trade, using the institutions developed in the 1930s and during the war.[83] The Communist Party inspired three-year plan that was actually implemented was widely regarded as a 'success'. Its economic targets were reached six months early, and success was clear to all in the rebuilding of Budapest's 'chain bridge'.[84] But it is difficult to state categorically that the Social Democratic three-year plan would have fared as well. It was premissed on foreign loans, and these were not forthcoming, although they might have been in a different political climate.

The inevitably of nationalization is equally problematic. Certainly, from 1947 onwards, Popular Front socialist control rather than nationalization was not given a chance. Nationalization was seen as a good in itself, as indeed it was in most socialist circles in Western Europe at the time. Popular Front control of industry was used by the Communist Party simply as part of the strategy of a 'dry road' to nationalization.[85] Reparations obligations, price, tax, credit and foreign trade policies necessitated by the financial chaos of inflation and stabilization were all used to drive companies into state hands. On the other hand, many of the pressures used to squeeze the private sector into state hands were socialist policies that most radical reformers would see as good in themselves, and would want to achieve independently of any ulterior motive. If such socialist goals as the establishment of the eight-hour day, the introduction of social welfare benefits, higher company taxation to fund them, and price controls to protect workers and consumers could not be achieved without the economy slipping into state hands, then perhaps nationalization was inevitable.

Certainly the combination of Popular Front policies and political uncertainty was sufficient to discourage foreign investment, either by companies or in the form of foreign loans. Even after the stabilization of the currency, or perhaps because of the nature of that stabilization, Western governments were, unlike after the First World War, reluctant to lend to Hungary. Foreign companies with Hungarian interests were also loth to invest significantly in such a climate. MAORT, the American-owned oil company, declared itself unwilling to prospect for more oil[86] (this was one of the issues in the show trial of 1948),[87] and General Electric of the USA proved reluctant to meet requests by United Incandescent's management for new investment funds.[88] There is also evidence that companies falsified figures: Goldberger companies presented costs figures four million forints too high to exaggerate the extent it was suffering from government wage control; and Shell declared a loss of 3.27 million forints when in fact it had made a profit of 1.69 million.[89]

Similarly, whilst Soviet foreign policy considerations above all else led to Hungary's rejection of the Marshall Plan, it is not clear that the Popular Front policies of the postwar years could ever have meshed with it. They certainly did not gel with the underlying economic assumptions of the plan as originally conceived. Pan-European aspects of the plan posed a threat to national sovereignty, and its assumption of maintaining existing comparative advantage within Europe excluded from the start any policy of accelerated industrialization or economic restructuring. Popular Front policies blended no better with the Marshall Plan as originally conceived than did the policies of the British left with the Economic Community in the 1970s. The Plan, amongst other things, required European countries to provide guarantees that private American investments in Europe could be converted back into dollars for repatriation to the USA and offset against European Recovery Programme (Marshall Plan) grants, and that 50 per cent of the goods shipped under the European Recovery Programme be carried in American bottoms at American freight rates, with 25 per cent (in 1949 12.5 per cent) of all wheat exports financed by the programme to be exported as flour milled in the USA.[90] On the other hand, the Marshall Plan was less onerous in its implementation than its conception; and, after the French government had taken the necessary political step of excluding communists from power, it was allowed significant economic leeway, and managed to implement the Monnet Plan, a combination of interventionist policies and indicative planning,[91] under the auspices of Marshall aid.

Although the Communist Party clearly manipulated the danger of right-wing conspiracies to its own ends, right-wing forces were nevertheless active in Popular Front Hungary. In Bibó's view, not only did reactionary forces exist in Hungary in 1945, but also the danger of the restoration of reaction was somewhat greater than that of the dictatorship of the proletariat. Bibó also accepted that Ferenc Nagy and the Smallholders' Party leadership had had discussions with people associated with right-wing extremist groups.[92] Given the international situation, the presence of the Soviet Army, and the strength of the Communist Party, such political conspiracies posed no significant threat. In a different climate, however, they could pose a genuine threat to a Popular Front government. The existence of extreme right-wing organizations in Western Europe is well known, as are their connections with government, especially such crucial areas of government as the secret service.[93] The ability of the right-wing establishment to soften the edges of radical left-wing governments is equally well documented.[94] Right-wing conspiracies constituted no threat to Hungarian Popular Front policies because the Ministry of the Interior and the police were under Communist Party control and protected by the Allied Control Commission under Soviet control. The situation would be altogether different if Popular Front policies were being implemented in the context of right-wing control of the Home Office and secret service.

The history of UK socialist local authorities' toehold in economic planning throws up interesting comparisons. The private sector in London in the first half of the 1980s was no more cooperative than it had been in Hungary in the 1940s: GLEB planning staff were refused entry to companies; workers were not given time off to attend GLEB-arranged meetings; and companies formed shadow subsidiaries not covered by GLEB contract compliance.[95] At the same time, some GLC administrators hindered GLC policy. GLEB 'project executives' did not always share the Board's non-commercial objectives, while the GLC's Valuation Department obstructed attempts to publicize the availability of industrial units in the ethnic and women's press. The council constantly suffered from an absence of 'red experts'.[96]

More than this, one of the constant themes of the experience is that the GLC had insufficient control. While the GLC itself did not call for the extra degree of control that is afforded by ownership and hence some form of nationalization, the ideas emanating from the Direct Labour Organization's Popular Planning Unit called for a solution that went beyond contract compliance to the creation of a National Building Corporation.[97] One problem that the GLC experienced which Hungarian socialists were saved from because of political control of the Ministry of the Interior was that of legal obstacles to socialist practice. In Hungary legal niceties could be and were ignored, and the opposition saw no purpose in making use of the law to further its interests. The GLC, on the other hand, faced both legal judgements (often inspired by court actions by right-wing councils) and a legislative framework which obliged services to be put out to tender, limited the conditions regarding union membership that could be built into contracts and, by permitting only 'reasonable' intervention into the economy, questioned the basis for subsidizing public transport and the acceptability of awarding pay rises to low-paid council workers.[98]

In the theoretical section of an article speculating about the socialist bodies necessary to cope with such non-cooperation, Diane Elson has suggested the formation of a Price and Wage Commission, a Consumer Union, a Regulator of Economic Planning and a Central Office of Economic Planning, all well resourced and with powers to enforce disclosure and seize company records.[99] Hungary, in the Popular Front period, dealt with the 'red expert' problem by removing the so-called 'B list'-compromised administrators in 1946,[100] and introducing trusted Party cadres in 1948. It dealt with economic cooperation via the Ministry of Reconstruction, the Supreme Economic Council, the Materials and Prices Office, an economic police, and works councils in monitoring price rises. The institutions were not so very different.

Mackintosh and Wainwright, in their account of the GLC experience, state that 'where the GLC failed to develop a popular basis for its policies by working with organized groups of Londoners, then the policies tended to founder or become captive to establishment wisdom',[101] but that 'efforts of the GLC to democratize economic policy were bedevilled by ... [the] assumption of consensus'.[102] 'To learn from the GLC would be to make democracy a central aim of Labour economic policy.'[103] But what sorts of institutions will administer that democracy, and can they remain democratic when strongly held differences of interest remain? Those active in the Labour-controlled GLC acknowledge that more questions were raised on the formal structures for industrial democracy than answers.[104] They note further that participation was always within the constraints of the GLC holding on to the final power of decision,[105] and that politicians, especially Labour ones, have a strong bias towards staying in control of what is going on.[106] Goodwill cannot be relied on. Many in the Hungarian labour movement had goodwill, yet this did not prevent the institutions listed above from turning into vehicles of oppression when a strong political interest (the Communist Party), backed by the security forces, decided to assert its will against that of others. Institutional and legal guarantees are also required. Discussion of such issues among Western socialists is not so well advanced that they can view Eastern European failings in this regard with complacence.

Neither the Social Democratic policy of continuing the Popular Front nor Bibó's 'Third Way' was a realistic alternative in the particular historical context of Eastern Europe immediately following the Second World War. In the Cold War, post-Yalta climate, there really were only two alternatives: capitalism and Soviet communism. But even at a more favourable conjuncture, many socialists will be dissatisfied with Popular Front policies, based on control rather than ownership, given the economic and political opposition they engender. In the context of non-cooperation, if not sabotage, by domestic capitalists and foreign bankers, it is understandable that the left demands extensive nationalization, if not Soviet planning, as a means of asserting greater control over the economy than that which was achieved by French-style planning of the Monnet Plan. This was as much the case in Hungary in 1948 as it might be for any future radical socialist government in the West. But, faced with such opposition and the urgency and overwhelming importance (for those carrying it out) of the task in hand, the descent into a disregard of alternative viewpoints is all too easy.

3

The Heroic Age of
Socialist Planning

The purpose of this chapter is to demonstrate that the traditional model of central planning does not seem inherently implausible and is quite consistent with popular variants of economic components of a 'socialist project'; but it does not and cannot work.

It seems so straightforward. Since the 'invisible hand' of the market manifestly does not meet automatically the needs of the population, socialisms's task must be to counter market forces and restructure production towards needs and the creation of socially useful products. And such production, if it is not to be subordinated to the market, must be regulated by planning. Thus, a GLC pamphlet states: 'It's only common sense: producing for need';[1] or the Lucas Aerospace Combined Shop Stewards Committee: 'We therefore evolved the idea of a campaign for the right to work on socially useful products';[2] or the Popular plan for London's Docklands: 'The plan will start from our needs, rather than developers' profits';[3] or the authors of *The ABC of Communism*: 'The communist method of production presupposes ... that production is not for the market, but for use';[4] or Soviet economists of the 1950s when asked what reasoning governs the plan: 'What is socially necessary'.[5] In addition, Marx's oeuvre has bequeathed an arsenal of non-market economic categories that might be used to build a needs-oriented, planned economic system. Marx's labour theory of value reveals the true engine of value creation behind the phenomenal forms of prices. All that is required to establish and plan a non-market, needs-oriented economy, then, is to apply these underlying value-creating rules in a rational manner.

But it is not that simple. There are two fundamental problems with the strategy. First, Marx's discussion of how needs might be first identified and then compared lacks realism. For Marx, such decisions are made by the social totality, or by its concretization as the 'association of producers'. But, under realistic social relations of large-scale production with an extensive division of labour and a differentiated market, in the context of a complex social environment, the arbiter of needs inevitably becomes the party which acts in the interests of the working class, whose interests, once capitalism has been transcended, are identical with those of humanity. Second, even if an arbitration scheme could be devised for identifying and comparing needs, there is the problem of what unit of measurement should be used in comparisons. Marx's labour theory of value is of little help. The most theoretically satisfactory solutions to problems associated with Marx's labour theory of value place value categories into an intellectual sphere entirely different from the mundane business of determining prices. Such theoretical rectitude is small comfort for those struggling to implement socialism in practice. All practical attempts to make use of categories derived from the labour theory of value to determine prices have degenerated into costs-plus pricing, and the debate has concentrated on costs plus what?

The theoretical and practical problems of implementing Marxist economic theory in practice will be considered below. First, however, the economic model introduced in Hungary following the Great Change of 1948 and the adoption of Soviet planning methods will be analysed and the degree to which they are consistent with a socialist project considered.

The Soviet Model Applied

The model of socialism Hungary's leaders introduced was one that their Soviet comrades had already developed; Hungarian planners, like their colleagues in Eastern Europe, simply had to implement an existing blue-print. This blueprint will be familiar to many, but it is worth considering some details of its Hungarian implementation. The model has had a bad press because of its association with Stalin, but it has much in common with models produced by other radical socialists who see the need for both nationalization and planning.

When examining planned economies, it is useful to distinguish three analytically distinct features: the planning system, the regulation system (the methods used to ensure actors behave in the desired manner) and the organization system (the physical form that the economic agents take).[6]

The planning system

The planning system applied in the Soviet Union of the 1930s and Hungary of the early 1950s consisted of the hierarchical disaggregation of needs drawn up in consultation with all levels in the planning hierarchy. The Council of Ministers, via the People's Economic Council, which was established at the end of 1949 to coordinate the planning bodies and the economic ministries, determined the overall framework of needs. The Planning Office then used the technique of 'material balances' (contrasting known sources of goods with requirements and determining how much more of that good and any necessary intermediary goods would be necessary to achieve balance) to construct approximate pre-plan figures. These pre-plans were then passed on to the ministries, which worked out more detailed yearly and quarterly plan directives for each of a number of (initially twenty-nine) industrial directorates. The directorates in turn drew up detailed plan directives for the enterprises under their control, which then drew up plan suggestions for their divisions, plants, and so on down the chain to workers at their benches. These plan suggestions were then reaggregated at every level in the hierarchy. From these reaggregated figures, the Planning Office constructed its actual plan figures which were subsequently disaggregated all the way down the hierarchy again. Thus, national needs were assessed by a process of consultation at all levels in the production hierarchy and then expressed in ever more concrete terms until they became the individual production quota for a certain good produced by a certain worker throughout the national economy.[7]

The targets passed down this hierarchy were predominantly in quantitative units. For example, the plan for heavy industry in the first five-year-plan period consisted of the following items:

(1) production value to reach 7,725 million forints, a 138 per cent increase on 1949;
(2) the value of machinery to increase from 185 to 610 million forints;
(3) the number of tractors to increase from 2,600 to 4,600 units;
(4) railway carriages and trucks to increase from 4,850 to 10,000 units;
(5) the number of lorries to increase from 3,200 to 9,000 units;
(6) the number of motor cycles to increase from 12,000 to 23,000 units;
(7) steam, electrical and diesel engines to be produced to the value of 520 million forints;
(8) the production should commence of, for example, trolley buses,

harvesters, diesel tractors, railway cranes, not then manufactured in Hungary;

(9) a total of 4,214 million forints should be invested in a smelting works, machine tool factories, milling industry machinery, machinery for the textile and light industries, oil extraction plants, diesel motor factories, crane factories, screw factories, radiator factories, other manufacturing industry plants;

(10) a new steel works and railway wheel factory should be created in the Borsod industrial region, and a new bridge and iron structure factory by the Danube.

The plan was enshrined in law; and at each level the responsible parties were under a legal obligation to implement it, even though both law and plan were silent about where the necessary resources to meet targets should come from. Plans included, in addition to increased production, sections on labour relations, materials supply, investment and renewal and finance; and separate administrative apparatuses existed for these plan components. There was, for example, a Wages and Labour Affairs Department of the Secretariat of the Council of Ministers, and labour affairs departments of the industrial directorates, and of each enterprise.

The regulation system

The most important element in the regulation system under the Stalinist model of central planning was the system of managerial premiums which constituted 'an extraordinarily powerful set of financial incentives'.[8] Top management could receive premiums of over a third of their basic salaries for successful plan completion. Workers' bonuses paid out of the enterprise director's special funds were, at 1.2–1.3 per cent of annual earnings, insufficient to provide an incentive, while the premiums of technicians were not clearly related to work done and depended largely on factors beyond their control. Those in overall charge of the enterprise had a clear incentive to fulfil plans; but what was meant by plan fulfilment? Kornai's work is the first empirical account of the operation of the Stalinist economy in Eastern Europe, and it describes the situation in 1955 after Hungary's New Course (see Chapter 4) and intense discussion by economists concerning the necessity of making the economic system more sensitive to costs. By this time, premiums depended not simply on the meeting of production plans, but also on cost reduction plans, the 'corrective condition' of ensuring planned wage and salary outlays were not exceeded, and special 'conditions of payment' established by the industrial directorate. Nevertheless, although other targets and indices such as profits plans or priority technical measures or over-time were included in plans, management only paid heed to those which were related to bonus payments. And, despite genuflexions in the direction of reducing costs, this really only meant fulfilment of quarterly and annual production plans.

Under such a system, prices did not play an 'active role' regulating behaviour by reflecting scarcity and balancing supply and demand. Rather they played an ultimately ideological role. Prices were not simply an accounting unit to help enterprises in the general business of quantification, they were also an expression of the fact that planning allowed the law of value to be subsumed to social and political goals. Sharp distinctions could be made between domestic producer prices and consumer prices, between domestic producer prices and foreign trade prices denominated in rubles, or foreign trade denominated in dollars, so allowing social policies such as the maintenance of low consumer prices for essential goods, or national political policies such as building up domestic industry, to take place in isolation from market signals.[9]

Interest rates and credit control mechanisms played no role in a regulatory system of this kind. Decisions about investment were made centrally and the necessary funds made available by central bodies to the enterprises at no cost. Similarly exchange rates played no active role because foreign trade was under the administrative control of the central planning bodies. In wages and incomes policy, state control was less direct. Although most wage-rates and norms were set centrally, a degree of indirect control was exercised between 1950 and 1956 by 'relative wage-bill' regulation. Under this system, each enterprise received, as part of its labour relations plan, a permitted wage bill based on the expected increase in the labour force and a planned, usually rather small, increase in wages. The relative wage-bill principle stated that for every percentage overfulfilment of the gross production value target, a similar percentage increase in the size of the wage bill was permitted. The wage bill also had to be reduced by any percentage by which the production value target was not met. Finally, and by no means insignificantly in the context of a regulatory system, the central authorities appointed enterprise management.

The organization system

The organizational system under the classic model of central planning is characterized by two features. First, productive activity was fitted into the branch ministry structure. Second, within that structure, enterprise activity was 'profilized' and rationalized to avoid 'wasteful' duplication.

In June 1949, the Ministry for Industrial Affairs, which had already been restructured along branch lines, was split into the Ministry for Heavy Industry, and the Ministry for Light Industry; and the Ministry of Commerce was split into Ministries for Foreign Trade and Domestic Trade. At the end of 1950, Heavy Industry was divided into the Metallurgy and Engineering Ministry and the Ministry for Mining and Energy Affairs. Beneath the ministry came the industrial directorates (*glavki* in Soviet terminology), twenty-nine of which had been created in 1948. For example, the Ministry of Light Industry supervised six directorates, for: cotton trades; flax and hemp trades; woollen trades; paper trades; printing trades; and leather and footwear industries. Each directorate in turn supervised a number of (in Light Industry up to eighteen) enterprises.[10]

Within each branch, 'it was necessary to reorganize rationally the various factories and divide production in such a way that they should specialize in their production in the most convenient lines for them ... for instance ... the production of agricultural machinery of MAVAG ... has been transferred to the plant Hoffer-Schrantz, and MAVAG concentrated on the production of transport equipment.'[11] In cases where a directorate inherited an enterprise division which did not fall within its sphere of activity, it had three courses of action. First, it could create an independent enterprise that could then be transferred to the appropriate directorate. Second, it could merge it with another enterprise under a different directorate. Third, it could simply wind it up and sell off its assets. Within its own economic profile, the desire to rationalize resulted in a single enterprise being created out of several scattered units which then began to specialize in a single product or group products. As a result of these two processes, there was an increase in concentration and a significant decrease in the number of independent enterprises. Between 1946 and 1948 there were over 4,600 independent units in manufacturing industry. In 1949, the figure had fallen to 3,937, and by 1950 the figure had reached 1,632.[12]

The Soviet Model and the Socialist Project

This is not the place to demonstrate in detail that the planning, regulation and organization systems of the Soviet model conformed in most crucial respects to the model of economic planning that can be derived from Marx. As Brus has argued convincingly, the works of Marx and Engels suggest five features for a socialist economy: (1) direct, ex ante regulation of the social division of labour; (2) direct determination of labour input coefficients for both living and embodied labour; (3) equilibrium of supply and demand in physical units; (4) the distribution of the social product in accordance with the satisfaction of general needs, and at the same time the allocation of the fund intended for individual consumption according to the amount of labour contributed; 5) centralization of the saving and investment decisions.[13] With the exception of the application of labour coefficients, which will be considered in greater detail below, these characteristics well describe both the Soviet and Hungarian planning models.

Rather, this section will draw Western parallels. The Soviet model is not dissimilar from that suggested by Mandel in his defence of socialist planning in 1986.[14] He too has a model of disaggregation from the planning office at the top to the enterprise at the bottom. The key difference between Mandel and Hungarian practice is that whereas Mandel refers to self-managed bodies at all levels in his hierarchy, Hungary followed Soviet practice and relied on a combination of one-man management and worker involvement via the Party organization. The issue of self-management and its assumed ability to transcend all inter-enterprise conflicts of interest will be considered below. Here we are considering models of planning and the relationship between levels in a hierarchy. Soviet practice and Mandelian theory are surprisingly similar in this respect. Likewise, the proponents of 'socially useful production', when they turn to concrete proposals that extend beyond asking the state to fund more social programmes or to take a less narrowly monetarist view, come close to advocating Soviet practice, although always with a caveat about the absence of democracy. One participant at a series of seminars at the Centre for Alternative Industrial Technological Strategies, for example, advocated Soviet-type banking.[15] Perhaps not surprisingly, those on the left who have been most critical of Labour's Alternative Economic Strategy or the GLC's London Industrial Strategy have been enthusiastic about adopting Mandel's (and by extension the Soviet) model of planning.[16]

In addition to the planning model, there are other features of the Hungary of the 1950s which are in line with the demands of various members of the radical left today. In Hungary social equality was stressed, as was the creation of a new socialist morality. In industry, wage and income differentials were small and were accompanied by a correspondingly high emphasis on moral incentives. This took the form of labour competition and movements to improve the quantity or quality of production, or the cleanliness of the workplace and so on. These began in earnest to celebrate Stalin's seventieth birthday on 21 December 1949 when numerous plants announced performance to match Zoltán Pozsonyi, a bricklayer who, a month earlier, had fulfilled his norm 1,000 per cent. By 1952, numerous movements were in existence: the socialist labour competition (to perform better tasks already allotted); the Stakhanovist movement; the Stakhanovist support movement (technicians who advised Stakhanovists); the innovation movement; ten- or five-minute movements (workers who had committed themselves to be ready to work five or ten minutes early); the Voroshin movement (to keep the workplace tidy); Nazarova and Kuznetsov movements (to keep the machine a worker used in good repair); the Gazda movement (to make use of waste products); the Deák movement for foremen (to look after their workers); the Roder movement (to help those who fell behind in their production tasks); the Loy movement (to increase production); the Csorba movement to save coal; a movement to reduce machinery downtime; the Lozinsky movement to prepare figures and statistics more quickly; and the 'look after yourself and your workmates' movement to encourage mutual concern for health.[17]

The new socialist culture enjoyed much of the excitement of creating something new. The building of the new towns themselves became a part of contemporary culture.[18] New university departments were created for topics – such as Marxist economics – which had not previously been taught and for which there were no professors.[19] The army had to be restructured with a new guard of politically trained officers. New publishing houses had to be set up to publish Marxist literature. New banks were established, as we have seen, untainted by capitalist practices. A whole new cultural apparatus had to be set up from scratch and those who were politically trustworthy found themselves rapidly in positions of responsibility. On the other hand, bourgeois science was rejected: psychology, for example, was abolished as a scientific subject on the grounds that class position was the true determinant of human activity; and cybernetics was rejected because the idea of self-governing systems was incompatible with class struggle.

Culture was to be brought to the reach of the working people,[20] and the cultural monopoly of the former ruling class was to be abolished by education. The new publishing houses produced an increased volume of books, mainly Hungarian and Russian classics, with a sprinkling of socialist Western authors. There was also an increase in the number of schools and universities, although there were proportionately even more new students than there were schools and universities to put them in. Between 1950 and 1952, 70 per cent of money spent on education went on building new universities – the heavy industry university at Miskolc, the chemical industry university at Veszprém, and the technical university at Budapest – although the percentage was reduced to 50 per cent in 1953.[21] There were increases too in the number of visits to theatres and cinemas, in the number of libraries, and so on. Cultural centres were built in small towns and music schools established in the provinces. And new priorities were introduced into medical training, with more attention being paid to preventative medicine and community health.

In terms of the method of planning and the goals of social policy in the Hungary of the early 1950s, there was much that Western socialists of today would find familiar. The model was internally consistent and, despite some Stalinist distortions, exhibited priorities which socialists still consider to be important. Yet it did not work. Indeed, as shall be argued, it could not work. In order to understand why, consideration must be given first to theoretical problems in Marxist theory and then to the empirical problems that developed in Hungary as theory was put into practice.

Theoretical Problems

Totality and needs

The first question raised by the notion of planning for need is: whose needs? How are needs determined? Marx has little to say on the topic, since, in his conception, under socialism needs simply do not compete. As Heller has reminded us, Marx's three major discoveries (that workers sell labour power not labour, that surplus value is the general form behind the phenomenal forms of profit, interest and ground rent, and the significance of use value) are all built around the concept of need, yet Marx never actually defines this concept.[22] Concepts of need are treated by him as historical–philosophical, that is, as anthropological value categories. As such, they are not defined within the economic system,[23] despite the fact that Marx's analysis of the society of associated producers is philosophically founded upon the concept of the system of needs:[24] 'How are needs and production matched? The "associated producers" ... will measure (a) needs and (b) disposable labour time and will fix (c) the labour time necessary for each activity.'[25] Yet,

> who makes the decision about how capacity should be allocated? ... Marx's reply ... is everyone.... But how can every individual make such decisions? Marx did not answer this question because for him it did not arise.... In his [Marx's] opinion the category of interest will be irrelevant in the future, and there will therefore be no group interests or conflicts of interest. The clear common interest of every member of society, apart from the satisfaction of necessary needs ... will be the reduction of labour time. This is possible only through the maximum of rationalization. Consequently every individual strives for the same thing, namely the maximum of rationalization; and the manner in which decision-making is carried out is of no consequence whatsoever.[26]

But conflicts of interest do arise.

> Efforts by the GLC to democratize economic policy were bedevilled at the
> start by the assumption of consensus between the GLC and what at first was
> seen as a relatively homogeneous constituency.... This assumption of
> consensus tended to run through enterprise planning, industrial democracy,
> and local plans for area development.... Issues concerned with anti-racism
> and women's employment led to the most drastic breaches in this assumption
> of consensus. The reason of course is that they illustrate most strongly a
> central problem for popular planning: that there are conflicts of interest
> among working people.[27]

These problems are magnified in the context of models of socialist
planning. The assumption of a unity of interest imbues 'Stalinist' one-
man management and 'Trotskyist' workers' self-management alike. For
the centralized Stalin model, one-man or one-party management is
unproblematic because all share the same real interest in any case. For
'Trotskyist' critics of central planning, conflicts of interest are recognized
between management (or the bureaucracy) and labour. But, it is
assumed, once these have been transcended by implementing workers'
self-management, inter-enterprise, inter-sectoral and intra-hierarchical
differences of interest will all automatically disappear. Following this
reasoning, the interests of a self-managed enterprise will never conflict
with the wishes of a national, democratically elected congress of
workers' councils. As Elson has remarked in reply to Mandel, ' "self-
management" functions rather as a *deus ex machina* to displace
"bureaucracy" '.[28] Much of the empirical evidence that will follow
demonstrates the fallacy of the assumption of an identity of interests
between planners and managers; and this conflict of interest does not
disappear simply because decisions within the enterprise are made more
democratically. Nor will a structural difference of interest of some kind
disappear once it has been demonstrated that the overriding factor in
defining enterprise interest in Hungary's (and other Eastern European)
model of socialist planning was the self-interest of enterprise top
management in its bonuses.

Even before the problem of costing alternative strategies is introduced, conflicting interests exist; and it is disingenuous to assume that
they will disappear under socialism, even if racism disappears, even if
sexism is abolished. Who will arbitrate such conflicts? Marx gives no
answer in his discussion of needs and the society of associated
producers, but one is implicit in the tenets of Marxism, especially as
extended by Lenin: the Party. If, as Marx and later Lukács argue, under
socialism the interests of the working class are those of humanity,[29] and
if the Party, which for Marx and Lenin and Lukács in its vanguard role

represents the real interests of the working class,[30] is still around,[31] the Party becomes the natural candidate for arbitrator between conflicting interests and needs.

Totality and value

The fact that the Party becomes the de facto arbiter of needs and competing interests in a socialist economy does not resolve the question of which criteria it should base its judgement upon. This is not a problem for Marx, because his society of associated producers is defined as one of abundance.

> Marx's assumption of a free association of producers where planning is merely technical organization of things in a marketless economy is only possible in a society where expenditure of technically and socially homogeneous labour constitutes the only scarce resource which needs to be economized, that is in a society of abundance ... [which entails] the very slow change – in practice constancy within the life-span of one generation – of the consumption need structure.[32]

Abundance entails

> a sufficiency to meet requirements at zero price leaving no reasonable person dissatisfied or seeking more of anything ... [it therefore] ... removes conflicts over resource allocation since by definition there is enough for everyone, and so there are no mutually exclusive choices.[33]

The assumption of unchanging needs and abundance contradicts Marx's anthropological concept of mankind as a self-creating social animal,[34] and lacks realism in any conceivable complex society, let alone the sorts of societies whose political situation is such that a radical socialist government has a chance of coming to power.

These problems aside, the notion implicit in Marx, and developed by his disciples, that such measurement as has to be made can, following the labour theory of value, be carried out in units of socially homogeneous labour has been open to much criticism, which began as soon as the first volume of *Capital* appeared.[35] When the third volume was published, Böhm-Bawerk used criticisms of the theory to deliver what he felt was the *coup de grâce* to the whole Marxist endeavour in his *Karl Marx and the Close of His System* (1896).[36]

Marx's materialist dialectic required him to put mankind and the social relations individuals enter into at the centre of his philosophical conception. Values were produced by societies; societies were not the concrete manifestations of immanent ideas. Not surprisingly, Marx took over the classical view of Smith amd Ricardo[37] that labour was the source of value. Despite the fact that, at a very general level, materialism required only that value be established somehow in the context of the play of social and production relations and mankind's struggle with nature (which would allow scarcity and opportunity cost to be included in the equation), he stuck to the labour theory of value because to abandon it would be to jeopardize two concepts central to his critique of capitalism: surplus value and, to a lesser extent, alienation. Marxism would lose much of its force if capitalist production relations did not lead to the extraction of surplus value[38] or mankind's alienation, because of the existence of private property, from its 'species being'.[39] But, in the view of Marx's critics, this critical force is gained at the expense of economic competence; that is, the theory is refuted by economic facts.

As Sweezy explains, for Marx, 'commodities exchange in proportion to the quantity of labour (stored-up and living) embodied in them. Surplus value (or profit) ... is a function of the quantity of living labour alone',[40] surplus value being the value created in the period between the time necessary to ensure the reproduction of labour power and the time actually laboured.

> This implies that equal investments of capital will yield different rates of profit depending on whether more or less is put into wages (living labour) or material accessories (stored-up labour) on the other. But this theory contradicts the fact that under capitalism equal investments, regardless of their composition, tend to yield equal profits.[41]

That is to say, Marx's theory expects more surplus value, and hence more profit, to be extracted from labour-intensive investment.[42] Yet this is simply not the case. It is in Volume III of *Capital* that Marx attempts to resolve the problem by recognizing the tendency towards equal rates of profit. He relates the resulting 'prices of production' to the value categories used in Volume I by taking an average, over different capitals with different organic compositions, of surplus value which he equates, by definition, with the average rate of profit.[43] He concludes that prices will equal the value of a constant plus variable capital, plus the average surplus value or (and this is identical) the average rate of profit.[44] Marx then shows that, whatever the proportion of constant capital converted into value in the production process, the price of the good will be (used-up) constant capital plus (used-up) variable capital plus the average rate of profit. His introduction of varying rates of used-up constant capital makes it even clearer that the price at which any individual good is sold will deviate from its value.[45]

Marx accommodates this theoretical modification in two ways. First, he increases the degree of abstraction in his value theory. The basic value equations still hold, but numbers can only be put to them at a high level of aggregation. At the level of individual capitals, the relationships still hold, but do so in the background unrelated to values at which goods exchange. Second, paradoxically, a level of abstraction is removed. Marx was not as consistent as his later commentators in separating 'value' and 'price' categories. In *Capital*, Volume III, the combination of constant capital (actually embodied labour) plus variable capital is mostly referred to as cost-price, and average surplus value as average profit. The price of production becomes 'its cost price plus the average profit'.[46] Labour might be the source of all value which determines ultimately the price at which goods will exchange, but in practice, even for Marx, it becomes a question of costs plus a rate of profit.

This leads on to the 'transformation problem' as defined by Sweezy.[47] The schematic tables used by Marx when he describes the problem of not wholly used-up capital do not hold when the prices of production of one circuit of capital become the (value) input to another. In his demonstration of how prices differ from values, the costs of production are given in value terms; but if the output of one process becomes the input of another, only its price is known. As Meek maintains, 'When values are transformed into prices, the ratio of price to value in a given commodity must be the same when the commodity is considered as input as when it is considered as output; and after the transformation, the rate of profit must come out equal in the case of each capital concerned.'[48] Solutions to the 'transformation problem' consist of demonstrating the formal possibility of a consistent derivation of prices from values.

The literature that these problems have stimulated is extensive.[49] Four general sets of conclusions have been drawn, and all are unpromising for those who, having rejected the market, attempt to build a system of prices or exchange ratios based on Marx's labour theory of value. These conclusions are that this project is wholly misguided because theoretically incorrect (Böhm-Bawerk, the Sraffians, Joan Robinson); or theoretically possible, but wholly arbitrary (Bortkiewicz, Winternitz); or essentially irrelevant, because abstract labour is only measurable in prices (the 'Rubin School'); or theoretically and philosophically correct, but only to be used at a highly aggregated level of analysis that either takes prices as already given, or does not consider price-determination its main task (Hilferding, Kliman and McGlone). And even if the project is successfully rescued and accepted theoretically, three practical problems remain: how to reduce skilled, complex labour to units of simple labour; how to value unproductive labour; and how to calculate quantities of dead labour already embodied in constant capital. Marx addressed these sorts of issues in principle, as Meek demonstrates,[50] but gives no realistic examples. Yet there can be little doubt, as Meek maintains,[51] that a pricing system derived from the labour theory of value and based on units of socially necessary labour time was what Marx intended for post-capitalist society.

It is perhaps not surprising that, after half-hearted attempts to introduce an economic system based on pricing in units of socially necessary labour time, pricing policy based on existing costs of production – the 'prices of production' interpretation of *Capital* Volume III – was adopted. In the years of War Communism in the Soviet Union the idea of a moneyless economy was taken seriously. Varga advocated a 'reduction method' for reducing complex to simple labour[52] and Kreve established a unit of labour time as one hour of unskilled labour fulfilling work norms at 100 per cent.[53] But little came of it. In the later 1920s and the New Economic Policy the chief issue dividing Soviet economists was the extent to which the law of values could be said to be the chief regulator of the economy considered as a whole.[54] Value was not an issue in the works of either Bukharin or Preobrazhensky during this period,[55] the New Economic Programme discussion focusing more on the differences between the state and the private sector, rather than on how either sector worked.[56] The debate between the 'idealists' such as Rubin and 'mechanists' such as Bazarov did not advance discussion of the practical application greatly. For the 'idealists' it was inappropriate to do so; for the 'mechanists' it was not, but they were more interested in technical and engineering problems such as measurements of quantitites of iron and steel.[57] In the 1930s Gatovsky continued this emphasis on natural measures, devoting little space to the issue of the labour-time based economy.[58] Batayev did address the question of a labour-unit based economy with his theory of the 'two regulators', and in his view the fact that the Soviet economy was surrounded by capitalist economies and was itself relatively underdeveloped meant that true labour allocation could not be used. Nevertheless, prices should be determined a priori as a matter of conscious policy.[59] Lapidus and Ostrovianov indicated what a priori pricing might entail when they noted that while the law of labour allocations was the basis of equilibrium, planning required unbalanced growth.[60]

In the 1930s, the main emphasis shifted to a study of the regularities observable in an economy where the 'principle of planning' predominated,[61] and there was no serious attempt to reintroduce questions inspired by the labour theory of value until the late 1950s. By 1938, the official line was the 'law of correspondence', the ultimate in a priori pricing, which held that the Soviet authorities always expressed adequately the objective laws of the development of the Soviet economy.[62] In 1943, an article appeared in a Soviet journal clarifying the official view. Although it criticized excessive voluntarism, by stating that the laws of socialism were fundamentally different from the economic laws of capitalism, it suggested the opposite and reinforced the 1930s practice. Economic law was virtually equated with government economic policy. It was thus unsurprising that the state plan should have the force of law.[63] Within the laws of socialist economics, the law of value distributes the social product on the basis of each according to his work and it 'sets as its goal the establishment of commodity prices based on the socially necessary costs of their production'.[64] This restatement of cost-based pricing does not just slip in. Accounting on the basis of labour-time units was consciously abandoned on the grounds that in the Soviet context labour was not qualitatively uniform in that differences still existed between worker and peasant, between skilled worker and unskilled worker.[65] Such an argument is clearly inconsistent with Marx, and must be interpreted as an acknowledgement that the practical problems in labour-unit planning had proved insurmountable. When the relevance of the labour theory of value to pricing was rediscovered in the later 1950s, despite extensive theoretical discussion of the differences between Volumes I and III of *Capital*,[66] the point at issue was not labour units or costs, but costs plus what? The argument in the Soviet Union centred on whether the plus element should contain a percentage of the value of the capital or should be related to labour costs only.[67]

By the time Soviet-type socialism came to Hungary it was no longer policy to attempt to make serious use of the labour theory of value. Pricing policy debates between 'value prices', 'average costs prices', 'producer price-based prices', 'two-channel prices' and 'income-type prices' focused, as in the Soviet debate, on using the theory to determine the precise composition of the 'plus' component in 'costs plus' pricing.[68] Likewise, consonant with a crude interpretation of the labour theory of value, the measure for productivity improvements initially considered labour costs only. Reformers called for a new indicator that took capital costs into consideration as well.[69] However much embellished by references to the labour theory of value, the demand was for savings and cost reductions of the most general kind.[70]

Totality and autarky

Foreign trade constitutes something of a problem for those trying to derive categories from Marx that can be applied in a real world of 'socialism in one country'. Theoretically, it is difficult to disagree with Meek when he says that goods entering into foreign trade would have to be classified as commodities and that therefore 'commodity production

... would finally disappear only ... when ... world production was controlled by a single international economic organization'.[71] In real world 'socialism' in a single country, when the single country was rich in resources and the size of the USSR, foreign trade could remain a very small island of commodity production within an otherwise non-commodity, planned economy. When 'socialism' is established in a trade-dependent small country, the significance of such commodity production is not small and its relation to other forms of economic activity is much more problematic. Yet, for Marx, the only way to avoid commodity production and achieve socialist relations, in the absence of the world socialist economic organization, is by moving more and more towards autarkic self-reliance.

The point of this digression into Marxist theory has been to show, on the one hand, that socialists in the Soviet Union and Eastern Europe took Marxist theory seriously, but, on the other, that planning for needs using Marx's concepts as a point of departure has two serious failings: the adjudicator of needs becomes the Party, and the armoury of non-market, economic categories that Marx's model of planning required, and which the Soviet Union and Hungary strove to implement, are theoretically ambiguous and proved impossible to apply in practical economic circumstances. In a telling footnote to his discussion of Lange, Meek says the following:

> And to his question 'what can Marxian economics contribute to the problem of the optimum distribution of productive resources in a socialist economy?' a Marxist might answer that it can at least contribute a knowledge of the fact that this would probably not be the basic economic problem in a socialist economy.[72]

Meek was both right and wrong. He was right in that the optimum distribution of productive resources was indeed never perceived as the basic economic problem of socialist economies; yet he was wrong in that, in reality, it turned out to be their central and unresolved problem. We should now consider how these problems of theoretical consistency translated themselves into practical problems of economic planning in Hungary.

Practical Problems

An enormous and constantly changing task

The problems associated with implementing Marxist planning methods can be grouped under two main headings. First, planning proved impossibly complicated to achieve. Second, the degree of planning that was achieved encouraged unintended, self-interested behaviour by enterprises which, although entirely rational from the enterprise perspective, must be considered 'irrational' in any concept of a national interest. These two major problem areas will be considered in turn. The technical problems associated with quantitative central planning can be grouped under four headings, all related to the complexity of the planning task when confronted with the plasticity and variability of human needs.

The first consequence of the size and complexity of the planning task is that the real planning period is very short, and consequently everything is done in a rush with no time to devote to detail. Plan directives for the coming year must be based on the performance of the year in progress; in the Hungarian case a ministry's proposals for the coming year, based on proposals received from enterprises under its control, had to be passed to the Planning Office by the end of October. The Planning Office then had only two weeks to present its plans to the People's Economic Council. Once passed by the Council, the detailed figures had to be passed back to the ministries by 20 November; the ministries then had a week to break down the plans to enterprises, which then had until 8 December to split these annual targets into quarterly plans. Thus by 1 January of the year to which the plan related, each workshop was in possession of a fully disaggregated plan.[73] In order to keep track of current production in relation to the plan, each month's actual production figures had to be published by the tenth of the following month so that they could be compared with those of the plan. As a consequence of these exceptionally tight time constraints, most of those involved in planning were totally absorbed in processing figures, while those concerned with the strategic and longer term could do so only on the basis of approximate figures. The more an element of feedback was incorporated into the planning process, the shorter the actual planning time-frame was.

A second problem with central planning, and the one most often cited, is the sheer size of the task. Nove cites Soviet sources which claim that a fully integrated plan for the Ukraine covering the twelve million separately indentifiable products in the USSR would take the labour of the world population for ten million years.[74] The population of Hungary is smaller than that of the Ukraine, but Hungary probably has more products and more enterprises per head of population. It makes no sense to try to scale down this problem by reducing the number of goods, as Mandel does, and saying that many are intermediate goods and spare parts, or variants of the same good. For the production plan to be met, it is the correct spare part, out of however many million, that is needed when a machine breaks down. Similarly, there may be thirty varieties of bread, but it is not all the same to most consumers whether bread is of the sliced white or brown wholemeal variety. Consumption pattern targets in planning either are too highly aggregated to address this problem, or, if they are disaggregated, run into the problem of mushrooming detail to be considered next.

As it becomes clear that highly aggregated targets result in insufficient breadth of choice, the logic of the model suggests that new targets should be added which ensure, to use Mandel's example, that sufficient quantities of white and brown bread are produced to meet needs. Plans inevitably become increasingly complex. The 1953 plan for the Hungarian Chemical Industry Ministry, for example, included 365 pages of figures; it was finally ready only on 20 June of the year to which it applied; on the following 4 July the ministry was abolished. The trend until mid 1953 was for ever more ministries and directorates to be created to respond to disaggregated needs. By early 1953 there were seventeen economic ministries, including separate ones for local industry, state farms and construction materials, while the heavy and light industry ministries alone supervised seventy directorates. Between 1950 and 1953, the four major official gazettes (Economic Planning, Construction, Metallurgy and Machine Tool, and Agriculture) published 710 decrees on accounting procedures, extending over 1,600 pages. In 1948, there were three appendices detailing the data enterprises should collect; by 1953, there were thirty-three. In 1951, 1,500 indicators were specified which enterprises had to meet; by 1953, there were 2,900. Each ministry processed on average 714,000 indicators. In November 1951, the National Planning Office required a daily report on plan fulfilment and data collection every ten days.[75] This mushrooming of figures required a similar increase in administrative staff to process them. In 1949, the number employed in state administration was 170,000. By 1953, it was 260,000, and in 1956 it had increased to 280,000 despite attempts to reduce numbers in 1954. In 1943, the economy employed five non-productive employees per hundred manual workers; by 1955, it employed thirty-five. In 1949, the wage bill for non-productive employees was 4.53 forints for each tonne of coal; by 1954, it had increased 184 per cent to 12.89 forints, even though the wage level for employees in this sector had hardly increased.[76]

The fourth, and in many ways the most important, manifestation of the complexity of planning is the fact that plans were subject to constant change. Needs are constantly changing, because conditions change. People fall sick; things break down; people make mistakes; winters are unexpectedly cold. All these have knock-on effects which must be catered for. The adjustment mechanism implicit in the Soviet model, as in Mandel's model (as Elson implies),[77] requires that the whole of the plan be readjusted at Planning Office level every time a minor change in needs occurs, certainly if the change affects another enterprise, since only the centre has sufficient knowledge to influence inter-enterprise relations. In Hungary in 1952, the then current five-year plan was changed 472 times, and the yearly plan for 1952 113 times. In 1953 the Council of Ministers and the Planning Office changed the plan 225 times, and plans as passed to enterprises were changed 71 times. Even if the initial planning task were possible within a reasonable time period, it would have to be repeated in full every time such a change took place so as to quantify all knock-on effects; and, in Mandel's model, the proposed changes would also have to go before various levels of democratically elected planning bodies before being accepted. None of this is possible even with today's technology.[78] But even if it were, an additional set of problems remains: the problem of enterprise behaviour and how to influence it.

Irrational enterprise behaviour

With plans getting more and more detailed and changing on average more frequently than once a week, it is not surprising that enterprises in Hungary began to be selective in ways which ensured that the most important targets for their self-interest were met, even if this meant going counter to the spirit of the plan. Even in the most democratically run organizations, constant change of goal can lead to disharmony. And in conditions of disharmony, enterprises are likely to do what is most convenient for them. But, as this section will illustrate, rational pursuit of self-interest by enterprises can have irrational consequences for the national economy, however all-pervasive the planning mechanism is.

Rational pursuit of enterprise self-interest which has irrational national economic consequences can be considered under five headings. The first of these is the absence of any incentive to cut costs, and the impact this has on the production of waste. The regulation system of centralized planning, as we have seen, placed most emphasis on meeting quantitiative gross output indicators. 'Directors of enterprises and top management generally are affected very indirectly by penalties via their premiums on cost reductions.'[79] Thus, while the output targets for the first five-year plan were met, by and large, targets for productivity

71

increase were met by only 60 per cent, and the targets for the reduction of industrial costs were met by only a third.[80] As Berend has noted, when costs are not important, the easiest way to increase the value of production is either to produce more or to use more costly materials.[81] This leads to waste in the sense of production forgone. Until 1951, there was also significant waste in the sense of production not completed. Until that date, production targets used for both premiums and labour competition included the value of unfinished goods. When regulations were changed to include finished goods only, enterprise interest switched to producing the more easily completed types of goods.

Waste was encouraged in the literal sense as well. 'From the point of view of premiums it may even pay to let quality deteriorate.' While in 1950, only 1 per cent of shoes for export were substandard, the substandard figure for the less exacting socialist market reached 25 per cent in 1951. By 1953, 20 million forints a month and 13,000 working hours were being lost because of scrapped materials, and between 30 and 50 per cent of export goods were not accepted by foreign trading partners because they were substandard. In his speech to the Central Leadership of the Hungarian Workers' Party at the end of 1952, Gerő, the member of the Stalinist triumvirate responsible for economic matters, could complain that the production of scrap had increased and the enterprise managers were not putting into practice the decree allowing them to reduce wages by up to 15 per cent to compensate for production that had to be scrapped. He pointed out that MÁVAG, the electrical engineering enterprise, had lost 9.9 million forints because of goods that had to be scrapped, but was fined a total of only 159 forints.

If economic indicators based on gross production value encourage waste and inattention to quality, they also discourage the production of a wide assortment of goods, a second category of irrationality. Before the Second World War eighty different types of shoe were produced in Hungary; in the first half of the 1950s there were only sixteen. In 1951, the Csepel Vehicle Factory fulfilled its output plan by 107 per cent, but its assortment plan by only 65 per cent. Shops were flooded with large items of crockery, for example, which nobody wanted, while the smaller items, which everybody wanted, were not to be had, because the plan was expressed by weight, and it was easier to produce a small number of bigger items than a greater number of smaller ones. Similarly, when, in the third quarter of 1952, the Underwear Factory was in danger of not fulfilling its plan, it spent the last day of the plan producing enormous numbers of footcloths (even though more than enough had already been produced) and successfully achieved its target. More generally, spare parts disappeared because production output was smaller, and more labour intensive, than in the production of finished goods.[82]

A third 'irrationality' is the technological conservatism that administrative central planning stimulates. Not only are enterprises under no pressure to innovate, but also the necessary funds for investment are hard to come by because all investment decisions are made centrally. More important, technological change introduces uncertainty, and uncertainty might jeopardize bonuses. Managerial bonuses were tied to current quarterly plans, not to long-term benefits. Despite the existence of an 'innovations movement' since 1948, by which workers were encouraged to suggest improved methods of production,[83] and despite the fact that enterprises were obliged to construct a plan for technical development, it was far easier to continue producing goods in the traditional way. To make matters worse, despite central planning of the economy, there was no systematic coordination of science and research policy in the early 1950s. The Academy of Sciences, the obvious central body, was weak, while the major economic ministries maintained their own research institutes which vied with each other for prestige and often duplicated research.

A fourth form of enterprise behaviour encouraged by the economic mechanism but 'irrational' from the perspective of the national economy is the 100 per cent fetish and its concomitant feature – 'storming'. As Kornai has noted, the plans were never so accurate that a few percentage points either side made any real difference – except that bonuses were tied to the achievement of the 100 per cent. Since delivery of the full 100 per cent by the end of quarter, or end of year, was all that mattered, production fell into a cyclical pattern, generally referred to as 'storming', whereby at the ends of each month, each quarter, and each year, there was intense activity to make the plan by the deadline concerned, while activity slackened off at the beginning of each month, quarter and year. For example, 40–50 per cent of deliveries took place in the last month of each quarter. Similarly, there was a tendency to concentrate in the last quarter of the year on goods with a higher production value. At a general level, it was in the interests of enterprises to hide from the directorates that controlled them just what potential they possessed so that plans could be met relatively easily. If it became clear that the plan could not be met in a given period and that 'storming' would not achieve the 100 per cent, it was in the enterprise's interest to fail by a long way, conceal its real capacities and build up reserves for the next period. As a consequence, the planning centre's theoretical omniscience was, in fact, based on systematically and increasingly distorted figures. Concealed, informal bargaining accompanied the formal bargaining that formed part of the disaggregation–reaggregation planning process outline above.

A fifth 'irrationality' from the national economic standpoint is the tendency towards 'limitless investment' and the exponential growth of uncompleted investment that this brings with it. In an economy where the central concern of each enterprise is the completion of the current plan, where new investments are determined by political considerations, with the only economic consideration being whether sufficient cash and materials are available to fund a given project at a given point in time, it is hardly surprising that the number of unfinished investment projects grew rapidly. The situation was exacerbated by the fact that investment plan targets did not include deadlines or quality considerations. At one and the same time, Stalinville (Sztálinváros) was being built, a mine and surrounding town were being transformed at Komló, the Budapest underground was under consideration, the Lenin smelting works at Diósgyőr was being reconstructed, and major works were taking place at the Borsod mines. The government devoted increasing funds to investment in vain. Either the necessary goods were not available, or only substandard goods could be obtained. As Table 3.1 shows, the proportion of unfinished investments grew alarmingly.

The consequences of so much unfinished investment were fourfold. First, investment gestation periods became increasingly long. In engineering, for example, projects that should have taken two to three years took six to eight. Second, the whole investment programme was more expensive than planned, by some 38 per cent. Third, inevitably, other tasks were given insufficient attention. According to a Central Statistical Office publication, renewal of existing plant was neglected, and this led to its deterioration. Finally, the ambitious investment plans in practice made only a small contribution to the actual increase in economic growth. New construction made up 20 per cent of all industrial

Table 3.1 Unfinished stock as a percentage of annual expenditure on investments 1950–55

	Unfinished investments
1950	24.0
1951	38.8
1952	49.5
1953	65.6
1954	91.3
1955	91.8

Source: I. Pető and S. Szakács, *A Hazai Gazdaság Négy Évtizedének Története 1945–1985. Az Újjáépítés és a Tervutasításos Irányítás Időszaka 1945–1968*, Budapest 1985, p. 190. Originally published in T. Bauer, *Tervgazdaság, Beruházás, Ciklusok*, Budapest 1981, p. 68.

investment, but produced only one-thirteenth of the growth in industrial production. The rest came from the exploitation of existing reserves.

A final dimension of irrationality, an extension of the general insensitivity to costs, was the effect of different sets of exchange rates on prices. As Liska recounts, when goods are purchased from the West at a rate of 40 forints to the dollar and sold at a rate of 100 forints to the dollar, materials can be bought for ten dollars, have (forint) value added to them, be sold at eight dollars, and still make a forint profit.[84]

When Marx's theoretical ambiguities are converted into the practical problems of planning, the weakness of the traditional model of centrally planned economies is revealed as follows. It is not simply that the task is too complicated (which it is, even with modern computers), nor that it cannot cope with constantly changing needs (which it cannot, even when it is allowed that there are fewer real world permutations than some abstract models might allow), but that, unless general and particular interests automatically coincide, it creates an economic system in which enterprises rationally pursue their particular interests in ways which are very far from rational when viewed from the perspective of the general interest.

Problems Peculiar to Hungary

Hungary's resource endowment and the policy of autarky

The above features are common to any economy which adopts the Soviet model for economic planning. Hungary, however, suffered from two additional problems during the early 1950s. The first concerned autarky and Hungary's resource endowment; the second concerned the degree of voluntarism that was used in applying the Soviet 1930s 'law of correspondence' between planned proportions and real social potential.

> While autarky is a feasible goal and may be attained without excessive costs in the Soviet Union, which has a large internal market and varied resource endowment, in Hungary both the smallness of the home market and the poor domestic raw material base call for participation in the international division of labour.[85]

However, as Liska and Máriás pointed out in 1954, certain economic textbooks equated autarky with socialism,[86] and autarky became a policy goal, despite the fact that the very policies aimed at creating economic independence by expanding heavy industry both led to an increase in imports of materials and necessitated importing foodstuffs that the newly disfavoured agricultural sector could not provide.[87] Hungary possessed few raw materials. As early as October 1949, it was recognized that import demands could only be met through the export of 'hard commodities'. But the structural transformation from an agrarian economy to a 'country of iron and steel' proposed by the first five-year plan adversely affected Hungary's traditional 'hard commodities'. From 1952 until the 1970s Hungary, formerly a major agricultural exporter, as we have seen, became a net importer of wheat.[88] To make matters worse, all its neighbouring countries in Eastern Europe were pursuing more or less identical policies, so reducing the possibility of finding export markets or import opportunities there. Autarky as a strategy was premissed on the assumption that trade would diminish and Hungary would become a self-supporting socialist economy. In fact, the reverse occurred. Trade increased. A domestic economy the size of Hungary could not produce everything it needed to stand still, let alone achieve economic growth. Between 1950 and 1954, although national income grew by 50 per cent, imports increased 100 per cent and exports, because of deteriorating foreign trade prices, by 150 per cent. Between 1950 and 1954, as a percentage of national income, imports rose from 12.1 to 16.3 per cent and exports from 13.7 to 20.9 per cent. Tables 3.2 and 3.4 demonstrate the following. First, the investment-created demand for imports prevented Hungary from establishing a positive trade balance on either the dollar or the ruble account in the first half of the 1950s (Table 3.2). Second, the foreign trade plan was not fulfilled in any year (Table 3.3). Third, Hungary fell into a pattern of importing materials and semi-finished goods and failing to export industrial products in significant numbers. As collectivization proceeded, this was not even balanced by agricultural exports (Table 3.4).

Table 3.2 Balance of exports and imports of goods of industrial origin 1949–55

	Dollar trade		Ruble trade		Total trade	
	Balance (thou. m. forint)	Exports as % imports	Balance (thou. m. forint)	Exports as % imports	Balance (thou. m. forint)	Exports as % imports
1949	−1,123	34.9	−326	78.2	−1,449	55.0
1950	−1,025	33.5	−281	85.7	−1,306	62.8
1951	−857	42.0	−474	82.1	−1,331	67.8
1952	−788	40.8	−898	74.2	−1,686	64.9
1953	−576	51.8	−56	98.4	−632	86.6
1954	−621	52.4	−411	88.8	−1,032	79.2
1955	−653	63.0	+193	106.2	−460	90.5

Source: Pető and Szakács, p. 164.

Table 3.3 Fulfilment of the foreign trade plan 1950–55 (Plan = 100)

	Import	Export
1950	95.8	90.6
1951	85.8	77.8
1952	90.7	90.9
1953	92.4	100.4
1954	95.0	92.3
1955	99.7	92.3

Source: Pető and Szakács, p. 167.

Table 3.4 The structure of export and import goods 1949–55 (%)

	Machines, machinery, instruments	Other consumer goods of industrial origin	Materials and semi-manufactured products	Products of agricultural origin	Total
EXPORTS					
1949	17.4	17.2	19.2	46.2	100.0
1950	22.5	19.8	14.8	42.9	100.0
1951	24.9	25.1	15.3	34.7	100.0
1952	28.1	21.9	16.3	33.7	100.0
1953	38.4	21.8	15.8	24.0	100.0
1954	37.2	20.1	16.2	26.5	100.0
1955	33.6	18.2	19.0	29.2	100.0
IMPORTS					
1949	17.4	2.7	75.1	4.8	100.0
1950	20.8	3.5	70.3	5.4	100.0
1951	22.3	2.0	71.5	4.2	100.0
1952	22.4	1.8	72.2	3.6	100.0
1953	19.5	1.8	67.6	11.1	100.0
1954	15.4	3.8	69.6	11.1	100.0
1955	12.6	3.7	69.6	14.1	100.0

Source: Pető and Szakács, p. 165.

Excessively distorted growth

As noted above, the major economic debates in the Soviet Union in the 1920s and 1930s centred the pace of industrialization and the extent to which the law of value should deliberately be broken by the 'law of correspondence' and a priori pricing in order to achieve primary accumulation.[89] The Hungarian leadership of the early 1950s pursued such 'voluntaristic' policies to an unprecedented extent. The official view was that 'investments are always determined by political viewpoints and economic indicators can only fulfil a secondary role'.[90] Initial targets for the five-year plan suggested a severe distortion of the law of value; and they were amended twice, both times in favour of investment and heavy industry (including military expenditure) as the international situation worsened. This was, after all, the era of the threat of war with Tito in Yugoslavia and the fact of war in Korea.

As Table 3.5 indicates, the targets of the first five-year plan were first changed in 1949 while it was still in conception, and again, in 1951, when it was under way. Direct military investments were also increased, from 14 to 18 per cent of the total investment budget.[91] The complete actual distribution of investments is given in Table 3.6. The effects of the New Course (which will be covered in the following chapter) can be seen in the 1954 figures. Agriculture and the infrastructure did very badly. The vast majority of the funds devoted to transport in fact went towards the (finally abandoned) Budapest underground which was planned with its air defence potential in mind.

Production targets were also increased. The 1950 production target for manufacturing industry went up mid year from 117.7 to 129.2 per cent of its December 1949 value. The 1951 plan revisions changed the planned percentage increase in output targets for manufacturing industry overall from 86.4 per cent over the five-year period to 310 per cent. In heavy industry, a 104.3 per cent rise over five years was increased to 380 per cent. Within these plans, the emphasis was on sector A (means of production), rather than sector B (consumer goods), even in the light and food supply industries. Yet despite these increased calls on resources, and the increased heavy industry and sector A bias,

Table 3.5 Three variants of the investment component of the first five-year plan (thousand million forints)

	April 1949	December 1949	1951
Industry	17.0	21.3	41.0
of which heavy industry	–	18.3	37.5
light industry	–	3.0	3.5
Agriculture	6.0	8.0	11.0
Transport	6.0	7.5	10.0
Social, cultural, house building	6.0	7.4	14.0
Other	–	6.7	9.0
Total investment	35.0	50.9	85.0

Source: Pető and Szakács, p. 156.

Table 3.6 Distribution of investments 1949–54 (%)

	1949	1950	1951	1952	1953	1954	1950–54
(1) Primary material production	–	25.0	29.8	34.4	34.5	30.6	31.2
(2) Engineering	–	10.0	12.2	8.7	8.9	5.9	9.5
(3) Heavy industry (1–2)	29.8	35.0	42.0	43.0	43.3	36.5	40.7
(4) Light industry	1.7	1.0	1.5	1.9	1.8	2.5	1.8
(5) Food supply	1.8	2.1	1.5	0.6	1.8	2.5	1.6
(6) Industry (3–5)	33.3	38.1	45.0	45.5	47.0	41.5	44.1
(7) Construction	–	4.1	3.1	3.0	2.4	0.9	2.7
(8) Agriculture	17.5	9.3	10.8	13.0	13.1	22.9	13.8
(9) Transport	21.1	18.6	14.0	15.0	10.7	6.8	12.8
(10) Commerce	3.5	3.1	2.3	1.8	2.4	3.4	2.5
(11) Communal services and administration	22.8	12.4	11.6	10.5	17.9	22.0	14.8
(12) Other	1.8	14.4	13.2	11.2	6.5	2.5	9.3
Total (6–12)	100.0	100.0	100.0	100.0	100.0	100.0	100.0

Source: Pető and Szakács, p. 160.

the modified plan also increased the targeted improvement in living standards from 35 to 50 per cent.

An increase in living standards of this size constituted wishful thinking of an absurd kind. As Table 3.7 indicates, with 25 per cent of national income devoted to investment, 51.7 per cent of which went to industrial investment, and 92.1 per cent of that to heavy industry and construction, Hungarian investment programmes were, by this measure, the most unbalanced in Eastern Europe.

Distorted socialist culture

If Hungary's economy was characterized by distorted growth in the name of a socialist ideal, socialist culture was equally distorted. The early 1950s was a period in which the new socialist culture and the new socialist 'science' of Marxism–Leninism had already become dogma. There was no equivalent period to that of the 1920s in the Soviet Union when attempts to establish a specifically socialist culture led to a flowering of artistic development and lively artistic debate between Constructivists and Suprematists, when Proletkul'tists invented new socialist sports which de-emphasized competition and promoted socialist pageants instead, and when the acronym 'agit prop' was associated with brightly coloured trains taking education and culture to the peasant masses. In the Soviet version of socialist culture which Hungary

Table 3.7 Comparison of industrialization plans

	Investment as % of national income	Industrial investment as % of total investment	Heavy and construction investment as % of industrial investment
Bulgaria 1st 5yr	19.6	43.1	83.5
Czechoslovakia 1st 5yr	22.3	40.6	78.1
Poland 6yr	21.6	45.4	75.0
Hungary 1st 5yr	25.2	51.7	92.1
GDR 1st 5yr	–	53.9	75.2
Romania 1st 5yr	–	53.4	82.6
Soviet Union 1st 5yr	–	49.1	85.7
Soviet Union 2nd 5yr	–	47.8	83.1
Soviet Union 1946–50 fulfilment	21.0	–	–

Source: Pető and Szakács, p. 168.

imported, 'agit prop' had become virtually synonymous with censorship.[92] Marxism–Leninism, the socialist science, was a compulsory part of all courses since it was a necessary skill for the building of socialism. Yet, as taught at the Party Institute, it consisted of courses on Stalin's economic writings and on the lives not only of Stalin but also of Rákosi, the Hungarian Party leader. The teaching of Russian was also compulsory in order to improve the quality of education by allowing students to read in the original Soviet science which they had been cut off from under the years of fascism. Art in the service of the people and socialism was reduced to art popularizing whatever the Party wanted.

Hungary's socialist culture was a confused amalgam. It consisted of the work ethic as encouraged by Stakhanovism (one of the Party's criticisms of the Church in the 1950s was that it belittled the Stakhanovite movement), new forms of language such as the encouragement of the familiar 'you' between comrades, use of the word 'comrade' itself, phrases such as 'fascist band' to describe Tito's regime; and imported Soviet culture. There were quotas for the percentage of films shown that had to be Soviet (57 per cent at one time) and all Soviet books had to be given long print-runs, irrespective of quality. There were also such curiosities as prohibiting policemen from carrying truncheons – because there is no need to hit people under socialism – yet requiring them to carry and use guns, permitting restaurants to employ gypsy musicians, but not female *chanteuses.* Kodály's Háry János was condemned as 'chauvinist' in 1951, although Kodály came back into favour in 1951 when Prokofiev visited Hungary in 1952.[93]

During this period, the political interests of the Party and its interpretation of socialism were paramount. The discipline which had evolved amongst a small group operating in exile and underground was imposed on a mass party. The Party's interference extended from the working lives of members (moving them between jobs for the Party's convenience) to their private lives (ordering individuals to divorce their wives if the wife had been implicated in a scandal).[94] There were large numbers of political prisoners and show trials. Prisoners such as the former Social Democrat István Riesz died under interrogation and were buried in quicklime.[95] To protect the country's food supply, peasants could kill pigs only with the permission of their local council. To alleviate the housing shortage the former 'ruling class' were expelled from Budapest, and people with large houses had parts of their houses 'nationalized'. (One local official even illegally nationalized part of his own house and asked to have it back when the political thaw came in 1954–55.)

Hungary's socialist culture of the 1950s was one in which the creation of a personality cult around the leader was obligatory. Rákosi was not only First Secretary of the Hungarian Workers' Party, he was also the nation's 'wise leader and teacher'.[96] To Hungarian youth he was a 'dear father and teacher'. His sixtieth birthday was celebrated as an important day not only for the Hungarian nation, but also for millions of people throughout the world. At Party conferences there was an applause-leader who stood up whenever Rákosi's name was mentioned, turned to face the delegates and started clapping loudly. Rákosi's contributions to socialist thought were published abroad in English, as were those of other Eastern European leaders. In Rákosi's case, these consisted of an account of his trial and re-trial in the 1920s and 1930s.

And a final characteristic of this new culture was secrecy about the real economic situation. The 1951 modification of the first five-year plan was produced in only 150 copies; decrees of the Council of Ministers were seen by only about one hundred people, and the incomplete, official collection of decrees was marked 'secret', 'very secret', 'confidential' or 'strictly confidential' for most of the early 1950s.[97] Party cadres mobilized the population to achieve plans that only the privileged few knew were unrealizable.

The Economic Background to 1956

The concomitant of the high level of spending on investments noted above was that insufficient funds were available to spend on maintenance and repairs. The average age of smelting machinery was forty to fifty years; that of cutting machinery in 1953 was 18.4 years (and in some important works it was 27 years), compared with a generally accepted maximum of 13 years; and some of the machinery used in the consumer goods industries dated from before the First World War. With little money spent on maintenance it is not surprising that 1953 witnessed a 60–70 per cent increase in machinery breakdowns over the previous year.[98]

The early 1950s were years of falling living standards as well as of shortage and disrepair. Table 3.8 reflects the extent to which both consumption and the share of investment which was not aimed at increasing capacity were de-emphasized during the first five-year plan. The emphasis on capital goods was reflected in the pricing structure. In 1949, the price index for consumer goods was 60 per cent higher than that for producer goods; by 1952, it was 166 per cent higher.[99] In the mid 1950s, clothes were between seventeen and eighteen times more expensive than they had been before the war; food was twelve times more expensive. And wages did not increase sufficiently quickly to keep up with these steeply rising consumer prices: while the latter rose by 78.3 per cent between 1949 and 1953, average wages increased by only 55 per cent. The effect of these price movements on nominal and real wages, and on real incomes, is given in Tables 3.9 and 3.10.

A survey carried out by the Trade Union Council in the mid 1950s found that a third of those living on wages or salaries had an income under the subsistence minimum. More telling perhaps, a representative survey carried out at about the same time by the Ministry of Domestic

Table 3.8 How national income was used 1950–56 (1950 = 100)

	1950	1951	1952	1953	1954	1955	1956
Consumption							
Population	100	103	98	100	119	125	135
Other	100	147	362	462	241	179	138
Total	100	105	112	119	125	128	135
Accumulation							
Increasing stock	100	174	194	225	178	195	175
Change in stock and other	100	169	81	122	68	91	–
Total	100	171	132	169	118	139	37
Total national income	100	116	114	128	122	132	117

Source: Pető and Szakács, p. 214.

Table 3.9 Index figures for wages of workers and employees (1949 = 100)

Year	Nominal wage	Real wage
1950	107.0	101.3
1951	114.5	89.7
1952	147.4	82.3
1953	155.0	87.0
1954	173.5	102.3
1955	178.3	106.0

Source: Pető and Szakács, p. 221.

Table 3.10 The real income of major population groups (1949 = 100)

Year	Per capita real income of worker and employee population	Real value of peasantry's per capita consumption without deducting taxes and working expenses
1950	102.8	112.7
1951	97.8	118.8
1952	87.5	106.6
1953	91.0	100.6
1954	115.0	111.0
1955	121.8	124.5
1956	129.3	131.2

Source: Pető and Szakács, p. 217.

Trade found that 13.3 per cent of workers did not have a winter coat.[100]

Living standards were not improved by the government's collectivization policy. The first wave of collectivization followed the Soviet pattern of the 1930s, and exhibited all the same tragic misunderstandings of the nature of peasant production.[101] First, it was carried out 'on the cheap' in that the policy assumed radical reform of production relations in a whole sector of the economy could somehow be achieved at zero cost – in fact at negative cost since a declining percentage of national investment was devoted to agriculture. Only 13.8 per cent of total investment was directed towards agriculture between 1950 and 1954, compared with 17.5 per cent in 1949, and 17 per cent on average between 1954 and 1957, and 18–20 per cent in the 1960s. Second, the only successful aspects of collectivization were the political and economic attacks on the supposed 'kulaks', who were excluded from all areas of political life, prevented from joining cooperatives, subject to high taxation and high compulsory deliveries, and restricted in their ability to employ outside labour. On the other hand, economic inputs designed to help agriculture were not forthcoming. Only half of the 22,000 tractors projected in the first five-year plan saw the light of day. Fertilizer use remained below planned levels, with the ration of fertilizer to hectare falling continually as cooperative landholdings increased. The original eleven thousand million forints of credit for cooperative farms planned for the years up to 1953 were reduced to eight thousand million in the course of the plan; and by 1953 only five thousand million had materialized. Collectivization, together with the consolidation of landholdings that accompanied it, led to a massive migration out of agriculture and the abandonment of much agricultural land. By 1953, cooperative farm membership had increased to 376,000, yet some 300,000 people had left agriculture altogether, abandoning some 820,000 hectares of cultivable land.

It is small wonder then that when Stalinist policies were reimposed in 1955, after the brief New Course interlude of rising expectations in 1954, the result was the revolution of 1956.

4

Economic Reform: Markets in the Present, Planning for the Future

This chapter is centred on Hungary's New Economic mechanism, which was introduced on 1 January 1968, the second best known and second most important date in Hungary's postwar socialist history. The chapter concentrates primarily on presenting the background to the introduction of the mechanism and examining the measures it entailed, before briefly attempting to locate the mechanism in the context of some other models of 'market socialism' presented in both the Eastern and Western literature.

The Background to and Origins of Hungary's New Economic Mechanism

Intellectual precursors

The aims of the 1954 New Course had not been radical: a greater emphasis on consumption rather than accumulation, a more balanced pattern of growth, the redirection of funds away from industry and back to agriculture and the services. Consumer prices were reduced, wages were increased, and the economic and political burdens on the peasantry especially were reduced, as can be seen from Table 4.1. There was also a concerted effort to reduce the size of the state apparatus.[1]

Despite this lack of radicalism, and despite the fact that by the autumn of 1954 it was already clear that Nagy and his New Course policies were losing the political battle, very radical proposals for economic reform were formulated that year. On the one hand, a government/Nagy-backed special committee report completed by the end of November 1954 called for prices to reflect true costs, for the law of

Table 4.1 The change of economic policy as reflected in the distribution of investments 1953–54 (%)

	1953	1954
Industry	46.3	35.2
of which heavy industry	41.3	30.6
light industry	1.4	1.7
electrical industry	1.4	1.8
construction	2.2	1.1
Agriculture	13.7	24.0
Transport	13.1	9.1
Commerce	1.8	2.6
House/flat building	6.2	11.1
Labour protection	1.3	2.3
Social, cultural and communal investments	8.3	11.4
Science and research	0.8	0.8
Other, remainder	8.5	3.5

Source: I. Pető and S. Szakács, *A Hazai Gazdaság Négy Évtizedének Története 1945–1985. Az Újjáépítés és a Tervutasításos Irányítás Időszaka 1945–1968*, Budapest 1985, p. 249.

value to operate more fully, for domestic prices to be influenced by world prices and for there to be a more banker-like attitude to money and credit.[2] (When Nagy was finally ousted and replaced by Hegedűs, all copies of the report were seized by the security police.[3]) On the other hand, the newly formed Economic Science Institute in its journal (*Közgazdasági Szemle*) published articles advocating reform, and listing nearly all of the problems with centrally planned economies which have since become commonplace: poor quality, waste, and shortage. The most radical solution to these problems was proposed by Győry Péter, president of the Central Statistical Office, and contained many of the components of the New Economic Mechanism which would be introduced some fourteen years later: enterprises to be made interested in indirect indicators, mainly profit; prices to be determined by supply and demand; capital charges to be introduced; and money to play an active role in economic management.[4]

The short-lived revolutionary government of Imre Nagy bequeathed two important features of economic policy and economic reform. The one lasting economic measure was the abolition of compulsory deliveries in agriculture which Antal Gyenes, Minister for Agricultural Deliveries, announced on 30 October.[5] This was to have far-reaching consequences since it effectively removed the standard feature of the planning system from a whole sector of the economy, a sector that was enormously important for both domestic demand and foreign markets, not to mention political stability. The removal of the traditional mechanism from this sector of the economy both questioned the viability of the whole and spurred agricultural specialists to investigate further possibilities for reform.

The second significant feature of the revolutionary government was the workers' council, and the discussion of its role in relation to economic reform. In the final months of 1956 the Greater Budapest Workers' Council produced a ten-page proposal for the future organization of the economy. In addition, five ministries (the Ministries for Construction, Metallurgy and Engineering, Light Industry, Finance and the Chemical Industry) responded to government prompting and produced similar sets of proposals.[6] The central feature of all was comprehensive reform of the method of economic administration. They all called for an end to the method of central disaggregation of plan directives and favoured forms of enterprise independence under which planning would be restricted to the middle term, or restricted to determining the annual budget and such tasks as establishing the proportions of national income to be spent on accumulation and consumption, the desired level of real incomes, and major investment projects. All proposals agreed that enterprise behaviour should be controlled by indirect methods – by price and tax policy, by deductions from profit, or by credit policy. Similarly, all proposals called for less control of prices, although the Ministry of Finance's proposal went into more detail and called for the freeing of prices for goods acquired through foreign trade and a realistic exchange rate. On the question of wages, all proposals started from the assumption that the workers' councils should establish wages, although all saw a need for some kind of wage control.[7]

The changed political climate of 1957 is well illustrated by the fate of attempts to synthesize these ministerial reform proposals of the final months of 1956, finally published in April 1957.[8] Pető and Szakács have compared the first version of the document to the original ministries' proposals, and the second, published version to the first. Even the first version differed from the original ministries' proposals in that, first, investment became again a task for central bodies, and, second, the need for administrative plan directives was retained in a number of areas. More significantly, workers' councils were no longer the centre of the model, being included only in the section considering 'organizational questions'. The work of what later became known as the Varga Commission was no more successful in influencing policy. Its final version was an even paler imitation of the original. The first suggestion for comprehensive reform prepared by Varga and Antos[9] followed the sort of proposals suggested by the ministries in 1956, except that investments remained in the hands of the state, and the workers' councils played no special role in the institutional system.[10] The committee's final document of June 1957 acknowledged that administrative planning would be necessary elsewhere in certain circumstances. On the other hand, it did retain its call for enterprise independence and for the intro-duction of indirect economic planning. Further, it gave enterprises a role in making suggestions for investments, and recommended that salaries should reflect the profitability of the enterprise. But the tide was turning against the reformers. The pressing need for economic reform dis-appeared as Hungary received aid from the Soviet Union and economic recovery from 1956 took place faster than expected. The reform plans of the Varga Committee were never effectively debated by any govern-ment or political body.[11]

Ignoring the writings of the small group of reform economists, the planners of economic policy after 1956 continued with a more balanced, more rational version of the traditional Soviet model. And, just as targets had become more ambitious in 1952 and 1955–56 following the initial successes in the first plan periods, so too did they become more ambitious in 1958, 1959 and 1961 as the economy recovered more quickly than expected, collectivization returned to the political agenda[12] and the Soviet Union called for a seven-year plan to catch up with and overtake the West. Despite this pattern of continuity, five new features emerged in the post-1956 period. First, the introduction of the profit-sharing system in 1957 gave management and workers alike a small indirect interest in profitability. Although profit was not the guiding indicator within the planning system, it was a factor affecting managerial bonuses, and, since the system extended to all members of the work-force, for whom a profit-share payment quickly became an expected element of income, was an indicator which no enterprise manager could easily ignore.[13] Second, the uniform wage tariff was abandoned and enterprises enjoyed some freedom to establish wages between centrally determined bands.[14] Third, autarky was no longer a policy goal, although cooperation was restricted to the CMEA countries, and here genuine cooperation was to prove difficult. Fourth, investment was no longer seen as an end in itself. Existing capacity was, in theory, now seen to have possibilities as a source of growth. The new goal was the development of fewer, more effective, investments. Fifth, in agriculture Nagy-like New Course pro-agriculture policies were reintroduced in tandem with forced collectivization.[15]

Concentration, independence, efficiency, 1958–64

Two minor and ultimately contradictory reform measures did take place in the late 1950s and early 1960s however (in the organization system and the regulation systems respectively): the concentration of industrial units, a continuation of moves since 1953 to simplify the planning system; and industrial price reform. The aim of the former was two-fold: to simplify the planning hierarchy by reducing both the number of levels within it and the number of economic units each administrative level controlled; and to grant the fewer, larger economic units greater independence and autonomy in economic decision-making. Despite official statements and a number of mergers in 1958 and 1959, little was done in this area for the next two years. It was only at the Central Committee meeting of 2 February 1962 that a final decision was taken to modify the organization system by abolishing the directorates and increasing industrial concentration.[16] In the event, concentration was achieved, but economic autonomy was severely restricted by the retention of some directorates and the creation of 'trusts' with administrative as well as economic duties.[17]

The effects of the mergers of the first half of the 1960s on enterprise size and concentration can be seen from Tables 4.2 to 4.4, the last of which is important since it implies that Hungarian industry was already highly concentrated before these mergers and questions whether the mergers were economically justified in the first place. All ten metallurgy works were merged into a single Metallurgical Enterprise, fourteen sugarbeet processing factories and a research institute were merged into the Sugar Industry Enterprise, and eight state wineries were merged into a single Hungarian State Winery.[18]

Industrial price reform was undertaken first in 1959 and again in 1965. The 1959 reform was in essence an implementation of the reform

Table 4.2 Distribution of enterprises and their workers by enterprise size 1950–69

Number of workers employed at enterprise	Number of industrial enterprises				Number of workers			
	1950	1960	1965	1969	1950	1960	1965	1969
Under 50	498	108	46	44	10,753	3,348	756	762
51–100	210	139	86	39	14,996	10,220	6,392	3,029
101–500	474	644	343	297	116,242	161,602	89,706	78,589
500–1,000	142	250	111	130	96,255	181,430	78,210	91,400
1,001–10,000	100	190	240	282	231,161	409,210	675,876	913,546
Over 10,000	1	7	10	11	10,491	89,747	144,390	160,520

Source: Pető and Szakács, p. 512.[19]

Table 4.3 Average workforce of industrial enterprises and cooperatives

	State enterprise	Cooperative
1950	337	38
1960	639	129
1965	1,335	218

Source: Pető and Szakács, p. 513.

Table 4.4 Percentage distribution of industrial employees in selected countries by plant size

	% of industrial employees at plants employing:	
	up to 500	over 1,000
Czechoslovakia (1960)	8.8	81.0
Hungary (1960)	20.5	58.3
Soviet Union (1960)	30.8	53.2
GDR (1960)	36.3	50.8
FRG (1964)	47.0	39.8
UK (1958)*	50.7	35.4
USA (1958)	55.6	31.6
Japan (1963)*	70.8	19.8

*excluding mines

Source: Pető and Szakács, p. 506.

already worked out by mid 1956 but not implemented because of the events of the October of that year. By 1963, it was recognized that price distortions were adversely affecting technical development. The principles of price formation introduced in 1953 predisposed enterprises towards high-cost technical solutions. Enterprise concentration meant that large mark-ups at each phase of production could be internalized and added to the final price, that is to say, it increased the scope for price manipulation. In the engineering sector for example, although producer price reform envisaged profits of some 2 per cent of turnover, in reality they were as high as 14.6 per cent in 1959, and had reached 22.7 per cent by 1963. On the other hand, prices of energy and foodstuffs turned out to be lower than expected. Actual prices, then, diverged increasingly from planned parameters based on government perceptions of 'socially necessary expenditure'.[20]

The government abandoned any idea of a general restructuring of producer prices on the grounds that it would take between five and six years to achieve. It switched the focus of the reform from encouraging technological development to re-establishing a 2–4 per cent profit margin.[21] The net effect on pricing of the producer price revision, when changes to the rate of turnover tax and very minor modifications to consumer prices were taken into account, was to further increase the discrepancy between producer and consumer prices.[22] An important consequence of the intellectual debate that accompanied this price reform was the introduction of capital charges, in January 1964, at 5 per cent of the value of the enterprise's fixed capital and affecting some 85 per cent of the capital equipment used in Hungarian industry.[23]

As the 1960s progressed, it became increasingly clear that the combination of an unreformed planning system, a slightly, but not significantly reformed regulation system and a highly centralized organizational system was not working. For an increasing number of people it became clear that without radical reform further economic growth could be achieved only at the expense of either reducing living standards or increasing foreign debt. As Tables 4.5 and 4.6 indicate, economic development in the second five-year plan did not proceed as planned, and was generally disappointing. The growth rate not only fell well below the levels planned, but went into a steady decline similar to, but not so dramatic as, that experienced by Czechoslovakia in the same period.[24]

The slowdown in growth was exacerbated by the fact that investment did not decline; indeed, as Table 4.5 indicates, its rate of growth was faster than that of both national income and the levels prescribed in the plan. And there were further worrying features concerning the nature of

Table 4.5 Plan fulfilment in the second five-year plan (% growth)

	National income		Socialist sector investments	
	plan	actual	plan	actual
1961	–	4.6	−10	−6.9
1962	7	6.0	10	15.5
1963	9	5.4	14	13.2
1964	7–8	4.3	10	4.8
1965	6–7	0.1	−5	0.4
1961–65	36*	24.0*	180*	210*

*thousand million forints

Source: Pető and Szakács, p. 403.

Table 4.6 National income and its use in the period of the second five-year plan (1959 prices)

	1961	1962	1963	1964	1965
National income					
thousand m. forints	148.1	155.1	163.9	171.7	173.7
% of previous year	106.2	104.7	105.7	104.8	101.2
Total consumption					
thousand m. forints	109.0	113.7	120.3	127.2	130.8
% of previous year	101.6	104.3	105.8	105.7	102.8
of which population's consumption					
thousand m. forints	103.9	108.1	114.3	120.8	124.4
% of previous year	101.4	104.0	105.7	105.7	103.0
Accumulation					
thousand m. forints	37.5	42.1	46.5	49.4	41.3
% of previous year	105.0	112.3	110.5	106.2	83.6
Foreign trade balance					
thousand m. forints	+1.6	−0.7	−2.9	−4.9	+1.6

− = import surplus, + = export surplus

Source: Pető and Szakács, p. 405.

these investments. First, there were signs that the post-1956 aim of intensive investment by means of improvements to existing capacity was not being met. A report to the Party on the nature of the investments proposed in the second five-year-plan found that 67 per cent of investments were concerned with either reconstruction or expansion.[25] Second, labour was being utilized less rather than more effectively. Between 1957 and 1967, the annual average increase in industrial production was 9 per cent, while productivity grew by only 6 per cent. The additional labour needed to fund these figures came from agriculture where collectivization had resulted in a large outflow of labour. The overall labour force in Hungary in the first half of the 1960s fell somewhat.[26] The propensity of socialist economies for excessive investment and extensive, labour-intensive development continued, even though plans now explicitly rejected this as a goal.

The measures introduced in the early 1960s also had very little effect on the recurrent problems of the centrally planned economy: waste and poor quality. A Party report on the state of the economy in 1965 noted that the proportion of goods for which 'there was no demand either at home or on the foreign market' had increased by 33 per cent between 1961 and 1963. Moreover, the proportion of national income wasted in this way eventually rose to a figure of twice the level of defence expenditure. Similarly, in 1961, 32 per cent of cloth produced for export by the Goldberger factory had to be returned; while in 1962 half of all refrigerators sold had to be repaired in the first six months, and all television sets had to be repaired on average three times within their guarantee period.[27]

A resistance to change and continued overwhelming focus on industry also characterized Hungary's industrial strategy and trade policy in the first half of the 1960s. Despite the shift of investment away from mining and electrical energy towards the chemical industry (an important sector in the second stage of industrialization throughout Eastern Europe) and food processing (Table 4.7), it is also clear that industry's overall share of resources by no means diminished. In fact, it increased.

Despite mounting problems and disappointments with the economy of the early 1960s, the government consistently adhered to its policy, begun in 1957, of ensuring a steady rise in living standards. As Table 4.8 indicates, real incomes increased steadily over the decade, with an impressive increase in the case of those involved in agriculture in the third five-year plan (1966–70).

The consequence of this rise in living standards in the context of a gradually stagnating economy and unreformed foreign trade structure was increased foreign debt. In the 1950s, the circle had been squared by

Table 4.7 Industrial groups as percentage of total industrial investments 1958–70

	1958–59	1960–65	1966–70
Mining	22.1	18.3	15.8
Electrical energy	19.1	14.2	12.3
Smelting	9.0	9.8	11.1
Engineering	18.6	19.1	18.1
Chemical	10.3	15.2	16.0
Light	9.3	9.3	9.8
Other	–	0.4	0.9
Food supply	5.9	7.7	9.5
Industry's share of all investments	35.3	38.3	35.9
Agriculture's share of all investments	–	15.7	18.4

Source: Pető and Szakács, pp. 533 and 425.

Table 4.8 Movements in the index of real wages 1955–70

| | Real per capita income of | | Real per capita value of peasant consumption* |
	population**	workers & employees*	
1955	–	118	110
1957	–	145	121
1960	100	168	143
1963	111	187	150
1965	118	119	117
1968	140	137	138
1970	159	154	150***

*1955–63 100 = 1950, thereafter 100 = 1960
**100 = 1960 throughout
***estimated figure

Source: Pető and Szakács, pp. 683 and 684.

reducing living standards. After 1956, this was not a politically accept-able option; but the alternative was debt. Hungary's convertible currency forint debt in 'devisa forints' grew from 1.6 thousand million in 1959 to 4.1 thousand million in 1964. In 1961 and 1962 taken together, the 'devisa forint' debt on the hard currency account had been 744 million forints. In 1963 alone, it had risen to one thousand million. This increasing debt 'put significant limits on economic development' at a time when, uniquely in Hungarian history, the terms of trade were moving in Hungary's favour. As a National Planning Office document stressed in 1966, 'foreign trade has become the central question in the industrial policy of our five-year plan'.[28]

Table 4.9 Main uses of national income in the second and third five-year plans (%)

	Second 5-year plan	Third 5-year plan
Consumption fund	77.6	77.9
Accumulation fund	22.4	22.1
increase in fixed capital	14.6	16.0
increase in circulating capital	5.0	3.7
increase in capital reserves	2.8	2.4

Source: Pető and Szakács, p. 416.

With these mounting economic problems in mind, the third five-year plan (1966–70) was modest in scope, its 19–21 per cent planned growth in national income being half that set out in the second five-year plan. The overall structure of the plan was similar to its predecessors, as Tables 4.9 and 4.10 indicate, although a novel requirement was included in the plan law, namely that the government was under an obligation to ensure the plan's implementation.

While the targets in this less ambitious plan were achieved more easily, as Tables 4.11 and 4.12 indicate, many worrying features remained. The foreign trade problem was clearly not solved; and crises of overinvestment continued. The yearly investment plan for 1967 was 18 per cent overfulfilled, and, perhaps most worrying of all, productivity did not improve as planned. The industrial labour force grew by twice as much as was intended, and industrial production per employee grew by only 20 per cent rather than the planned 24–27 per cent.[29] The hoped-for move towards intensive economic development and technology-produced growth was clearly not taking place.

By the middle of the 1960s, then, it was becoming increasingly clear that there were problems with the traditional model of central planning, even when balanced growth had been restored, and when the more obvious excesses of autarkic voluntarism had been abandoned. By 1962, the political situation was stable, the plans to catch up and surpass the West had been quietly shelved, and plan targets were not outrageously ambitious. Yet even these targets could not be met. The growth rate declined. Foreign debt increased. The policy of increasing living standards was under threat, and with it political stability.

Table 4.10 Distribution of investments in 1961–65 and in the third five-year plan (%)

	1961–65 (actual)	1966–70 (plan)
Industry	44.3	46.7
Agriculture	18.6	17.1
Transport and communications	13.8	14.2
Commerce	2.0	1.9
Non-productive branches and remainder	21.3	20.1

Source: Pető and Szakács, p. 417.

Table 4.11 Plan fulfilment in the period of the third five-year plan

	National Income (annual increase)		Investments (thousand m. forints)	
	plan	fact	plan	fact
1966	4	8	45.1	47.7
1967	4	8	49.0	58.0
1968	6	5	56.9	55.4
1969	5	8	72.8	74.7
1970	6	5	79.2	87.2
1966–	19–21*	31*	250–260	323.0

*as % of 1965 actual figures

Source: Pető and Szakács, p. 420.

Table 4.12 National income and its use in the period of the third five-year plan (comparable prices)

	1966	1967	1968	1969	1970
National income					
thousand m. forints	203.0	218.4	229.3	247.6	260.0
% of previous year	108	108	105	108	105
Total consumption					
thousand m. forints	157.2	167.1	176.4	187.6	201.5
% of previous year	105	106	106	106	107
of which population's consumption					
thousand m. forints	140.8	150.0	156.8	165.9	177.9
% of previous year	105	107	105	106	107
Accumulation					
thousand m. forints	199.6	223.3	231.5	240.8	268.6
% of previous year	112	132	98	97	126
Foreign trade balance					
thousand m. forints	−2.3	−4.8	−2.2	+6.8	−8.6

− = import surplus, + = export surplus

Source: Pető and Szakács, p. 429.

Continued reform writings and agricultural reforms in practice

The problem of economic stagnation and increasing debt acted as a new stimulus for discussion of far-reaching economic reform both in Hungary and throughout Eastern Europe. Libermann's celebrated article recommending economic reform in the Soviet Union was published in *Pravda* in September 1962, and the Soviet Union made its first international grain purchase in 1963. In that same year, the German Democratic Republic not only announced its intention to introduce its Libermann-inspired New Economic System in January, but actually implemented it in July. A general Eastern European climate in favour of economic reform was confirmed in October 1964 with the downfall of Khrushchev and the ascendancy to power of Kosygin and Brezhnev.

In Hungary, movements towards renewed economic reform began at about the time of the VIIIth Party Congress in November 1962, when Kádár's supremacy was confirmed by the expulsion of Marosán and other factionalists from the party, and by the passing of such reformist measures as opening the universities to all irrespective of political and class background. The preceding Central Committee plenum had expelled Rákosi and Gerő from the Party because of their pre-1956 activities. At the November Congress, Rezső Nyers, who had been Minister of Finance since January 1960 following the death in office of the former incumbent, joined the Political Committee and became secretary to the Central Committee. As a former Social Democrat, he was considered an appropriate replacement for Marosán. Nyers was immediately given responsibility for economic affairs as chair of the newly founded State Economy Committee, which, in addition to Nyers, included Lajos Fehér, who was to become a leading figure in the so-called 'agrarian lobby'. In early 1963 Nyers and Fehér started their work by considering the economic mechanism in agriculture.

Renewed academic interest in economic reform was signalled in September 1963 by the publication of an article by Tibor Liska which caused a storm because he not only insisted that socialism required a market economy, rather than one that was geared to the direct satisfaction of needs, but he also went further and suggested that within this market economy, domestic prices should be determined by world prices, and the currency should be fully convertible.[30]

Towards the end of 1963, Nyers put together an informal 'brains trust' to consider economic reform more generally, which included such 1950s reformers as György Péter and Imre Vajda. Formal recognition of the need for reform came some six months later. On 21 July 1964, the State Economy Committee attached to the Central Committee drafted a decree which was then passed at the Central Committee session of 10

December 1964. The State Economy Committee was given two years in which to draw up a comprehensive proposal for modernizing the economic mechanism. The task of coordinating the project work was placed in the hands of a three-person Mechanism Committee consisting of Nyers, István Friss and Imre Pardi. The practical work was carried by a three-member independent secretariat headed by Tamás Nagy of the Economic Science Research Institute, helped by Péter Havas of the Central Statistical Office and Tamás Morva of the National Planning Office. Eleven work teams in all took part, involving some 130 economists and other experts. Submissions were received from many of the economists who had been advocates of reform to the economic mechanism since the term was first mooted in 1954.[31]

The first draft of the reform was prepared, in two versions, as early as the summer of 1965. These were presented to the Central Committee session of 18–20 November 1965, and the more radical of the two was accepted. In retrospect, it is perhaps surprising that the proposals should have been accepted by the Central Committee without opposition, but as Nyers recalls, the document was not aggressive or alarming in tone, but well argued and convincing. In addition, the second five-year plan was then coming to a close with, as demonstrated above, very poor results. '[T]he existing mechanism was difficult to defend.'[32] The next step in implementing the reform was the elaboration of detailed directives. These were completed in the spring of 1966, and the final decision to implement them was taken by the Central Committee at its session of 25–27 May. As far as specialist economists were concerned, the New Economic Mechanism of 1968 was fully elaborated by mid 1966.

An additional impetus for the introduction of the New Economic Mechanism was the experience of agriculture. While the unreformed planning system, and only slightly modified regulation system and organizational system, of industry were leading the country into economic stagnation, and while economists were theorizing about the possibilities of economic reform, there was growing empirical evidence that the reformed planning, regulation and organizational systems in agriculture were having some success.

As early as 1960, before collectivization had been completed, János Hont, Deputy Minister of Agriculture, could argue that events had proved the political correctness of replacing administrative planning in agriculture with 'economic methods (price, tax, credit and purchasing policy)'.[33] Five years later, in a submission to the committee considering economic reform, he made similar points. The introduction of economic measures to control agricultural producer cooperatives, their greater flexibility, and more direct interest in material incentives had resulted in a much more successful collectivized agriculture than previously, despite a whole panoply of negative features.[34] In his contribution to the same committee, Ferenc Erdei, former representative of the pro-communist wing of the National Peasant Party and prolific writer on the situation of the Hungarian peasantry between the wars, recommended more cooperatives in industry generally and suggested that enterprises should be more cooperative-like.[35]

The New Economic Mechanism

Key components

The New Economic Mechanism introduced on 1 January 1968, but finalized conceptually in mid 1966, was a detailed elaboration of the sort of model conceived by Péter and others some twelve years previously. Central planning in quantitative units was abandoned entirely. Enterprises were instructed to maximize profits, and enterprise guidance was in the form of a complex system of indirect indicators, predominantly taxation and subsidization, which performed a role akin to Smith's 'invisible hand', but with an explicit, socialist intent. In addition to its role in setting the necessary parameters to control and steer this market environment for static equilibrium and simple reproduction, the state retained a determining role for strategic issues and larger-scale investment decisions. There were two further characteristics of the reform. First, in the early years at least, enterprises were to operate in an environment shielded from movements in world prices. Second, the organization system, the structure of economic administration and the size and degree of concentration of enterprises, remained intact. The only change in this area was a further shift of emphasis towards the 'functional ministries' at the expense of the branch ministries, and a relative increase in the independence of the enterprises from the centre.[36] Crucially, branch ministries continued to appoint the three main directors in the enterprise, the managing, financial and technical directors;[37] and branch ministries continued to be the only bodies that could found, liquidate and determine the sphere of economic activities of enterprises in the state sector.[38] Furthermore, proposals to revamp the workers' councils which had so dominated the 1956 discussion were rejected. One of the New Economic Mechanism's preparatory committees headed by András Hegedűs (the one-time prime minister and later dissident) suggested a model which gave the workforce, in the form of workers' councils, a greater role in economic management. But its recommendations were not accepted. This was partly because trade unionists on the committee opposed giving increased powers to new bodies such as workers' councils and so the committee was unable to present a united case; but it was also because Nyers was unwilling to resurrect the political hot potato of the workers' councils.[39]

Under the New Economic Mechanism, the state's role in relation to planning was restricted to setting the main national economic objectives and the important proportions of economic development.[40] Three levels of planning were considered necessary: long term (fifteen years), medium term (five years), and short term (one year). The medium-term plan was the most important of these and had to be passed by parliament.[41] Plan disaggregation stopped at branch level and was not extended down to enterprises.[42] Decisions concerning technological development, product pattern, the introduction of new commodities, the use of enterprise resources for development purposes, investments, the raising of credits and the distribution of personal incomes all devolved to the enterprise manager.[43]

The long-term plan was directed towards larger economic considerations such as the growth rate, both overall and between branches, Hungary's international situation, and the planned improvement of living conditions.[44] The five-year, medium-term plan specified the principal objectives of development and the means of achieving them. It covered areas such as the rates of growth of national income and the social product, the relative proportions of consumption and accumulation, the total amounts of investment and its distribution between branches, a list of major individual investment projects, a list of Central Development Programmes (aimed at realizing major coordinated development across several branches of the economy), the principles of price, financial, credit and labour policies. The short-term, one-year plan related to adjustments only, necessitated by either internal or external conditions which had not been foreseen at the time of drafting the five-year plan, such as relatively minor adjustments to credit or pricing policy, or amendments to labour market regulations.[45]

Clearly, enterprise autonomy increased dramatically; but the centre's influence remained strong in two areas of considerable importance. First, the 'founding organ' (in most cases the branch ministry, the body that exercised ownership rights in that it could create and liquidate enterprises under its control) was still in a position to issue instructions to enterprises in exceptional situations such as in the interests of national defence, or of foreign trade obligations undertaken by the government, which included the majority of CMEA trade. Second, in the area of investments, in addition to indirect instruments such as credit policy, a significant number of centrally determined factors continued to coexist alongside indirect planning in the form of the larger investment projects and the Central Development Programmes.[46] Although the latter were drawn up independently of the national economic plan, they had to be in harmony with it and were implemented by separate special government acts which extended into areas of economic life not covered in the national plans.[47]

The guiding principle of medium-term planning was the encouragement of enterprise profit maximization within state-administered market parameters. In consequence, the rationale underlying pricing policy became of determining importance. The essence of pricing policy under the New Economic Mechanism (NEM) was that prices should take on a more active, allocative role than previously, but within clear limits determined by notions of social justice. Three broad categories of price were introduced: those whose level continued to be fixed centrally, those where the state controlled levels in one way or another, and those which were free from all central government control. Within the controlled category, there were four separate types of price: 'maximum' (established by the state), 'limited' (where the state established the base level and permitted margins above that, usually between 5 and 15 per cent), 'minimum' (used for certain agricultural commodities only), and 'orientation' (mainly used for services provided by the private sector).[48] In the case of producer prices, the government required enterprises to construct price levels using an accounting scheme agreed by their controlling ministry and consistent with guidelines issued by the National Prices and Materials Office (reproduced in Figure 4.1). In so

Figure 4.1 General structure of price formation cost calculations

(1) Direct material cost
(2) Direct wage cost
(3) Taxes on direct wages, additional payments and extra wages
(4) Extra production and selling costs
    Total direct costs (sum of items 1–4)
(5) Overheads (plant, factory and enterprise)
(6) Amortization
(7) Taxes on assets
    General costs (5+6+7)
    Production prime costs (sum of items 1–7)
(8) Costs of technical development
(9) Guarantee repair costs
(10) Other expenses
    Total prime costs (sum of items 1–10)
(11) Profit
(12) Taxes
(13) Subsidies
    Price (sum of items 1–11, minus 12 & 13)

Source: P.G. Hare, 'Industrial Prices in Hungary II', *Soviet Studies*, vol. XXVIII, no. 3, July 1976, p. 372.

far as both factors of production (labour and capital) were taxed separately and at different rates, this schema corresponded to the 'two-channel' theory of pricing.[49] The profit category was the only area of significant difference between controlled and uncontrolled prices. In the case of free prices, the profit component was determined by market forces. In the case of prices fixed or variously controlled by the National Prices and Materials Office in conjunction with the industrial ministries, the level of profit built into these prices depended on these central agencies' estimation of investment needs and social justice.[50] An additional consideration introduced at this time was the attempt to set relative prices in fields closely related to foreign trade according to world market prices, and to link domestic to foreign prices via proxy exchange rates (see below).[51]

A central concern of the NEM was that 'the relative prices of consumer goods and services should correspond more or less to the relations existing between their prime costs'.[52] In order to achieve this closer linkage between producer and consumer prices, the structure of consumer price formation followed the following equation:

Consumer prices = industrial wholesale prices, plus wholesale trading margin, plus retail trading margin, plus turnover tax, minus subsidies.[53]

The original conception was that consumer prices using this formula would be some 6–10 per cent higher than producer prices.[54]

Table 4.13 Types of producer prices relating to domestically produced raw materials and typical intermediary products (% of production affected)

	Fixed	With maximum	With limits	Free
Sources of energy	75	10	–	15
Other minerals and raw materials for heavy industry	10	25	–	65
Metallurgical products	–	85	5	10
Textile thread	–	75	–	25
Leather	–	60	–	40
Building materials made from silicates	–	40	–	60
Wood and paper materials	10	30	–	60
Total	30	40	2	28

Source: X. Richet, *The Hungarian Model: Markets and Planning in a Socialist Economy,* Cambridge 1989, p. 78.

Table 4.14 Types of prices in the processing industries (% of production affected)

	Fixed	With maximum	With limits	Free
Chemical products	10	35	5	55
Engineering products	–	30	5	65
Textile and clothing	–	10	–	90
Finished wood and paper	–	–	–	100
Building structures	–	–	–	100
Food products	5	5	5	85
Total	3	16	3	78

Source: Richet, p. 79.

The sectoral usage distribution of the various types of price (fixed, controlled and free) can be seen from Tables 4.13 and 4.14. Roughly speaking, 30 per cent of prices were fixed, 30 per cent were free and 40 per cent were controlled in some way. Looked at from one perspective, only 30 per cent of prices remained fixed centrally by the omniscient central state. On the other hand, despite the greater market orientation of the economy, 70 per cent of prices remained administered in some way or another, and even nominally free prices of many final products were largely determined by the fixed prices of most raw materials and semi-finished goods.[55] Furthermore, even free prices were affected by taxation and subsidies, that is, by central government's indirect indicators aimed at achieving national plan objectives. In order to appreciate how these operated, the basic principles underlying enterprise accounting and the various funds constructed within each enterprise's budget should be presented.

One significant consequence of the price reform and reduction in turnover tax levels that accompanied it[56] was that a greater proportion of sales income remained with the enterprises. This was the essence of increased autonomy – that funds generated by enterprises could be disposed of as enterprise management saw fit. But the architects of the reform felt the need to guide enterprises in the use of this increased income, and established regulations concerning burdens on it and the manner in which they had to be met. Enterprises first had to cover rents, wage costs, and a number of taxes before establishing three obligatory enterprise funds, as illustrated in Figure 4.2.

The latter two funds were the most important in terms of enterprise autonomy and warrant further comment. The Development Fund was

Figure 4.2 Enterprise taxation and fund formation under the original
NEM

(1) Rent on industrial sites: 5% of site value;
(2) Wages costs (including 17% wages tax and 8% employers' national insurance);
(3) Production Tax (a rent equivalent depending on sector of economy and nature of products);
(4) Charge on assets (5% of gross value of fixed assets and working capital);
(5) Depreciation (centrally determined, on average 40% of value of assets. Average enterprise would retain 60% of depreciation allowance);
(6) Reserve Fund (50% of value of assets plus 8% of wages bill);
(7) Development Fund;
(8) Sharing Fund.

Source: Törvények és Rendeletek Hivatalos Gyűjteménye 42/1967 (X.22)
Korm sz r.

used to cover enterprise-funded investment, and was taxed at a linear 60 per cent (although special rates existed in the commercial sector – 70 per cent – and agriculture – 45 per cent). The Sharing Fund funded enterprise profit shares and, during the first few years of the reform, all increases in salary over the 1967 level. It was taxed progressively (after a tax-free element: 3 per cent of the value of the wage bill in 1968, 2 per cent per year thereafter) from 0–70 per cent according to the ratio of the apportioned to the sharing fund relative to the wage bill. Apportionment between the Development and Sharing Funds was decided according to a formula relating to the value of assets (fixed and circulating) to the wage bill modified by a standard 'wage multiplier'. The standard value of the wage multiplier in 1968 was two, although it was four in metallurgy, aluminium and the paper industry, and six in coal mining and forestry.[57]

The proportions of the sharing fund used for profit shares and increases in employee and management incomes were subject to additional regulation. Wage levels continued to be controlled by the average-wage principle which had first been introduced in 1957, but in a rather different context. The absolute ceilings on the total wage bill were removed.[58] Under the new regulations, any increase in an enterprise's average wages had to be financed out of the Sharing Fund and included in its taxable value. For 1968, there was also a one-off 4 per cent ceiling on average increases.[59] Increases in average wages over the annual 2 per cent tax-free amount were thus effectively subject to highly progressive taxation. This became even clearer when the wage regulation system was modified in 1971. The use of 1967 as a base year was abandoned, an annual 4 per cent tax-free increase in average wages introduced, together with a new, exceptionally progressive 'wage-development payment' on wage payments in excess of the tax-free level.

The profit-sharing system distinguished between three groups of employee, and rewarded them according to their perceived degree of responsibility for enterprise performance. Enterprise directors and top management, some 0.5–1.0 per cent of the workforce, could receive a profit share of up to 80 per cent of their salaries. Middle-level management and foremen, some 4.5–12 per cent of the workforce, could receive profit shares of up to 50 per cent of their salaries. The remaining 87–95 per cent of the workforce could receive profit shares of only 15 per cent of their salaries. On the other hand, while this latter group was guaranteed full salaries however poorly the enterprise performed, the former two categories could experience a drop in salary of 15 and 25 per cent respectively if the enterprise made a loss.[60] This distinction between workers and managers was subject to a great deal of criticism in the first year of the reform and was withdrawn in 1969, although other measures taken at the time ensured that the total possible additional income as a percentage of basic salary accruing to top management under whatever heading (profit share, bonus, premium) did not diminish and exceed that available to the average worker by a considerable extent.

The Development Fund proportion of enterprise profits was used to fund enterprise investment. The New Economic Mechanism envisaged two basic types of investment: enterprise and state. As originally conceived, some 40 per cent of investment was to fall within the competence of enterprises or cooperatives, which were to be funded half from internally generated sources such as the Development Fund and half from bank loans.[61] In reality, no clear equivalence of source of funding and area of authority developed. Enterprise investments included a degree of state funding and vice versa. Indeed, some 85 per cent of enterprise investments involved state funds of some sort.[62] The notionally state investments fell into three types: individual large-scale

Table 4.15 Distribution of investment by decision-making authority (%)

	Government	Enterprise
1970	41.7	58.3
1975	32.0	68.0
1980	36.7	61.0
1985	31.6	68.5

Source: Richet, p. 122.

Table 4.16 Structure of investment by type (%)

	1970	1975	1980	1985
Major investments	15.4	13.8	30.4	21.5
Group investments	20.4	20.6	7.5	8.5
Other investments	9.1	10.7	0.8	0.8
Total state investments	44.6	45.1	38.7	30.8
Socialist enterprise investments	37.9	42.9	58.3	60.2
Cooperative investments	17.5	11.8	3.0	
Total enterprise investments	55.4	54.9	61.3	60.2
Total investments	100.0	100.0	100.0	100.0

Source: Richet, p. 122.

projects such as the Budapest metro, atomic power stations and so on, which were too large for a single enterprise; 'aimed-group' investments, projects such as rural clinics, and minor road developments which required a degree of central coordination of enterprise activity; and other state investments, either in the enterprise or public sector, where the Planning Office dealt in the traditional fashion with the branch ministries.[63] The distribution of these types of investment is given in Tables 4.15 and 4.16.

Bank credits for enterprise investment were determined by the Directives of Credit Policy established annually by the government. These directives selected investments according to two main criteria: conformity with plan objectives, and economic efficiency and profit maximization. In 1968, the directives established exceptionally favourable conditions, such as low rates of interest and extended repayment periods, for agriculture, the development of the services and the production of certain building materials.[64] The interest rate for short-term (one-year) loans was 8 per cent, that for medium-term loans (2–3 years) and long-term (up to 10 years) was not fixed, but was generally above the 5 per cent charge on assets.[65] A condition for granting investment credits was that projected profitability of the investment reach a prescribed minimum.[66] The National Bank expected returns on investment of 20 per cent for engineering, the aluminium and building industries, 15 per cent for metallurgy and light industry, and 7 per cent for transport, communications and agriculture.[67] In comparing the efficiency of competing investment projects which met the rate of return criteria, the so called 'D-index' was established following a procedure essentially similar to the 'net present value' formula used in the West, but with a prescribed fifteen-year evaluation period.[68]

In the area of foreign trade, the overriding concern was to bridge the 'abyss which formerly separated inland producers and consumers from foreign markets'. This was achieved by using actual foreign prices in foreign trade, modified by one of two 'foreign trade multipliers', or commercial exchange rates.[69] These multipliers were established by reference to the average (rather than marginal) cost of earning units of foreign exchange in terms of actual, existing exports.[70] Marer refers to these as 'proxy exchange rates', since they were based on prices determined in the actual current pattern of Hungarian trade rather than computing the purchasing power of the currency for a representative bundle of goods and services produced at home and in selected foreign countries. Two multipliers were introduced, one for ruble trade and one for dollar trade. If the application of the appropriate multiplier resulted in a loss, but the good in question was considered necessary for national economic reasons, a system of state refunds existed to support that enterprise's production. In the event, such subsidies became an important part of exports to the West, so undermining one of the central goals of the New Economic Mechanism, namely increasing efficiency.[71]

The state continued to keep a tight control over foreign trade activity, which could only be conducted by enterprises with permits or licences issued by the Ministry of Foreign Trade. Preferential customs tariffs were available to protect domestic industry. Import quotas continued, but only in accordance with guidelines laid down in the national plan. In 1968 they covered such items as electrical energy, fertilizers, cars and consumer goods, extending to 10–15 per cent of total imported materials.[72] There were cash limits on consumer goods imported from the West, but enterprises were allowed to obtain investment goods from the West after depositing with the National Bank a forint sum equivalent to the foreign exchange price multiplied by a special coefficient.[73] The latter restriction was regarded as a temporary measure, however, one of the many 'brakes' or 'financial bridges' modifying wholesale introduction of market policies which it was originally intended would be removed in the first decade of the operation of the NEM.[74]

The achievements of the New Economic Mechanism

Chapter 5 will consider in some detail how the NEM was modified over the years that followed, why further reform was considered necessary, and why the proponents of the reform later came to see the 1968 paradigm as 'naive'. Here it is appropriate to summarize briefly what the 1968 measures achieved.[75]

First, perhaps the most significant negative feature of the NEM was its reluctance to move the majority of investment decision-making away from the centre. The state, by means of its control of banking and credit, retained the overriding say in investment. Second, the reform left the 'organizational system' – the structure of economic administration – untouched. Third – and a consequence of the second feature – the reform achieved very little in the field of economic policy and development strategy. Economic discussion remained 'mechanism-centred'.[76] In certain crucial respects the economy remained committed to extensive development, to large-scale, long-term production within an autarkic CMEA market. The centrally funded Central Development Programmes dictated a different path of economic development from that required by a regulated market economy. Finally, also to some extent a consequence of the second feature, the NEM was essentially technocratic in character. Although part of its aim was to bring to the surface conflicts of interest that had previously been concealed, little progress was made in developing effective new bodies either to defend group interests or to develop democratic institutions. In the absence of such bodies, when tensions developed on the labour market the only response possible was increased state control and restriction. Central control over investment and the right to establish and liquidate enterprises rendered the mechanism inflexible to changes in world markets and new technological developments.

Turning to the reform's positive achievements, first, and uniquely in Eastern Europe, the NEM succeeded in establishing a form of decentralized planned economy where the centre no longer issued commands and directives concerning volume and range, and which was at least as effective in meeting centrally determined aims as the traditional method of quantitative plan disaggregation had been. Second, a concomitant of the first, the reform created a system of trade and choice in capital goods at least as effective as their distribution via administrative channels. Third, more generally, the reform recognized the multi-sector nature of the economy, the fact that state, cooperative and private small-scale economic activity all had an equal right to exist within a socialist economy. Fourth, although this was implemented less fully in practice, the NEM established the principle that domestic and foreign markets should be closely linked.

But fifth, the real success of the New Economic Mechanism was in the field of consumer choice, in the creation of something approaching 'consumer sovereignty'. As Kornai stated in the late 1980s, 'All observers agree that the supply of food and of many industrial consumer goods is much better in Hungary than it is in other Eastern European economies'; 'Hungary today is less of a shortage economy than it was before reform'; 'The great achievement of the reform is the significant extension of choices.'[77] With the New Economic Mechanism, uniquely in Eastern Europe, Hungary developed market relations in small plots of land (for housing or market gardening), building materials, foreign currency for tourism, and cars.[78] As a result, goods were available for sale along the whole spectrum from once-in-a-lifetime purchases, through occasional luxuries, to everyday items, even if the price was relatively high. Unlike the rest of Eastern Europe – which suffered from the traditional problem of centrally planned economies, 'not the lack of money but the lack of goods' – for Hungarians after the introduction of the NEM the problem was not 'lack of goods, but lack of money'.[79]

The New Economic Mechanism was, inevitably, a child of its place and time. Its essence was the 1968 paradigm of market socialism of 'markets in the present and planning for the future', that is to say, major investment and other future-oriented decisions concerning enterprise establishment and liquidation, market entry and market exit remained predominantly under the control of central planning bodies. In retrospect, its most characteristic features were institutional conservatism and a 'naive' assumption that simple reproduction could be left to the market, but extended reproduction must be kept for the plan.[80] The institutional structure was not seen as a problem at the time. If enterprises were responding to market signals, what did it matter if legally they were still owned by a branch ministry on behalf of the people? Similarly, the extent to which the state apparatus would resort to direct interference in investment decisions was not a self-evident consequence of the proposed investment structure. It is hardly surprising, therefore, that the 'mechanism-centred' reformers failed to predict that enterprise management and the branch ministries would continue to bargain over the definition of national interest, and bend the functioning of financial indicators to further their own ends.

Finally, it should be noted that, just as the renewed interest in economic reform from 1963 onwards formed part of a more liberal political climate, so too the New Economic Mechanism was originally conceived as part of a wider-ranging reform. Political events in Czechoslovakia put paid to such developments, but not before a modest electoral reform could be introduced in 1966. Law III of that year introduced single-member constituencies aimed at strengthening the link between constituents and their deputies and, more significantly, allowed for multi-candidate elections.[81] In elections in 1967, 9 out of 349 seats were contested.[82] To a limited extent, the principle of market competition had been extended to politics.

The New Economic Mechanism and 'market socialism'

The 'naive' conception of the 1968 paradigm, that is to say leaving simple reproduction to a regulated market but retaining central control over extended reproduction, is common to much writing on market socialism. Here the works of three writers will be considered very briefly to illustrate the point. Their choice is not entirely random. Brus is in many ways the intellectual mentor of the tradition. Liska deserves to be better known and, as we shall see in Chapter 6, saw more of his model implemented than he thought. Elson's article, on the other hand, represents a serious Western attempt to develop a market socialist model without reference to developments in Eastern Europe.

Brus's major writings have appeared widely in the West,[83] and exerted a significant influence on the creators of the NEM.[84] Indeed, Brus refers to the New Economic Mechanism's mixture of central control with a regulated market mechanism as his 'favourite idea'.[85] He took as his starting point the fact that, in reality, it has never been a question of all plan or all market, of all centralized and all decentralized. Even when the Stalinist model was at its height, labour and consumer markets did exist since there was freedom of career and place of work, and choice, however limited, in consumer goods. Next he identified three types of activity in a socialist economy: basic macro-economic decisions such as rate of growth, share of investment and consumption, principles of distribution of the consumption fund; current or section decisions such as size and detailed structure of branch or enterprise, source of supplies, and form of remuneration; and individual decisions such as the composition of consumer goods in household, choice of profession and so on. Market relations already obtained in the Stalinist model at the third of these levels, and Brus's model of a decentralized socialist economy simply called for their extension up a level to current or sectional decisions. The centre's role was to determine macro factors such as the rate of increase of productive capacity, its structure, total demand, interest rates, tax systems, wage-control mechanisms and long-term investment decisions. Enterprises would then take autonomous decisions with the objective of profit maximization under the influence of the centrally determined market magnitudes. Monetary relations were to be active instruments in the operation of the economy, presenting real choices and influencing enterprise decisions. Money and commodity forms would constitute an active, basic form of resource allocation.[86] Very similar ideas were put forward in Hungary in a lecture by Tamás Nagy in 1964 which drew extensively on Brus's work, and argued that the market could not establish socialist preferences, but that once these had been established, the law of value was the most appropriate mechanism for distribution.[87]

Tibor Liska's *Ökonosztát* (finally published in 1988 although written almost twenty-five years earlier) can also be seen as firmly rooted in this paradigm, although his proposed reform is certainly much more radical than the New Economic Mechanism.[88] Liska's argument is subtle. His point of departure is that, as cybernetic theory suggests, the best sort of economic system is one that works by itself, where all countervailing forces balance each other out. Such systems are able to cope with the unexpected in a way which no ex ante planned economy can. For such a system, the key ingredient is information, and the key element of information in an economic system is price. But prices must give real information, hence they must be based on world prices, which reflect real scarcities, and, less crucially but nevertheless importantly, should be open to scrutiny.[89] His ideal, then, is a decentralized, self-balancing economic system, the key ingredient of which is the adoption of world prices and, as a consequence of this, a fully convertible currency. Commodity production, and production for the market, rather than some centrally predetermined notion of need, is essential to socialism.

Liska isolates three fundamental types of activity: labour force or work-undertaking, capital or social ownership, and entrepreneurial, all three of which necessarily have conflicting interests. In Liska's view, both socialism and capitalism are commodity-producing market societies. The advantage of socialism over capitalism lies in the fact that, under the former, the most appropriate functions of labour power, capital, and entrepreneurial activity can be performed by the most appropriate individuals and institutions. Under capitalism, all three of these functions were distorted by a set of ownership relations which reflected past historical power rather than the needs of society. Under socialism, because all capital is essentially credit capital and not based on property, everyone can perform an entrepreneurial function, and everyone will have financial security because Liska also advocates a basic wage for all, irrespective of place or nature of work.[90] The real advantage of socialism, then, is that 'it has developed a higher degree of commodity production and has made it more all-pervasive than under capitalism'.[91] The 'econostatic' system, of which the introduction of world prices is the first step, allows these three spheres to balance each other out.

At the abstract level, Liska's conception requires a radical departure from precedent. But the more concrete he gets about institutions and actors in the model, the clearer it is that he is still working in the 1968 paradigm. This is especially the case in the section describing the 'socialist plan market'.[92] True, he talks of banks (a bank?), under an obligation to function profitably, owning industry rather than ministries.[93] Nevertheless, the setting of the 'rules of the game' for the whole system is seen as a political task,[94] to be carried out by the ministries.

And, as with the other writing in this paradigm, the relationship between the 'ownership' and 'entrepreneur' functions is fuzzy. In places, Liska seems to be simply asking for a new breed of manager who is professionally competent and not restricted by the ties of either political interference or historical accident (ownership).[95] Elsewhere, he describes a new organizational system where all enterprises appear to be subsidiaries of one or more banks which act as holding companies. But the ownership of these banks is not resolved in any detail, nor is the question of how new enterprises are founded and others liquidated.[96] Though he is at more pains than most to stress that all influence must be via indirect indicators, he sees no need to abolish branch ministries (simply change their role), and he suggests a strong role for the state in the sphere of investment. Investment capital will be distributed via bank credits to the enterprises offering the most advantageous project; banks, which enjoy a credit monopoly,[97] are in some rather imprecise way owned by the state; and political factors are to be taken into consideration in investment decisions. The state's monopoly of credit puts Liska's theory very much in the Brus paradigm. Furthermore, for Liska, as for the other 1968 paradigmers, there is nothing problematic about the combination of decentralized production units and some form of ultimate state ownership of their assets.

In the Western literature, the outline of a socialized market suggested by Diane Elson twenty years after NEM also conforms with the 1968 paradigm, although her model is closer to Liska than to Brus. On the one hand she assumes, quite reasonably in the UK context, that the prices a socialist economy would use are world prices. On the other, she places similar emphasis on the importance of information and the need for the process of price formation to be open to scrutiny.[98] She and Liska also share the view that the state should provide a basic minimum income to all. Finally, again like Liska, her model consciously rejects the traditional form of branch ministry. Unlike the Eastern European writers, however, she places much more emphasis on worker-management. This, as she says, 'means that the total labour costs of an enterprise will generally not be treated simply as a cost to be minimized'.[99] Similar concerns led the Czechoslovak reformers to suggest gross income as their basic success indicator,[100] an indicator which was also adopted throughout Hungary's cooperative agriculture where the social obligations of the production unit were considered to be more extensive than in industry,[101] and which Cornforth et al. suggest (using the Western term 'value-added') for evaluating the performance of cooperatives in the UK.[102] Elson makes it clear that, while enterprises would buy their materials and equipment and sell their output in 'socialized markets' (that is to say, where all have equal access to information on how prices were determined), reconstruction of enterprises would be the responsibility of a Regulator of Public Enterprises.[103] Investment decisions are decentralized to the enterprises, but her secretariats of buyer and seller networks interacting with a national planning agency to generate an overall agreed strategy for the national economy leave some scope for creeping centralization in investment decisions.

In areas other than pricing, the structure she suggests ends up looking more like Hungary's New Economic Mechanism than the institutions of French and Japanese strategic planning to which she refers. The duties performed by her Wages Commission are analogous to those of Hungary's Ministry of Labour or State Office for Wage and Labour Affairs. The democratically controlled job evaluation exercises are analogous to the Hungarian trade unions' rights of consultation and veto discussed below in Chapter 7. Her obligation on public enterprises to share technology information has no direct analogy but is reflected in Eastern Europe's general reluctance to recognize intellectual property rights. Even her requirement on the disclosure of information on pricing is met, although not in the way she suggests, since the principle of price formation was in the public domain, and the majority of prices were controlled centrally in some way. More fundamentally, as with the Eastern European reformers of the 1960s, there is a lack of clarity about ownership. Enterprises are publicly owned and subject to the Regulator of Public Enterprises. Employees of public sector enterprises would exercise use rights, but not property rights, and enterprises would be self-financing. The state, in the form of the Regulator of Public Enterprises, retains property rights. Enterprises are free to make investment decisions, yet they can be influenced by the Regulator exercising its property rights.

The 1968 market socialist paradigm is one that is shared by socialists from both sides of what used to be called the Iron Curtain. Chapter 5 will consider the problems encountered by the paradigm when put into practice.

5

Market Socialism in Practice: Large Enterprises and the Mechanics of Planning

The period between 1968 and the mid 1980s in Hungary is usually split into three phases. Marer, for example, presents a 'golden age' (1968–72), a period of illusion (1973–78) and a 'period of realism' (1979–85), to be followed by a period of 'all caution to the winds' (1986–88).[1] Galasi and Sziráczki refer to the period 1968–71 as one of rapid increase in national income and living standards and improvement in economic performance, to the period 1972–78 as one of continued growth, but accompanied by inflation and a slowdown in the rise in living standards, and the period 1979–84 as one of high inflation, slow growth and declining real wages.[2] Here only two major periods will be isolated: retreat from reform, which began well before 1972–73 and recentralization in favour of fifty 'privileged' enterprises, and culminated with the XIth Party Congress in 1975; and reform reluctantly reborn which began in agriculture before the onset of more general Party realism in 1978. The chapter first considers retreat from reform, before addressing the economic problems encountered by the 1968 paradigm. Finally it considers renewed moves towards reform which, however, failed to solve key problems and resulted in a paradoxical combination of radical reform and voluntaristic planning.

Retreat from Reform

Although the New Economic Mechanism was introduced as a comprehensive measure, a single package rather than a series of piecemeal reforms, the use of 'brakes' and 'bridges' between producer and consumer, and domestic and world prices indicated a commitment to further reform. This second stage of reform would, according to Nyers, over a fifteen-year period[3] address two central sets of issues: first, the active use of world prices and the convertibility of the forint; second, the need to create some sort of capital market, and the possibility of enterprises issuing bonds. The theme of foreign trade reform, a convertible forint and a more active use of world prices figured in a speech made by Nyers in 1968,[4] and in an article published by Csikós-Nagy in 1970.[5] Meanwhile, in the spring of 1969, the Economic Committee decided in principle on further price reform which would take account of world prices. The same session also acknowledged that, at some later date, the forint should become convertible.[6]

At the same time, the Central Committee's summer session addressed the additional problem of large enterprise: the need to break up monopolies, and undo the results of the 1962–64 merger campaigns.[7] Meanwhile, the Economic Policy Department of the Central Committee had organized a working party, which reported in the autumn of 1969, to consider the question of more decentralized investments.[8] It suggested new forms of commercial credit, granting enterprises the right to issue bonds, and the creation of an institution which would organize and carry out the planned movement of capital.[9] In 1970, the attention of the Economic Committee turned to the question of labour and such fundamental and intangible questions as what the concept of a high income means, whether it can be determined in absolute terms, and how excessively high incomes might be controlled indirectly.[10] In an article published in 1972 and later regarded as seminal, Márton Tardos continued the theme of the need for changes to the organization system. His solution called for an ending of ministerial ownership of enterprises and the transfer of their assets to 'production and commercial banks' which would act like holding companies and direct funds between enterprises on the basis of commercial considerations.[11]

But the planned second stage of the New Economic Mechanism was not to be, despite minor measures – such as lifting some price controls and relaxing credit controls in the first years of reform – which Portes interpreted in the early 1970s as hopeful signs.[12] As Table 5.1 indicates, the economy performed quite well in the first years of the reform. Indeed, as Portes argued in 1970, 'Recentralization would ... require a conscious, open political decision.'[13] Despite Kádár's statement at the Xth Party Congress of November 1970 that the decision in favour of reform had been correct,[14] a conscious political decision to recentralize was in fact made, although it could not be described as open.

Politically the turning point was the removal of Dubček in Czechoslovakia in 1969,[15] a year which also witnessed the rejection in Hungary of 'Marxist pluralism', and the removal of Hegedűs as head of the Sociological Research Group of the Hungarian Academy of Sciences.[16]

Table 5.1 Hungarian economic performance under the reforms (% increase)

	1968	1969	1970	1968–70 average
National income	5	8	5	6
National income from industry	6	4.5	8.5	6
Industrial production	5	3	7.5	5
Industrial employment	4	3	0.5	2
Industrial productivity	1	0	7	3
Exports (foreign exch. prices)	5	16	11	12
Imports (foreign exch. prices)	2	7	30	11
Fixed investment (current price)	1	7	15	7.5
Balance of trade (million for exchange forints)				
ruble	+400	+1200	−1380	+70
rest of world	−540	+670	−900	−260
Ave. earnings state industry	2	4	6	4
Industrial producer prices	0.5	2	2	1.5
Retail prices	1	1.5	1.5	1.5
Per capita real income (workers and employees)	5.5	6.5	6.5	6
Real wages (workers/employees)	2	5	3.5	3.5
Stockbuilding (thou. m. fts)	17	10.5	15	14

Source: R. Portes, 'The Strategy and Tactics of Economic Decentralisation', *Soviet Studies*, vol. XXIII, 1972, p. 654.

Following this, when Nyers and others visited the Soviet Union in 1970, they came under pressure to reintroduce compulsory indicators based on the Soviet model.[17] By 1972, Soviet concern with developments in Hungary increased further. The recentralization lobby had gained clear supremacy by the Central Committee session of November 1972 which issued a statement noting that the reform 'in places ... was operating not in the desired direction'.[18] A succession of 'salami tactics' followed during which politicians opposed to the reform, supported by their Soviet colleagues,[19] removed all prominent pro-reformers from positions of influence.[20] The final defeat of the reformers came in March 1974 when Nyers and Lajos Fehér were removed from their Political Committee posts.

Despite the good economic performance of the first few years following 1968,[21] the 'golden age' of the reform, two problems (one evergreen, the other entirely new) offered powerful economic arguments to the anti-reformers. The evergreen problem was a growing crisis of overinvestment which peaked in 1970–71;[22] the new problem was labour mobility, and this proved to be the single most important card in the anti-reformers' hand. Increased market relations, in an area where market rather than central allocation had always been the norm, gave unprecedented opportunities to the working class to pursue its group interests. As never before, it began to vote with its feet and move to better paying jobs. Discussion of increased labour mobility reached the status of a 'moral panic' against 'migratory birds', the term invented for workers who constantly changed their jobs. In reality, the situation was more complex than this. Labour turnover between the beginning of 1968 and the end of 1969 was twice that of the preceding four years, but the evidence suggested that although more people were changing jobs, those who did change were doing so fewer times. There was no 'irresponsible' flitting from job to job; rather, more people were availing themselves of the new opportunities for changing jobs.[23]

As early as 1969, the profit-share system with its three categories of reward for top, middle and non-management had to be altered because of 'widespread dissatisfaction' with the too visible distinction between managers and workers.[24] In some cases, the 1969 profit share for top managers was ten times that of workers, despite the fact that the total income of the top managers was only 2 per cent higher than in previous years. The new system returned to the former policy of camouflaging income inequalities under a variety of bonus headings, thus simply making them less visible. Instead of receiving a disproportionately large profit share, managers received a new 'profit premium'. In the same year, the government also outlawed the practice of collective farms hiring out their surplus labour to labour-starved state enterprises, and, responding to pressure from the latter, mooted the possibility of regulating collective farm salaries more closely.[25] In the summer of 1970, the Economic Committee of the Central Committee discussed the need for more active intervention to make labour more expensive and staunch demands for investment,[26] and, in 1971, such measures were introduced. On 1 June 1971, a blanket credit stop for a year was declared to arrest the spiralling investment crisis,[27] and restrictions were placed on labour turnover. Workers who terminated employment without giving adequate notice were deprived of their rent subsidy, and local councils were encouraged to use their powers to direct labour in the cases of workers who changed jobs more than twice a year or who were dismissed for indiscipline.[28] In June 1972, additional taxation was levied on collective farms which engaged in non-agricultural activities.[29]

The most significant point in the retreat from reform came some months later with the Central Committee meeting of 14–15 November 1972. Reacting to the overinvestment crisis and the labour shortage with its associated high levels of labour turnover, it determined to reassert central control over the economy. The most important consequence of this was the creation, in 1973, of fifty 'exceptional' or 'privileged' enterprises under the special control of the Council of Ministers for which the full rigours of market discipline no longer applied. These enterprises accounted for 64.6 per cent of socialist industry's fixed capital, 50 per cent of total production, and 60 per cent of exports. They employed some 700,000 people, and were already heavily subsidized.[30] Although the management of these large enterprises did not engineer the process of recentralization alone, they clearly benefited from it. Symbolic of the renewed emphasis on central planning, the government created a new State Plan Committee and upgraded the status of the National Planning Office such that its chair, who had not even had ministerial status previously, was now a deputy prime minister.[31]

Central intervention in the sphere of investment continued in 1974 with the first major amendment to the New Economic Mechanism's investment regulations, which introduced a new requirement for investment requests to complete all necessary documentation, made explicit reference to the need for conformity with the National Plan and the Central Development Programmes, and gave wider powers to the branch ministers.[32] A new Central Development Programme in association with the fifty 'exceptional' enterprises was also introduced,[33] covering such areas as public vehicle (bus) production, aluminium, computers, pharmaceuticals and electronics. The government also increased centrally the wages of industrial and construction workers in the state sector of the economy in 1973 by an average 8 per cent for skilled workers.[34] In 1974, this increase was extended to those performing state sector industrial or construction work but not employed in these two sectors of the economy.[35] The rhetoric of the period stressed the principle of equality and the necessity of increasing wages in the state sector, especially in heavy industry, in relation to the cooperative sector. On the other hand, the measures also explicitly increased differentials between skilled and semi-skilled workers by giving the latter a smaller rise.[36] The return to the former methods was symbolized by the fact that, in 1974, a labour competition was introduced to greet the XIth Party Congress in 1975 and the thirtieth anniversary of the liberation.[37] The final step in the reimposition of central control over wages was the introduction on 1 January 1975 of a national wage table to ensure that wages depended on the type of work performed, and not on the branch or economic sector it happened to be performed in.[38] Any payment of a wage outside the upper and lower levels of the wage band for each type of work had to be reported to both the branch ministry and the trade union concerned.[39]

This reassertion of central control of labour and investment coincided with the 'first oil shock' of the early 1970s which adversely affected Hungary's terms of trade by some 20–30 per cent. Worse, the political climate of the times interpreted the shock as part of an international crisis of capitalism which would have no effect on Hungary.[40] Growth rates were not reduced, necessitating continued extensive imports from the West, which could be paid for only by increased foreign loans. Tables 5.2 and 5.3 taken from Kornai illustrate this process clearly.

The XIth Party Congress of March 1975 marked the culmination of this wave of recentralization. Its proclamations were full of the rhetoric of an earlier era: the need to develop socialist morality, the need for discipline, the need for continued unbroken growth, the danger of petty-bourgeois attitudes developing.[41] Its targets for the fifth five-year plan (1976–80) stressed the need for a further centralization of national income.[42] In addition, its prescriptions for the plan took little notice of the changes in world trade. Despite a recognition of the deteriorating foreign conditions, the plan called for 'continuity in every important field of the economy', as Table 5.4 illustrates.[43] Traditional voluntarism was reflected not so much as ever-increasing targets but in aggressive maintenance of continuity in the face of a world climate that required less dynamic growth. The traditional penchant for the grandiose was reflected in a renewed emphasis on large enterprises. From 1971

Table 5.2 Growth in Hungary 1967–78 (annual rate in %)

	1967–73	1973–78
	(in real terms)	
National income	6.1	5.2
Investment	7.0	7.8
Wage per wage earner	3.1	3.2
Consumption per capita	4.6	3.6
	1971–73	1973–78
	(at current prices)	
Gross convertible currency debt		
on forint base	13.8	20.0
on US$ base	23.8	26.8

Source: J. Kornai, 'The Hungarian Reform Process: Visions, Hopes and Reality', in V. Nee and D. Stark (eds), *Remaking the Economic Institutions of Socialism: China and Eastern Europe*, Stanford 1989, p. 78.

Table 5.3 International comparison of growth rates in construction activity
(a proxy for investment activity)

	Annual growth rates (%)	
	1968–73	*1973–78*
Austria	5.5	1.0
Finland	3.9	1.1
Portugal	8.9	0.9
Spain	5.9	−2.1
Hungary	6.6	5.7

Source: Kornai, 'The Hungarian Reform', p. 79.

onwards, a move towards amalgamating industrial enterprises in the
state and cooperative sectors had begun, and this reached its peak in
1976–77 following the XIth Congress.[44]

Although agriculture did not escape the consequences of the changed
political climate of the mid 1970s, in areas specific to agricultural
production (that is to say, excluding the non-agricultural ancillary
activities), the retreat from reform was much less marked. The agricultural sector in many ways benefited most from the economic climate
created by the New Economic Mechanism.[45] In a sector dominated by
over a thousand collective farms, the cosy relationship of ministry to
monopoly supplier could not develop to such an extent. Farms enjoyed
considerable autonomy from central control, which some developed to

Table 5.4 Major indicators of the development of the Hungarian economy,
fifth five-year plan (% growth)

Indicator	1971–75 preliminary	1976–80 planned
National income	35	30–32
Gross output (industry)	37	33–35
(construction)	26	30–33
(agriculture)	18	16–18
Per capita real income	25	18–20
Real wages per earner	18	14–16
Total personal consumption	28	21–23
Exports, total	67	53
Imports, total	54	36
Investment in social sector	50	26

Source: O. Gadó, *The Economic Mechanism in Hungary – How it Works in 1976,* Leyden
and Budapest 1976, pp. 26–7.

good effect, diversifying into food-processing, marketing, non-agricultural products, and disposing of product lines that were insufficiently profitable. The major significance of agriculture during this period, however, lies in the structures developed for creating opportunities for small-scale production and integrating them within the larger-scale socialist production unit.

Two processes were at work in the decade and a half that followed successful collectivization. On the one hand, in the major product areas, large-scale, mechanized agriculture was established, employing a labour force which earned guaranteed wages at almost industrial levels, with pensions and other social benefits equivalent to industry's (together with paid holidays), in the context of financial regulations more or less identical to industry's (see Figure 5.1). On the other, significant steps were taken to encourage, and then incorporate into the collective farm the labour of farm members and outsiders based on the 'self-exploitation' typical of peasant and other forms of family economy (see Figure 5.2).[46] It was later recognized that such activity formed part of a 'second economy'.

By the mid 1970s, then, the second stage of the New Economic Mechanism had not been implemented and much of the original reform had been retracted. What remained was the absence of compulsory targets, and thus a degree of genuine enterprise autonomy, something

Figure 5.1 Stages in the growth of the institutional and financial context for 'socialist wage labour' on agricultural producer cooperatives

Publication of Agrarian Theses	1957
Cooperative ownership of capital equipment	1957
Introduction of pensions	1958
Introduction of depreciation funds	1966
Establishment of National Prod. Co-op Council	1967
Cooperative ownership of land	1968
Reorganization of cooperative funds	1968
'Work payments' treated as production costs	1968
Introduction of maternity allowances	1968
Introduction of production tax (non-agricultural prod.)	1971
Introduction of increase in income tax	1971
Obligation to form Reserve Fund	1972
Near parity of wages industry and agriculture	early 1970s
Recommendations for length of working day	1974
Recommendations for national table of wage rates	1975
Ministerial decree on national table of wage rates	1977
100% wages recommended rather than 'wage payments'	1977
Introduction of overtime rates for night work	1977
Introduction of mandatory qualifications for certain jobs	1977

Source: Swain, *Collective Farms Which Work?*, Cambridge 1985.

122

Figure 5.2 Stages in the integration of 'family labour' on to producer cooperative farms

Publication of Agrarian Theses	1957
Concessions in regulations concerning size of household plot and no. of animals held on it	1959
Role of household plot in commodity production acknowledged	1960
Extensive use of 'sharecropping'	1960s
Household plots given to individuals not families	1968
New emphasis on General Consumer and Marketing Co-ops	1968
Beginnings of purchasing arrangements between small-scale agriculture and state enterprises	1968
Abolition of restrictions on animal numbers on household plots	1970
Recommendation that cooperatives hire household plot agronomist	1971
Work on household plot with animals marketed via co-op counts towards social benefits	1970
Establishment of Agricultural Specialist Groups	1971
Co-ops recommended to form household plot committee	1971
State aid in purchase of machinery for small-scale production	1971
Cooperatives receive state aid to encourage integration of household plot animal husbandry	1972
State aid in purchase of polythene sheeting for small-scale vegetable production	1974
Work on household plots with vegetables marketed via co-op counts towards social benefits	1974
Small-scale producers allowed to lease state land	1977
Co-ops obliged to form household plot committee	1977
Prohibition on members' horse ownership abolished	1977
Improvement of household plot production becomes criterion on which part of management bonus can be based	1977

Source: Swain, *Collective Farms*, p. 67.

akin to consumer sovereignty since management bonuses still depended on profits and ultimately sales, and an agrarian reform which suggested how reserves of private family initiative might be liberated and incorporated into the socialist sector of the economy.

Problems with the 1968 Paradigm

Soft budget constraints

The retreat from reform of the mid 1970s was to have disastrous economic consequences. Before documenting them, we should pause to consider the more general problems associated with the 1968 paradigm and its inherent tendencies towards recentralization. It is important to do this before turning to the rebirth of reform at the end of the 1970s, so as to be well placed to appreciate why the series of measures which culminated in the enterprise reform of 1985 and the banking reform of 1987 in fact did little to solve the problems, even though in many ways they constituted, a decade and a half late, the rejected second stage of the New Economic Mechanism.

The problems with the 1968 paradigm can best be conceptualized in terms of Kornai's designation 'soft budget constraints'. The term has been subjected to considerable criticism by economists, and Nuti has even labelled it a 'soft concept';[47] but it is its very malleability that makes it useful. As Hare has argued in an extensive elaboration of Kornai's work and its criticisms, there are gaps in Kornai's formal modelling of 'soft budget constraints', and its associated concepts of 'expansion drive', 'quantity drive', and norms of shortage, which are only adequately addressed in his descriptive account.[48] In addition, the evidence which Kornai uses to demonstrate his case is ambivalent and may simply reflect the irrationalities of the price system.[49] But irrational prices and soft budget constraints are not unrelated. 'Soft budget constraints' must be taken as a descriptive-analytical rather than an abstract-theoretical term. It refers, under a single heading, to a constellation of conceptually linked, empirically observable features which characterize only partial commitment to market relationships. In this sense, it is a useful conceptual shorthand. Its essence is that, for key sectors of the economy, when it comes to the crunch, market forces do not apply. Enterprises are not permitted to go bankrupt, and pricing levels, taxation policy and subsidy policy will all be modified accordingly to make sure they do not. Because enterprises know this, tax and price policies are not treated as an 'effective constraint, but only act as an accounting relationship over which bargaining is possible'.[50] Socialists will not necessarily see much wrong with 'soft budget constraints' in this sense. After all, one of the main aims of socialists is a society in which 'the market' or the 'law of value' does not dominate every sphere of human activity. Kornai's point is that where 'soft budget constraints' are an all-pervasive feature of an economic system, severe negative consequences ensue, which undermine the efficient and effective operation of the economy, and result in persistent shortage.

The kernel of the 'soft budget constraint' case is that exceptions to financial regulators can always be found. A central factor in this is the persistence of monopolies, exacerbated, in the 1970s at least, by the absence of institutional reform in the organization system. Management of the large, virtually monopoly producers that were created in the early

1960s was well placed to demand special status, even before 'exceptional' status was formally granted to the fifty large enterprises in 1973. As early as 1970, Portes noted that state subsidies were awarded mainly to a small group of large enterprises.[51] Five years later, Bauer gave what has become the classic statement of problems associated with the unreformed institutional structure and the contradictory position this places enterprises in.[52] Enterprises remained informal subordinates of the branch ministries which owned them; and continued to be large monopoly suppliers:

> While, on the one hand from the point of view of formal interest and general financial regulation, the situation of the enterprise was characterized by the abolition of plan disaggregation, an interest in profit maximization and uniform regulation, on the other, it appears that in the informal decision-making mechanisms of the economy, *in essence, the direct dependence of enterprises on the state apparatus remains*, and enterprises remained parts of an extensive branch-area hierarchy of economic administration.... In order to bridge this duality ... there developed ... certain financial preferences. These include various forms of price support (including support for imported material), concessions to enterprises to increase wages, export subsidies, tax reductions, tax exemptions ... investment support etc. ... obtaining privileges... is nowadays often an easier way of increasing profitability ... than greater efficiency.[53]

As Hegedűs and Tardos demonstrated in an empirical study of the Budapest stocking factory, 'The dependence of executives on the industrial ministry and the freedom of the enterprise contradict one another ... it is no longer worthwhile for the enterprise to assert its original point of view developed on the basis of profits, since bargaining with the centre may yield as much profit.'[54]

'The basis of the bargaining position', as Laky has noted, 'is the place of the enterprise taken in the national economy.'[55] Monopoly enterprises are susceptible to pressure from ministries to meet the supply needs, or export obligations within the CMEA of the economy;[56] and they are well positioned to bargain with this pressure to obtain concessions, especially in the field of investment, from the central authorities. As one manager put it, 'Even the ministry is careful with an enterprise in which fifteen thousand men work and when two priority programmes of special importance are underway – you must not fail here, and the ministry is well aware of it.'[57] On the other hand, the locus of ultimate power is clear, as can be seen from the following remarks made to Szalai:[58]

> The ministry does not give orders as a sergeant does to the soldiers, and the

enterprise does not wait to be instructed, but goes, by its own will, to meet [expectable wishes] ... The ministry states its conditions in advance when negotiating with us, and they listen to and observe also our conditions. We ask for certain things from each other and try to fulfil requests on both sides. But the money is in their hands, thus all that is, on their part, just a polite, proper and cultured form of instruction. It would be illusory – even theoretically – to oppose the ministry.

The traditional model of 'plan bargaining' between enterprises and ministries identified by Kornai in the 1950s was replaced by 'regulation bargaining'.[59] Rather than ask for easily achievable output targets, enterprise management sought concessions in relation to one or more of the economic regulators such as price, tax, subsidy, in return for performing an unprofitable task deemed by planners to be in the national interest. Profit became a falsifiable plan indicator rather than the centre of interest in a controlled market economy.[60] Large enterprises returned to direct bargaining with ministries, for enterprise funds as well as extra bonuses and the privilege of foreign travel, in return for providing the extra output that was demanded of them;[61] while smaller ones concentrated on accommodating themselves to ministry-approved larger projects in order to be guaranteed funds.[62]

The nature of the bargain changed over the years. First, the overriding national interest used to justify central intervention changed from duty to supply in the 1970s,[63] to duty to export, especially to the West, in the 1980s. Second, the contours of the bargaining process changed considerably when, as we shall see below, the branch ministries were abolished in the 1980s. Enterprises lost their ready ally in the sector's branch ministry who, as Szalai notes, could help further a case against the 'functional ministries' such as the Ministry of Finance which controlled the financial regulators under the New Economic Mechanism. Despite this loss of their natural ally, enterprise 'regulation bargaining' continued.[64]

In an economic climate where the norm became making exceptions to the rule and softening budget constraints, it is not surprising that planners developed, or rather maintained, a 'lack of confidence in the ability of directors to manage their enterprises efficiently'.[65] Richet's account of this process is remarkably similar to the description of the traditional planning process given in Chapter 3.

Initially, when the national plan is being prepared, the Planning Office sends enterprises a series of methodological directives setting out how to start preparing the plan, what it should contain and how it should proceed, and the basic principles to be applied in the relations of the enterprise and the controlling bodies with other enterprises. These recommendations are supplemented with others from the branch ministries, which are more technical in nature and spell out the main categories and indicators in the enterprise plan....[66]

A further dimension to this continued absence of enterprise autonomy was simply the number of instructions that passed from ministries to enterprises. Kornai has shown that the number of economic regulations issued in each year between 1971 and 1981 increased (319 in 1971, 399 in 1976, 433 in 1981), while the numbers employed by the central bureaucracy decreased by only an insignificant amount (10,791 in 1971, 11,046 in 1976, 10,069 in 1981).[67] He also shows that administration expenditure grew faster than GDP between 1979 and 1981.[68]

One of the most important topics over which enterprise bargaining takes place is access to investment funds. After three brief years of 'genuine autonomy' between 1968 and 1970,[69] access to investment funds became a central feature of bargaining, as Laky makes clear. Of the twenty-four investment projects she included in her study, only four were financed by enterprises entirely from their development funds, and in a further one the majority funding came from enterprise sources. In all the remainder, funds came wholly (eight cases) or mainly (eleven cases) from external sources. In all cases of central support return on investment stipulations were made. In thirteen cases, capacity and sourcing requirements were also made, and these were subject to constant change.[70] Soós estimates that nationally, by the early 1970s, only 12 per cent of investments were funded wholly from enterprise sources compared with the 60 per cent originally conceived for the New Economic Mechanism,[71] a figure which held into the mid 1970s.[72] The corollary of this process was that projected rate of return became decreasingly important in investment decision-making, although with some justification since, as Soós has noted, with a price system distorted by subsidies all investment proposals could seem equally profitable.[73] Indeed, one result of the bargaining process and multiple, mainly central, funding of investments was that subsidies themselves became a major determinant of creditworthiness: 'enterprises can raise credits for some investment project because another one is financed from state subsidy ... moreover ... subsidy and credit are simultaneously used for financing the same investment ... it is the subsidy that makes it creditworthy'.[74]

A further consequence of the fact that access to investment funds depended increasingly on success in bargaining rather than the demonstration of financial soundness was that it became of paramount importance to cultivate good enterprise relations with external bodies.

Because conditions are so uncertain and subject to change, personal, subjective judgement in decision-making inevitably gets a great emphasis. We therefore try to establish good personal relations with the higher authorities, to give them a good picture of our enterprise because that increases our chances of sharing in external funding and concessions.[75]

While the branch ministries still existed, there was, as Richet notes, an additional dimension to investment bargaining. The functional and branch ministry contributions to the bargaining process served different goals. The branch ministries were motivated by developing their particular industrial sector; the functional ministries had more global goals such as equilibrium or efficiency.[76]

The overall consequence of this pattern of investment sourcing and the bargaining strength of the small number of large monopoly enterprises was far more significant than the fact that creditworthiness can become dependent on the size of subsidies. A systematic redistribution of funds from the profitable to the unprofitable took place, to the benefit of the large enterprises. This process is considered in great detail by Kornai and Matits,[77] who develop a concept of 'original profit', that is to say the profit that would have been achieved without any cross-subsidization,[78] and consider how it is related to the level of subsidy and the net effects of redistribution. Having demonstrated that there is a close correlation between 'original' profit and redistribution which operates in the direction of supporting loss-making enterprises and diverting funds from profitable enterprises,[79] they show how this had an overall levelling-down effect. Table 5.5 demonstrates this effect, and while it does not in itself indicate that the larger enterprises were the main beneficiaries of this transfer of resources, we have already seen that large enterprises were consistently the main beneficiaries of subsidies.

Table 5.5 Enterprise profitability before and after redistribution 1982

Degree of profitability	% of enterprises in each category:	
	before redistribution	after redistribution
Loss-making	14	1
Low	22	76
Average	40	17
High	24	5

Source: J. Kornai, 'A vállalati nyereség bürokratikus újraelosztása', in Kornai (ed.), *Régi és Új Ellentmondások és Dilemmák*, Budapest 1989, p. 128.

The traditional problems continue

With the continuation of enterprise bargaining (albeit 'regulation bargaining' in place of 'plan bargaining') and an economic model, the essence of which remained to deny the force of the 'law of value' (albeit the application of 'soft budget constraints' rather than deliberately distorting growth in the interest of primary accumulation or rapid industrialization) it is not surprising that many of the negative features associated with the traditional planning model persisted. Central amongst these were two problems in the area of investment (the tendency to investment cycles and over long gestation periods), the continuance of 'storming', and continued foreign debt.

The Hungarian economy, like others in Eastern Europe, had long been prone to a three-to-five-year cyclical pattern in the rate of growth of investment.[80] Bauer describes the cycle in terms of four stages:[81] *run-up*, a general build-up in the number of investment projects; *rush*, when the 'approval coefficient' for new investment projects falls, existing projects are continued rather than abandoned, and the rate of investment and accumulation within the economy as a whole increases at the expense of other possible uses of the national income (either consumption on its own, as was the case in the 1950s, or consumption in conjunction with the balance of trade); *halt*, when physical capacity has been reached, either in terms of the balance of trade crisis, or in terms of the readiness of the population to tolerate a further reduction in consumption, as happened in 1956; and finally *slowdown*, when there is a fall in the planned and actual growth rate in investment outlays, some projects are abandoned, the percentage of unfinished investments decreases, the efficiency of investment is improved, the 'approval coefficient' begins to increase again and the cycle restarts. Two consequences follow from this cyclical pattern. First, it inhibits technical innovation. None of the four stages in the cycle allows for the normal scrapping of existing plant. In both the run-up and rush periods the investment is always additional new plant. In the halt and slowdown periods, investments are left on ice, but rarely abandoned. There is thus an inbuilt tendency for obsolete plant to remain alongside the new. Second, the joint consequence of the postponement of investment during the slowdown phase and shortage of material in the rush is that gestation periods for investments are excessively long, which in turn means that investment projects can become technologically obsolete before they are completed, and enterprises lose the technological monopoly that being first with an innovation gives.[82]

In the 1950s, the causes of investment cycles could be located in overambitious planning and the trade crises which ensued. In the 1960s, the political mystique of rapid growth disappeared from central plans, but enterprises and their branch ministries pursued growth in their bargaining with the functional ministries in the one-sided belief that it was in the national interest.[83] Enterprise appetite for investment remained large, but now the pressure was less clearly from above: inbuilt pressures from below were becoming manifest. Enterprises attempted to 'hook on to the plan' so as to guarantee stocks and increase enterprise prestige, and if necessary they would underestimate investment costs in order to do this.[84] The change to overinvestment resulting from pressure from below was clear after 1968.[85] Investment cycles persisted in Hungary despite the introduction of the New Economic Mechanism, but the post-Stalinist cycles differed from the original ones in two ways. First, increasingly over the 1960s and 1970s pressure came 'from below', from the enterprises themselves, rather than from the political leadership; and second, after 1956 they were not paid for by a reduction in living standards, even if this inevitably meant increasing foreign debt.

Another characteristic feature of the traditional Stalinist model which did not disappear as expected with the introduction of the New Economic Mechanism was the practice of year/month-end 'storming', especially in branches related closely to investment and foreign trade. As with the persistence of investment cycles, the forces at work were rather more sophisticated than those of the 1950s, but the key variables were shortage and the need to spend time simply obtaining materials at every point in the chain, the holding of reserves, continued central intervention, and attempts to meet centrally imposed deadlines. The particular operation of the regulators in force at the time that Laki was investigating the persistence of 'storming' made it so disadvantageous for enterprises to hold high levels of stocks that, come the year end, it was cheaper to give goods away in order to bring stocks down to the expected level.[86]

By the mid 1970s, the inherent tendency of the 1968 paradigm towards recentralization and 'soft budget constraints' had combined with political developments in favour of recentralization and the imposition of a set of unrealistically optimistic planning targets which the recentralizers favoured. This combination had disastrous results. The political changes brought about by the XIth Party Congress, and the successful pursuit by large enterprises and their management of an expansion drive to meet politically established targets, initiated a further investment boom which, by 1978, was adversely affecting the balance of trade.[87] The increase in foreign debt, especially convertible currency (CC) debt, over the mid 1970s is clearly visible from Table 5.13. As Marer notes: 'during 1968–73 total trade and trade with the West were approximately in balance; the cumulative CC deficit represented less than 2 per cent of total CC imports during the period. By contrast, in each of the five years from 1974 to 1978 Hungary ran a large CC trade deficit, totalling more than $3 billion.'[88]

Reform Reluctantly Reborn

Crisis in agriculture and its consequences

Events in agriculture signalled the beginnings of a swing back towards reform even as the anti-reform movement reached its peak in 1975. The success of the recentralizers at the March 1975 Congress was followed by a government-inspired campaign against money-grubbing peasants and other small-scale agricultural producers.[89] A wholesale slaughter of pigs ensued which, by chance, coincided with the low point in the natural cycle in small-scale pig farming; this necessitated a reversal of the policy towards small-scale agriculture and precipitated the replacement of the Minister of Agriculture.

Generally, however, in the years immediately following 1975 recentralization predominated. In 1976, measures were taken in three areas: a greater proportion of enterprise funds was channelled to the centre, decision-making in the field of investment was centralized further, and additional restrictions were placed on labour mobility. The first task was achieved chiefly by a reduction in import subsidies and an increase from 25–35 per cent in the tax on wages, the latter measure having the additional beneficial effect of making labour relatively more expensive and discouraging labour-intensive development. These measures reduced enterprise profits by some 30–35 per cent. Further centralization of incomes was achieved by the introduction of a new compulsory enterprise reserve fund, and modification of the base figure for the charge assets to net rather than gross value. While some flexibility was introduced by abolishing the centrally determined formula which split profits into the Sharing and Development Funds and introducing a flat tax of 36 per cent, on all profits, the government imposed a strict sequence in the order of enterprise tax payment and fund formation. In the field of investment, the government continued the principles introduced two years earlier, but determined to increase the share of state investments within the total and widen the scope for influencing enterprise investment by a new scheme of budget grants specifically for investments in line with national economic policy objectives. On the labour side, in addition to a centrally imposed freeze on the hiring of white-collar staff,[90] the restrictions on labour mobility introduced in 1971 were now given the force of a government ordinance,[91] and a number of enterprises were brought under a new system of 'centrally determined' wage control.[92] In the face of this recentralization, dissident intellectuals decided to form themselves into a more cohesive 'democratic opposition', and from 1977 samizdat began to appear on a more systematic basis.

Despite the increase in central intervention in 1977, a number of minor developments took place which signalled the beginning of a new wave of reform. Three significant concessions were made to encourage small-scale private endeavour. In agriculture, collective farm members were allowed to expand (virtually double) their household plots by leasing additional unused state and cooperative land, the prohibition of horse ownership was abolished, and the 'symbiosis' between communal and private sectors developed further as increasing the value of production on members' household plots became a criterion on which collective farm management's bonuses could be based (see Figure 4.2). Second, for private traders generally, taxation was reduced in that the tax on their incomes was made linear rather than progressive on the first 100,000 forints of income.[93] Third, the legal system was amended in ways which, on the one hand, reduced the barriers, albeit rather marginally, to market entry, and, on the other, removed potential legal barriers to risk-taking in the state sector. The Civil Code was amended to allow individuals wishing to pursue joint economic endeavour to form civil law partnerships; 'legal persons', that is to say enterprises, were permitted to create economic partnerships between themselves with essentially the same rights as the civil law partnerships;[94] and a new law on state enterprises referred to their obligation to husband and increase state property rather than simply preserve it.[95]

By 1978, a radical change of policy had become inevitable. A Central Committee statement was issued in April calling for a more active price policy, a credit squeeze, and an only moderate increase in living standards.[96] The new policy aimed at reducing domestic consumption while measures were taken to restructure the economy towards goods that could be profitably exported to the West, so permitting renewed economic growth. In the original conception, the years 1979–81 were to be characterized by restriction, a reduction in foreign debt, and restructuring before renewed growth was possible in 1983. In the event, this timetable was upset by a short-term credit crisis in 1981–82. Over the 1970s, Hungary had been successfully raising many hundreds of millions of dollars from consortia of European and Japanese banks. Suddenly, with the declaration of martial law in Poland and the prospects of the Reagan presidency in the USA, Eastern Europe became an unattractive investment. To make matters worse, many Middle Eastern governments that had money on deposit in Hungary withdrew their funds, partly as a result of the Iran–Iraq war. The events, in conjunction with higher interest rates generally, created a severe liquidity crisis which in 1982 obliged the Hungarian government to join the IMF and World Bank.[97] It also precipitated, in September 1982, the introduction of tight import controls which imposed severe restrictions on investment.[98] Renewed growth was postponed until the XIIIth Party Congress of 1985; and when it took place, there had been reform, but no restructuring.

The years between 1978 and 1982 were characterized by reform measures which focused not so much on decentralization as on the stimulation of restraint and financial realism. The major new elements in policy were a further round of price reform in 1980, followed in 1981 and 1982 by the beginnings of institutional reform to the organization system. There was also a change in labour policy, with the emphasis switching away from restricting labour mobility, as was done in 1971 and 1976, to increasing supply by removing limits on overtime working, encouraging pensioners to remain in work, and postponing a reduction in the working week.[99] In addition, a directive in 1979 on the implementation of the early 1970s regulation concerning joint ventures with Western companies resulted in an increase in their number (from three to seven) in 1980.[100] Both the financial restraint associated with price reform and the organizational reform strengthened the hand of the 'functional ministries' in their dealings with the large enterprises.[101] In this climate, the opposition flourished. In fact, János Kis (later leader of the Free Democrats) described 1980–81 as the 'best years of the democratic opposition'. At the beginning of the period, in 1979, the Poor Support Fund was set up by Ottilia Solt in an opposition attempt to do something more concrete than signing petitions; and at the end of 1981 samizdat was transformed from occasional publications to the production of a regular periodical, *Beszélő*.[102]

The 1980 price reform took a further step in bringing domestic prices in line with those pertaining elsewhere in the world.[103] Two pricing spheres were introduced: 'competitive', covering some 65–70 per cent of the total; and non-competitive. Enterprises with 5 per cent or more of output against convertible currencies were obliged to use 'competitive prices' and were prohibited from building into their domestic prices a level of profit greater than that achieved in exports.[104] In all, some two-thirds of Hungarian prices were affected.[105] The overall tax burden on enterprises was reduced in compensation for the higher producer prices this entailed: the wages tax was reduced, and the charge on assets removed. On the other hand, continuing the trend towards financial constraint, modifications to various aspects of the tax system ensured that some 60 per cent of enterprise profits were centralised.[106]

The first institutional changes to the organization system were also taken in 1980. In the summer, the government set up its own economic committee to replace two interdepartmental committees, one of which – the Interdepartmental Committee for Financial Commodity Circulation – had come into prominence since 1976 as a body to allocate centrally certain goods where prices no longer reflected supply and demand.[107] More important, in the enterprise sphere steps were taken to break up some of the large enterprises created in 1962–64. Between mid 1980 and early 1981, four trusts and two other large enterprises were broken up, resulting in the creation of seventy independent enterprises.[108]

In 1979, the government had initiated moves to bring commercial and tourist exchange rates closer together, and from October 1981 they were merged into a single exchange rate, thus ending, as Berend reminds us, a policy that extended back to the 1930s.[109] Foreign trading rights were also extended to a number of larger enterprises.[110] The most decisive change in 1981, however, again concerned the organization system: the abolition of the three industrial ministries (Heavy Industry, Light Industry, and Metallurgy and Engineering) and their replacement by a single Ministry of Industry.[111] In addition, the non-governmental Hungarian Chamber of Commerce was given a role in the mediation of inter-enterprise disputes,[112] and, on 30 September, the Ministry of Labour was abolished. Its responsibilities passed to a new State Office for Wages and Labour Affairs and the existing National Planning Office, and Ministries of Finance and Health.[113]

Although some of the functions of the former branch ministries were taken over by the Planning Office, the Price Office and local party organizations, this move had tangible – and negative – consequences for the bargaining positions of the large enterprises.[114] Their position had already been significantly weakened since 1978 by the austerity policy. Branch ministries had been less able to defend their clients, and less willing to support their expansionary plans, obliging some enterprises to turn directly to the functional ministries for support. The new Chamber of Commerce immediately came under large enterprise influence, but the Ministry of Industry, the Chamber of Commerce and the Party organizations together were initially too weak to counter the financial discipline imposed by the functional ministries.[115]

Reform initiatives in the areas of pricing and modifications to the organization system in the early 1980s were accompanied by renewed discussion of economic reform. In 1981, an Economic Arbitration Committee was set up, behind closed doors, to consider further comprehensive reform, and the credit crisis of the following year coincided with the publication of a number of articles in the weekly *Heti Világgazdaság* which called for a new wave of reform.[116] The debate continued in the Party's *Social Review*, in one issue of which Tamás Bauer stated that the crux of the problem was the need to cut enterprises, as business under-takings, from the hierarchical umbilical ties of the state administration. Another significant moment in this renewed discussion was a debate in 1982 on the work of Tibor Liska and his concept of 'entrepreneurial socialism'.[117]

The contributors to these debates all agreed that the essence of the problem lay in ownership. What was needed was a form of ownership of productive assets which would render them completely independent of the state administration, so minimizing opportunities for 'regulation bargaining' and imposing 'hard budget constraints'. Three analytically distinct approaches evolved, although individual contributions combined various elements. These were the 'management socialist' view of Tardos, Antal and Kopátsy, and 'workers' self management' view of Bauer and Lengyel, and the 'personal socialist entrepreneurs' view of Liska.[118] Under 'managerial socialism' the assets would be owned by an indepen-dent organization such as a holding company, the position of workers would be that of wage labour, and the enterprise interest would be long-term profit. Under the 'self-management' model, the assets would be owned by the collectivity of workers, who would therefore be property owners, and the enterprise interest would be in gross income or value added. Under the 'socialist enterpreneurs' model, the assets would be owned by the leader, the workers would be middlemen (jobbers) and enterprise interest would be in short-term profit. Three additional views were put forward to counter the possibility of holding companies becoming huge, state-run conglomerates: Soós's self-managed holding company, Matolcsy's limited right trusts, and Kopátsy's idea of pension funds becoming large-scale owners of enterprise shares. The reformist buzzword of the period was the 'holding company'. But, by the end of the 1982, Ferenc Havasi, secretary of the Central Committee, took the expression off the political agenda,[119] and, by 1983, the idea was unac-ceptable even when presented in a translated form by a circumlocution such as 'property centre'.[120] In a statement of 30 April 1983, Kádár made a television and radio statement emphasizing that 'This manage-ment system will not be radically exchanged for another.'[121] Neverthe-less, organizational reform at the Liberation collective farm in Szentes in 1981 had already implemented a self-consciously 'Liska-type' reform with the collective centre acting as a holding company operating ten independent entrepreneurial units.[122] And far-reaching, if conceptually less radical, reform was introduced at the beginning of 1982, based very much on the experience of agriculture.

Reform to the organization system modelled on agriculture

Towards the end of 1980, István Gábor, who, along with Péter Gaslai, had invented the term 'second economy' and done most to theorize its role in socialist economies, published an article in *Figyelő* calling for the legalization and co-option of the second economy using the methods already proven in agriculture.[123] This coincided with the moves to break up trusts mentioned above. On 1 January 1982, the government sought to both legalize 'second economy' activity, and create a new small business sector, by introducing three new broad categories of small enterprise. The first of these comprised the Small Enterprises and the Small Cooperatives. Both had a maximum of 100 staff or members, and differed from one another only in terms of their internal administration along enterprise or cooperative lines. They were distinguished from standard enterprises and cooperatives in that, because of their smaller size, they could operate according to 'simplified accounting procedures' involving 70 per cent less paperwork. The two forms within this category differed from the others created at this time in that they constituted separate legal persons. Although statistical practice did not include them in the state or cooperative sector, they had an independent identity under socialist law.[124]

The second broad category of new economic undertaking was the Economic Work Partnership. These could comprise a maximum of thirty partners and differed from the Civil Law Partnerships permitted by the 1977 legislation in that local authority permission was required to establish them and they could operate in a wider compass. The third category covered the Enterprise Economic Work Partnerships, and Industrial and Service Cooperative Specialist Groups. These were essentially special cases of the second category which operated entirely within an existing enterprise or cooperative, and consisted exclusively of its present or retired members or staff. The latter had to have a minimum of five members, while the size restrictions on the former were as for the standard Economic Work Partnerships.[125]

Since 1982, as can be seen from Table 5.6, the growth in Economic Work Partnerships – and especially Enterprise Economic Work Partnerships – was exponential. The increase in Small Cooperatives was more measured, with a rapid increase in 1985 for reasons which will be discussed below. Laky studied all three of these new forms of economic undertaking in considerable detail. She was particularly critical of the Small Enterprises, in which category she included the subsidiary companies of larger enterprises for which the same 'simplified accounting rules' apply. Rather than create background industrial activity, they were concentrated in the service sector. The majority were

Table 5.6 Evolution of the new forms of economic unit introduced in 1982

	1982	1983	1984	1985
Small enterprise		13	19	25
Subsidiary enterprise		44	102	136
Small cooperative		221	349	659
EC work partnership	2,538	4,851	7,868	10,002
Enterprise EWP	3,575	9,989	18,299	20,878
Specialist group	512	1,347	2,387	2,704

Source: T. Laky, *Az Új Típusú Kisszervezetek 1986-ban*, Budapest 1987, pp. 141 and 155.

formed from the break-up of the AFIT car repair and GELKA house-hold appliance repair enterprises. They exhibited no tendency for greater profitability, and were as dependent on their 'supervisory organ' (in this case the local council) on baling them out in times of hardship as were the larger enterprises on theirs.[126]

The consequences of these new forms of economic unit for both the labour market and labour behaviour will be considered at length in Chapter 6. Here it is necessary to stress only that, as might have been inferred from the comments surrounding their formation, they were more successful in introducing into the industrial and service sectors of the economy the sort of 'symbiotic' relationship between first and second economy that had already been created in agriculture, than they were in developing a dynamic independent small-scale industrial sector. As can be seen from Table 5.6, by far the most dynamic growth from 1982 onwards was in the Economic Work Partnerships and Enterprise Economic Work Partnerships, both of which were characterized predominantly by part-time employment.[127] Only in exceptional cases, such as computing, did a dynamic, more or less independent small-scale industrial sector develop.[128]

There is extensive debate amongst economists and sociologists as to how the 'second economy' should be defined, yet underlying the disagreement there is a general, if imprecise, consensus that it has some-thing to do with non-socialist sector economic activity; that the new organizations introduced in 1982 were something to do with legitimizing this and incorporating it into the socialist sector; and that what tradi-tional private-sector artisanal and petty-trader activity shares with activity in the 'black economy' and the new post-1982 organizations is something to do with the way in which participants treat their own labour. For István Gábor, Péter Galasi and their associates, the second economy is 'income-creating activity outside the sale of labour to the socialist sector'.[129] Laky adopts the more conventional Western distinction between 'first' and 'second' economy, namely between legal and illegal activity.[130] Pál Juhász adopts a Chayanov-type definition[131] when he characterizes the distinction as follows: 'The enterprise active in the first economy buys the labour power of the producer and puts it to productive use under separate management; the individual or group active in the second economy employs himself/itself, his own wits and labour power (work organization is not determined by law or separate management), and sells only its products and services.'[132] The advantage of this approach is that it allows the postulation of 'second economy' relations wholly within the socialist sector which, as we have seen, is the case in both the Enterprise Economic Work Partnerships of 1982 and the 'symbiotic' combinations of family and wage labour in agriculture of the early 1970s. By the 1980s, three types of 'second economy' activity could be distinguished in Hungary, differentiated by the degree of intensity of their interrelationships with the 'first economy': part-time labour actually within an enterprise; part-time labour outside enterprises but subcontracting to them; and full-time self-employment where the only link with the socialist sector was via the market.[133] But, despite two additional measures taken in this period to boost the legal private sector (the placing of local authorities under an obligation to issue licences to all suitably qualified artisans, leading to a 20 per cent increase in their number between 1981 and 1983, and the encouragement of the leasing of retailing and catering facilities such that by June 1983 a fifth of all restaurants were leased by private individuals),[134] the majority of this private sector, 'second economy' activity was of the first two types. It was intimately tied in with the pattern, structure and practices of the state sector.

Semi-monetarized reform: financial reform and large enterprise interest

Although the political leadership unambiguously rejected the reform economists' 'holding company' proposals, piecemeal reform continued. The organization system of the economy was further modified to create a capital market, and market exit was facilitated by moves to tighten bankruptcy regulations. That is to say, very limited attempts were made to introduce market relations to future-oriented aspects of the economy. However, in all these processes, the large enterprises succeeded in capitalizing on their strategic importance to the economy and reasserting their status as privileged exceptions to the rule. The credit shock of 1982 increased austerity, and the centralization of enterprise funds which accompanied it increased the possibilities for enterprise bargaining.

From 1983 onwards especially, there was an increase in individually specific, rather than general, regulations. Institutions such as the Wage Club and the Price Club (enterprises for which special regulations obtained) strengthened the bargaining process and, with it, the role of the large enterprises. In a situation of acute balance of payments crisis, the relative strength of the Ministry of Industry and especially enterprises with significant exports to the capitalist market increased. The functional ministries, the Ministry of Finance and the Hungarian National Bank were obliged to take an understanding view if these enterprises got into financial difficulties. The weaker large enterprises became noticeably 'anti-market'.[135] In the mood of financial austerity, however, the more successful ones did not come to their rescue to form a single interest group. They remained 'ambivalent', thankful for the cushion provided by bureaucratic redistribution.[136] The reform moves of these years acted as window-dressing, giving the international financial community the illusion of market relations but creating what has been characterized as a 'semi-monetarized economy'.[137]

The chief characteristics of the years between 1982 and the renewed reform of 1985 were bonds and bankruptcies. The right of enterprises to issue interest-bearing bonds was granted from the beginning of 1982.[138] At first, only enterprises were permitted to purchase the bonds, but from autumn 1983 certain less expensive bonds were offered to individual investors. The number of bonds available to individuals and enterprises increased quite quickly, but, as Table 5.7 suggests, even by 1986 they played only a minor role in savings and investment credit, and enterprises proved rather reluctant to buy them.[139]

Trading was in bonds only: no shares were offered for public sale. Nevertheless, as Table 5.8 reveals, a considerable growth took place in the number of joint enterprises of various types between state companies

Table 5.7 Availability of bonds, May 1986

Available to:	Total nominal value* (bn ft)	Yield (%)	Relative size (%)
Private citizens	4.5	7.13	2.0**
Firms and institutions	2.0	7.15	9.7***

*covers all bonds issued prior to May 1986
**total nominal value/stock of household deposits in savings banks
***total nominal value/stock of outstanding bank investment credit

Source: Kornai, 'The Hungarian Reform', p. 65.

Table 5.8 State sector new enterprise forms

	1979	1985	1986	1987
Joint enterprise	146	206	210	214
Limited partnership	0	18	24	26
Association	22	44	47	51
Public limited company	3	11	14	28
Private limited company	6	42	54	92
Total	177	321	349	411

Source: Figyelő, no. 31, 4 August 1988, p. 3.

or cooperatives that legislation had made possible in 1978.[140] Their number increased dramatically from the end of 1986 when measures were passed removing the restriction that public and private limited liability companies could only be formed in the case of joint ventures with foreign companies,[141] or with special ministerial permission.

In 1983, a further element of institutional reform was introduced when it was announced that enterprise directorships should be open to tender.[142] Enterprise directors were still responsible to their 'supervisory body', but were no longer its appointees. In 1984, the issue of bankruptcy and the inadequacies of the 1977 law and 1978 ordinances that controlled it were given a high profile and applied with greater rigour.[143] The much-discussed bankruptcy law was finally introduced in September 1986 when a receivership organization was established under the supervision of the Ministry of Finance[144] and provisions were made for redundancy payments to be made when ten or more employees were sacked during the course of the bankruptcy and receivership procedures. These payments took the form of a salary extension for up to six months at 75 per cent of salary for the first three months and 60 per cent for the final three.[145]

The key event of 1984, however, was the announcement in April of a new Action Programme, which had been in preparation since late 1983,[146] and which would come into force at the beginning of 1985.[147] The introduction of this reform, described by Bognár as the culmination of the first period of the reform,[148] was accompanied by both pre-congress euphoria leading up to the XIIIth Party Congress and some improvement in economic performance. The balance of payments became positive,[149] and the increase in indebtedness was stopped.[150] Commenting from the United States, Balassa reflected this optimism, noting that 'between 1978–85 Hungary succeeded in transforming a deficit in convertible currency trade to a surplus'.[151]

The 1985 reform was indeed in many ways the long-delayed second stage of the 1968 New Economic Mechanism. To, albeit restricted, capital markets and, albeit rarely enforced, bankruptcy was added virtually total autonomy from the centre. Only two features of the 1968 paradigm of market for the present and planning for the future remained: the continued existence, despite the break-up of trusts, of near monopolies; and restrictions on external ownership of enterprise assets. Enterprises finally owned their assets and chose their own management; but there was little scope for the ownership of productive assets by outside bodies or individuals.

The key elements in the 1985 system were as follows. Between the beginning of 1985 and the end of 1986, all enterprises, outside a new non-profit sector where there would be no significant change, were obliged to transform themselves into one of two types: those run by an enterprise council, and those run by an elected leadership. In addition, the majority of rights stemming from the ownership of state property passed formally to the enterprise. The only intervention rights retained by the 'founding organ' related to defence interests. The National Materials and Prices Office could also intervene in relation to the domestic market, and the Foreign Trade ministry could intervene in relation to international obligations; but in such cases enterprises were able to claim damages against losses incurred because of external intervention.[152] Administrative control of investment was reduced in that less documentation had to be approved by fewer committees. The system of Central Development Programmes was ended. A general market intervention fund administered by the National Materials and Prices Office was introduced. Enterprises were free to determine their own plans and change their sphere of activity, provided the 'founding organ' and appropriate ministry were informed. The enterprise fund system was also radically reformed, to create a single fund the use of which, after obligations to the state had been met, was entirely in the hands of the enterprises. The profits tax was reduced from 45 to 35 per cent, but a new 10 per cent wages tax was introduced to make labour more expensive.[153] In addition, a gradual relaxation of the system of wage regulation was introduced, making enterprises less interested in retaining unnecessary labour. In two of the three methods of wage control introduced at this time, the 'average-wage' principle, which had existed since 1957 in one guise or another, even when it was the 'wage bill' rather than the 'wage level' that was technically controlled, was to be phased out by 1987.[154]

But alongside these reforms, which created genuine autonomy within a 'semi-monetarized' economy, came measures aimed directly against the market competition. In order to control the mushrooming growth since 1982 of new small-scale economic units, a 10 per cent tax (increased to 15 per cent in 1986 and 20 per cent by 1987)[155] was levied on all purchases from the second and third categories of small undertakings mentioned above.[156] The tax did not extend to the Small Cooperatives, occasioning their increased popularity after 1985 and the levelling off in the growth of Economic Work Partnerships. Two-thirds of the Small Cooperatives active at the end of 1986 were formed in 1985/6.[157] In tune with this attack on the small-scale sector, much of the small print of the 1985 reform measures and the economic orientation of the seventh five-year plan favoured large enterprises. The large enterprises benefited most from short-term tax concessions that accompanied the introduction of the new regulations; and the large enterprises benefited most from the renewed emphasis on energy and basic materials in domestic and foreign investments.[158] Indeed, the XIIIth Party Congress in advance of the seventh five-year plan resembled the XIth in many ways. As in 1975, statements at the Congress favouring renewed reform were low key,[159] while the renewed calls for dynamic growth reflected a Ministry of Finance uncertain in the face of the success of the large enterprises and their allies, the Ministry of Industry and the Chamber of Commerce, where the large enterprise lobby was most effective.[160]

This apparent contradiction in the 1985 measures – aspects of recentralization in the midst of decentralization – can be resolved. What was happening was that monopolies, newly independent from central control, were pursuing the sorts of anti-competitive policies that came naturally. This new enterprise autonomy needs to be placed in context. The 1985 measures merely created in industry and the services what had long existed in agriculture. Collective farms had for some time enjoyed genuine autonomy and the ownership of their assets. They had long been able to draw up and pass their own plans without ministerial intervention, and been able to change their economic 'profile' by diversifying out of agriculture.[161] Yet the lesson from agriculture was that despite autonomy, despite ownership, and despite institutions of cooperative democracy which matched those suggested by cooperative supporters in the West, collective farm managers enjoyed autonomy without responsibility, either to the market or to the membership, and that extensive 'regulation bargaining' remained.[162] The likelihood was that in industry too, autonomy had been granted 'in a way that created no effective form of social control'.[163]

Despite relatively good short-term economic results in 1984, the optimistic tone of the XIIIth Party Congress and the success in controlling wages (see Table 5.9), three longer-term problems remained. First, the state sector was in decline. While the contribution of the state sector to national income was 73.3 per cent in 1975, by 1980 it had dropped to

Table 5.9 Index of real incomes and real wages compared to previous year

	Per capita real income		Real wages of workers and employees
	Workers and intellectuals	Peasants and households with dual income*	
1966	105	107	102
1967	106	109	104
1968	106	108	102
1969	107	105	105
1970	107	109	105
1971	105	104	102
1972	103.3		102
1973	104.7		102.8
1974	106.2		105.6
1975	104.4		103.8
1976	100.8		100.1
1977	104.9		103.8
1978	102.9		103.1
1979	100.1		98.3
1980	100.4		98.4
1981	102.9		101.1
1982	100.3		98.8
1983	101.1		96.8
1984	101.1		97.6
1985	101.9		101.3
1986	102.3		101.9
1987	100.7		99.6
1988	99.2		95.1

*per capita personal real income

Source: Hungarian Statistical Pocket Books, various.

69.8 per cent and by 1984 to 65.2 per cent.[164] Furthermore, the degree of state enterprise dependence on subsidies was increasing, not decreasing. In 1980, 43 per cent of profits came from subsidies; by 1983 the proportion was 83 per cent.[165] Second, the fundamentals of the foreign trade situation were not improving because no significant restructuring had taken place. Both the structure of Hungarian industry (Table 5.10) and the structure of foreign trade changed little in the first half of the 1980s (Table 5.11). Hence, despite the steady growth visible in Table 5.12, the foreign debt continued to rise alarmingly (Table

Table 5.10 The structure of Hungarian industry (% sales at current prices)

	1981	1982	1984	1986	1988
Mining	6.7	7.2	6.9	6.9	6.5
Electrical energy	4.7	5.0	5.3	6.1	6.1
Metallurgy	8.5	8.4	8.4	8.2	8.5
Machine tool	22.7	23.2	23.1	25.5	25.9
Building materials	3.2	3.1	3.1	3.0	3.3
Chemical industry	20.4	20.6	21.1	19.0	19.7
Light industry	13.4	12.9	12.7	13.0	12.9
Other	1.4	1.3	1.0	1.0	0.8
Food processing	18.4	18.3	18.4	17.3	16.3
Total	100.0	100.0	100.0	100.0	100.0

Source: Hungarian Statistical Pocket Books, various.

5.13). Third, in the political sphere, despite the regime's success in preventing noted dissidents from standing in the first elections where a choice of candidates was obligatory,[166] some prominent politicians were defeated (such as Fock, prime minister from 1967 to 1975),[167] and a number of genuinely independent deputies elected, most notably Zoltán Király.

In the absence of restructuring, despite almost two decades of constantly adjusted market socialist reform, the improved economic performance of 1984 proved short-lived, and the seventh five-year plan turned out to be 'just as unfulfillable as those of the 1950s'.[168]

Silent Expansion

While the 1985 reforms brought to its final conclusion the original intention of the 1968 reforms to increase enterprise autonomy from the centre, they also continued the bias towards large, virtual monopoly enterprises within the organization system. They further indicated that significant managerial and political pressures existed in favour of ending the deflationary policies in force since 1978 and returning to a period of economic growth. Although the declared principles of monetary policy did not change over the decade, in 1985 and 1986 there was a significant 'silent expansion'[169] in the money supply, as Table 5.14 reveals.

This expansion coincided with a political offensive on the part of large enterprises, with little distinction made between enterprises which were 'good' and 'bad' in terms of profitability.[170] The peak of this offensive

Table 5.11 Commodity structure of foreign trade (%)

	Imports						Exports					
	(ruble)			(non-ruble)			(ruble)			(non-ruble)		
	1982	1986	1988	1982	1986	1988	1982	1986	1988	1982	1986	1988
Fuel and electric energy	30.0	32.4	27.4	10.3	7.2	2.3	0.8	0.6	0.4	9.8	6.4	3.9
Raw and basic materials	12.8	13.6	12.9	12.9	12.1	13.8	2.2	2.2	2.3	6.8	9.8	12.0
Semi-finished products	12.9	11.9	14.3	33.8	31.4	33.9	10.8	10.0	9.5	21.5	25.4	26.4
Spare parts	8.7	7.8	8.3	10.9	12.1	14.8	9.8	10.4	10.3	2.3	3.1	3.9
Machinery, transport and other capital goods	21.8	20.3	20.9	13.9	13.4	13.7	42.4	46.0	47.5	14.9	13.6	12.5
Industrial consumer goods	10.4	11.2	13.6	7.8	12.1	10.2	18.6	16.7	16.6	12.5	15.6	15.5
Agricultural products	0.3	0.5	0.5	3.0	4.8	3.7	5.1	4.2	3.9	12.6	10.5	10.0
Food industry products	3.1	2.4	2.1	7.4	6.9	7.6	10.3	10.0	9.6	19.6	15.6	15.8
Total	100.0	100.0	100.0	100.0	100.0	100.0	100.0	100.0	100.0	100.0	100.0	100.0

Source: Hungarian Statistical Pocket Books, various.

Table 5.12 Indices of national income, production and investment
(previous year = 100)

	(1)	(2)	(3)	(4)	(5)	(6)	(7)	(8)
1965	100	–	101	101	88	101	–	102
1966	108	–	105	105	112	96	–	111
1967	108	–	106	107	132	130	–	120
1968	105	–	106	105	98	97	–	102
1969	108	–	106	106	98	112	–	108
1970	107	–	109	108	122	145	–	117
1971	105.9	111.3	105.4	105	130.4	101.6	–	110.5
1972	106.2	96.3	103.1	103.4	78.6	108.9	–	99.2
1973	107.0	102.0	103.7	103.9	96.2	105.5	–	104.0
1974	105.9	112.7	106.9	106.1	134.2	94.4	–	108.9
1975	106.1	106.4	104.7	104.9	111.5	139.7	–	113.2
1976	103.0	101.2	102.1	–	98.6	–	103.6	99.9
1977	108.0	106.2	104.6	–	111.0	–	107.6	113.0
1978	104.2	110.0	104.9	–	123.8	–	104.4	105.0
1979	101.9	94.5	102.9	–	75.1	–	102.7	101.9
1980	99.2	98.1	101.1	–	88.7	–	100.2	94.2
1981	102.5	100.7	103.0	–	91.4	–	102.9	94.4
1982	102.6	98.5	101.2	–	86.0	–	102.3	97.4
1983	100.3	97.3	100.6	–	79.6	–	100.7	97.0
1984	102.5	99.4	100.9	–	88.7	–	102.7	97.1
1985	98.6	99.4	101:1	–	86.1	–	99.5	97.7
1986	100.9	103.9	102.0	–	121.4	–	101.5	102.3
1987	104.1	103.2	103.1	–	102.7	–	104.1	107.6
1988	99.9	97.2	96.4	–	93.8	–	100.1	91.7

(1) = National income (net material product)
(2) = Domestic consumption
(3) =   of which material consumption
(4) =   of which consumption of the population
(5) =   of which net capital formation
(6) =   of which net fixed capital formation
(7) = Gross Domestic Product
(8) = Total investment

Source: Hungarian Statistical Pocket Books, various.

came in 1986 when the Chamber of Commerce suggested that the
biggest exporters should be excluded entirely from the normal system of
economic regulators.[171] The Chamber further opposed ideas, mooted in
the late summer of 1986, of imposing restrictions on growth,[172] and in
the autumn of 1986 floated the idea of reintroducing 1972-style 'privileged' status for large enterprises, although this was opposed by the
Planning Office and the Ministry of Finance.[173]

Table 5.13 Balance of trade, balance of payments and foreign debt in convertible currencies (US$ million)

	Balance of trade	Balance of payments	Total currency flows	Gross debt	Net debt	Gross debt as % GDP
1970	−77	35	35	1,000	−424	–
1971	−218	−252	−285	1,511	−694	–
1972	−59	−92	−70	1,867	−853	23.7
1973	109	65	256	2,315	−846	23.6
1974	−426	−540	−100	3,105	−1,381	27.9
1975	−292	−528	−482	3,929	−1,925	32.0
1976	−176	−363	−459	4,531	−2,267	33.2
1977	−359	−753	70	5,227	−2,870	34.2
1978	−782	−1,242	482	7,586	−4,461	38.2
1979	−167	−825	−141	8,300	−5,016	41.4
1980	276	−368	430	9,090	−5,388	39.1
1981	445	−727	−526	8,699	−5,474	39.2
1982	766	−77	−1,168	7,715	−4,943	35.6
1983	877	297	443	8,250	−4,594	38.2
1984	1,236	330	305	8,836	−4,083	42.2
1985	295	−457	992	11,760	−5,018	49.8
1986	−540	−1,419	49	15,086	−7,790	56.6
1987	3	−847	−904	17,739	−10,904	62.9
1988	670	−592	−161	17,349	−11,069	63.2

Source: Figyelő, no. 16, 20 April 1989, p. 15; 41, 12 October 1989, p. 4.

Table 5.14 The economy's money and credit supply

	Money supply per 100 ft GNP	Credit supply per 100 ft GNP	Increase in money supply per 100 ft increase in GNP	Increase in credit supply per 100 ft increase in GNP
1983	8.5	4.8	3.9	3.9
1984	8.3	5.2	5.1	8.6
1985	9.0	5.5	22.9	13.7
1986	10.2	6.3	29.8	22.5
1987	9.9	6.0	12.3	1.4

[1] 'Money supply' = MI measure
[2] 'Credit supply' refers to short-term credits of enterprises and cooperatives

Source: E. Várhegyi, 'Monetáris politika és gyakorlat 1987–88', in I. Csillag (ed.), *Jelentések az Alagutból II*, Budapest 1988, p. 15.

As has already been indicated, it had been intended that the deflationary policies introduced in 1978 would be accompanied by the restructuring of industry, but such restructuring did not in fact take place, nor did productivity improve.[174] When, in response to the offensive orchestrated by the Chamber of Commerce on behalf of the large enterprises, the brakes were silently lifted from repressed domestic demand in 1985–86, the finances necessary to fund it could only be provided by increased government borrowing, as indicated in Table 5.15. This increased borrowing exacerbated what was already an unacceptably high level of debt. A change of policy became unavoidable, and demands for renewed radical reform became increasingly loud.

Meanwhile, in 1987, the banking system was radically reformed. The aim of the new system was to introduce 'two-tier' banking, to make a clear separation between the functions of the National Bank and commercial banks, and, by moving investment financing to the commercial banks, to introduce much tighter market relations in the provision of credit and the financing of investment. The reform both redefined the terms of reference of the National Bank, and introduced a new set of commercial banks. The Hungarian National Bank became the central bank of issue, with a responsibility for monetary policy and the obligation to 'assist the implementation of economic policy objectives through regulating money in circulation'.[175] Initially five commercial banks were created out of the previous specialist banking system, with names reminiscent of those used prior to the bank nationalization in 1947: the Hungarian Credit Bank, the National and Commercial Credit Bank, the Budapest Credit Bank, the Hungarian Foreign Trade Bank and the General Banking and Trust Company. The main savings banks continued to be the National Savings Bank, which was also permitted to involve itself in commercial lending on small ventures, and the local Savings Cooperatives. The banking scene in 1987 also included a number of specialist financial institutions and three banks in which there

Table 5.15 Changes to net deposits minus credits of enterprises, the population and the state budget

	1985	1986	1987	1984–87
Enterprises	−14	−8	−13	−35
Population	11	18	5	34
State budget	−9	−68	−42	−119

Source: Várhegyi, p. 16.

was foreign participation. In anticipation of changes to the company law, all the new banks were established as public limited companies.[176]

Despite its radical appearance, the 1987 banking reform had little success in hardening budget constraints. Companies were assigned initially to their banks in a predetermined way, and were only allowed to choose freely between them from 1 July 1987. In consequence, although the banks were supposed to operate according to commercial principles, they could not choose their customers on a commercial basis. And since the banks were obliged to take over existing debts run up to the end of 1986, they inevitably became the slaves of the large enterprises which had monopolized investment credits. Big enterprises, as big debtors, were in a strong bargaining position; furthermore, the banks were given conflicting signals from government as to whether they should impose the new bankruptcy regulations or not.[177] The real economic independence of these nominally independent banks was thus severely restricted, and, in addition, the central bank retained an ability to intervene directly in monetary flows via its system of county offices.[178]

The Stabilization Plan of 1987

The stabilization plan introduced in September 1987 following the July Central Committee statement was in many ways a rerun of the plan introduced in 1978. The brunt of the adjustment was placed on consumption, in that the rate of inflation was to be allowed to substantially exceed wage increases.[179] As in 1978–84, the emphasis was on administrative restrictions, on limiting imports and encouraging exports, and on reducing living standards. And, just as before, this opened the way for increased intervention, and the making of exceptions for important enterprises through 'regulation bargaining'.[180] No measures were taken to stimulate the restructuring of the economy, and the CMEA large investment programmes were continued.[181] However, as Table 5.15 reveals, the reimposition of restrictions on the money supply were not very successful. Enterprise profits and incomes were higher than expected; anticipation of the increased inflation after the tax reform to be introduced in 1988 meant that the population's savings were lower than expected; the budget deficit was greater than expected; and in addition there were technical problems connected with the introduction of the bank reform. All these factors increased the money supply above the planned limits.[182]

Budget constraints remained as 'soft' as ever, and the pattern of cross-subsidization to the large enterprises continued unchanged up to 1987,[183] as Table 5.16 indicates.

Table 5.16 Economic return before and after redistribution and net deductions
1984–87

ORIGINAL RESULT	1984	1985	1986	1987
Socialist industry	13.4	13.2	8.8	8.9
(a) Over 1,000 employees	12.9	12.4	8.4	7.1
(b) Less than 1,000 employees	18.9	20.3	10.6	17.8
(b) as % of (a)	146.5	163.7	126.2	250.7
POST-REDISTRIBUTION RESULT				
Socialist industry	7.1	7.4	8.4	8.8
(a) Over 1,000 employees	6.6	6.8	7.6	7.9
(b) Less than 1,000 employees	11.6	12.6	13.0	13.5
(b) as % of (a)	175.8	185.3	171.1	170.2
NET DEDUCTIONS (DEDUCTIONS LESS SUBSIDIES)				
Socialist industry	12.7	12.9	7.7	8.3
(a) Over 1,000 employees	12.4	12.3	7.3	6.6
(b) Less than 1,000 employees	15.9	18.0	9.6	17.1
(b) as % of (a)	128.2	146.3	131.5	259.1

Note: The concepts of original and post-redistribution results are explained in Kornai (ed.), *Régi és új*, pp. 92–173.

Source: E. Szalai, 'Válság és nagyvállalati érdekervényesítés (1984–88 első félév)', in Csillag, pp. 75–6.

Although it had salary continuation and retraining programmes on the statute books, the government was unwilling to remove subsidies which might adversely effect the large enterprises, their managers and their employees. Despite the fact that in December 1987 the government promised a reduction in subsidies, little of substance had happened by the autumn of 1988, and what reduction there had been – some 22 thousand million forints[184] – had been nullified by either allowing enterprises to raise prices, or, as in the case of attempts to 'rationalize' the mines, giving extra financial support to the miners after they went on strike.[185] Nor were the bankruptcy and receivership regulations of 1986 used aggressively. Despite the fact that the Planning Office had been working on restructuring measures since the summer of 1987,[186] in the two years following the introduction of the 1986 law, 121 closure proceedings were set in motion (three state enterprises, eight other enterprises, fifteen Economic Associations, three collective farms, 21 cooperatives and 71 Small Cooperatives), but only six of these were because of insolvency.[187] The only really significant bankruptcy was that of the Veszprém State Construction Enterprise which its banker, the

Hungarian Credit Bank (in which the state did not hold the majority of shares),[188] forced into liquidation after it had refused merger terms offered by the Alba Regia State Construction Enterprise.[189] This bankruptcy, and that of the Cigand collective farm, were the only ones to result in final liquidation and cause temporary local employment problems.[190] Nevertheless, as a result of closures and the wage regulation reforms discussed above, by mid 1988 unemployment had reached 11,462, 24.7 per cent up on twelve months earlier,[191] and the government was obliged to introduce unemployment benefit from 1 January 1989 in the face of predictions that put possible unemployment at 60–80,000.[192]

By the middle of 1988, the government had proved itself incapable of countering effectively the offensive of large enterprise management, who could play on the justified concerns of workers potentially threatened by unemployment to give an acceptable socialist rhetoric to their self-interested concerns. Subsidies might keep some workers in jobs, but primarily they made life easy for enterprise management and, as Chapter 7 will amply demonstrate, they significantly reduced social service provision for all workers, including those threatened with unemployment. The net effect of this failure to restructure can be seen from Tables 5.9 to 5.13. Persistent stagnation is apparent in all areas except one: foreign debt, which kept on increasing until Hungary's per capita debt was the highest in Eastern Europe.

Further worrying features of the economy, which had showed no sign of changing in the intervening two years, were summarized in *Turnabout and Reform*.[193] Although Hungarian exports had doubled since 1975, their share of world trade was constantly falling. While the exports of the newly industrializing countries to developed industrial countries had increased six times since 1973, those from CMEA countries had increased only two and a half times. The commodity structure of Hungary's exports increasingly consisted of energy-intensive, and low-valued, mass-market products, while its technology-intensive products were increasingly squeezed out of export markets. The export of machinery from all of the CMEA countries to the developed capitalist countries was exceeded by Taiwan (more than three times as much), Mexico (two and a half times as much), South Korea and Singapore (both twice as much) and, in 1985, by Malaysia (20 per cent more). Hungary had proved simply incapable of switching to producing the sorts of exports the world was willing to pay for in order to finance its borrowing. But, as 1956 had demonstrated, neither could it survive by retreating to autarky.

Production Relations in Hungarian Socialism: Bureaucratic Control, Shortage and Second Economy

Management, Bureaucrats and Labour in the State Sector

External constraints

The previous chapters have presented, very broadly, a picture of the Hungarian economy as characterized by bureaucratic control, shortage and the emergence of a 'second economy'. The first two, in the form of central quantitative planning followed by 'soft budget constraints' and 'regulation bargaining', were recurring themes in Chapters 3 to 5; the third came to the fore with its incorporation discussed in Chapter 5. In this chapter, the focus is on labour in relation to these three features, in terms of production relations and the labour market. Chapter 7 will turn its attention to labour as a consumer of the social product.

The first topic to be addressed is bureaucratic control. It is clear from preceding chapters that the term is very much a shorthand. The central bureaucracy dominates the economy and makes 'soft budget constraints' possible; but it is far from unitary. Conflicts of interest exist between enterprises and ministries, between functional ministries and branch ministries, and between all of these and the Party. This section considers the place of labour within this complex of forces. The central question when considering production relations in Eastern European socialist economies is not whether it is 'owners' or 'controllers' of the means of production who have ultimate control, but who within the hierarchy of command has control over what, and what freedom of action within that hierarchy does any given individual enjoy. The nature and scope of control are the crucial questions, not its ultimate location. The powers associated with ownership might reside in the branch or industrial ministry. Decisions regarding finance might be determined in the

Ministry of Finance, or the Hungarian National Bank. Ultimate strategic decisions might be taken by the Central Committee. But what freedom of action remains for those whose power to control, although limited, is exercised immediately at the point of production? How free is management from central, local government, and Party agencies, and what are the consequences for the individual's labour and for the labour of others? A full understanding of production relations in Hungary requires the location both of management in relation to the Party–State apparatus, and of labour in relation to management. This section first considers the constraints imposed on management by bodies not directly involved in production: the Party and the trade unions. It continues with an examination of management autonomy in relation to meeting its primary obligation, that is to say plan fulfilment, before focusing finally on the direct management–labour relationship.

The role of the Party in economic planning and management has been characterized as follows:

> It is common knowledge that the main directives of the national plan are elaborated and accepted by Party forums (the Congress and the Central Committee). The national plan, together with plans at different levels are prepared on the basis of these directives. These plans are therefore the concrete expression in figures of the Party, its economic programme.[1]

But this indicates little about the role of the Party within the executive when making lower-level decisions. The role of the national and county Party organization in day-to-day economic decision-making was one of supervision. Party officials were instructed to concern themselves only with essential economic questions which had significant political and social implications.[2] According to a 1975 Central Committee ruling – admittedly the high point of economic recentralization – each Party organ was obliged to vet four general areas of policy: planning, economic activity, both general and specific, internal management, and the personal behaviour of management.[3] It also had to ensure that the Party's overall economic programme, the balance of national economic interests, and the principles of socialist distribution were not being violated, while additionally ensuring that appropriate individuals occupied managerial posts, people who were able and willing to fight for the implementation of Party policy.[4]

Party supervision was achieved in three ways. The Party monitored enterprise plans; it monitored, vetoed, and in some cases made appointments; and it required economic leaders, whether they were Party members or not,[5] to report regularly on their performance and indicate how their plan targets conformed with central interests.[6] But it did not decide day-to-day economic policy. The Party exercised clearer, although still essentially negative, control via the appointment of staff. As was noted in earlier chapters, for the majority of the socialist period enterprise directors and other senior management were appointed by the relevant industrial ministry. An additional requirement was the approval of the county Party organization, which also vetted middle-management appointments as well as Party secretary posts within the enterprises of a given county.[7] The enterprise Party organization enjoyed powers of a similar nature. It too had a duty to make decisions about general policy goals, on the basis of the decrees of bodies above them in the Party government hierarchy, and about questions having a fundamental effect on workers' working and living conditions. It used its right of supervision and its right to receive reports from economic leaders to ensure that the spirit of the plan was being adhered to in both its economic and social aspects.[8] But it was under the same obligation as the national and regional committees not to interfere in economic decisions themselves. Enterprise Party committees, like their national and county counterparts, prepared 'action programmes' for their members.[9] At the bottom end of the hierarchy, the workplace groups were encouraged to busy themselves with propaganda work, with competitions, and with socialist brigade activity on the basis of six-monthly plans. At this level, Party meetings consisted mainly of hearing reports and suggestions made by the Party apparatus. The workplace organs also had a supervisory function in that members were under an obligation to inform the relevant Party organs of the atmosphere among, and opinions of, the non-Party members in the workplace. The Party made influential recommendations, but legally enforceable decisions could only be made by government or by the economic leadership.[10] Its influence at both national and enterprise level took the form of negative control.

The second external constraint on enterprise management was the trade union movement. Trade unions were powerful political institutions in their own right. They had extensive formal rights of suggestion and veto in relation to many decisions which affect labour. They were active in taking up cases of individual injustice in relations to workers.[11] However, certain factors prevented them from acting as an independent force with the primary purpose of defending workers' interests within the enterprise.

Trade unions had extensive formal rights to contribute to enterprise decision-making. In addition to their traditional role in areas of social benefits and working conditions, regulations in 1968 gave them the right to express an opinion both on the appointment of managers and on policy matters which affected the workforce.[12] They also enjoyed a right of veto in the case of breaches of the 'collective agreement', failure to consult the unions when required to do so, or contravention of socialist morality.[13] Amendments to the 1968 law in 1972 required that the National Trade Union Council be consulted on drafting five-year plans,[14] and in 1975 the unions gained the right to express an opinion on the distribution of profits within enterprises,[15] in addition to an effective veto on wages, norms, bonus and disciplinary decisions at the workplace, in that such decisions could only be made with union agreement.[16] In 1980, the areas in which shop stewards could express an opinion were extended, and they were encouraged to give an annual evaluation of their managers' performance.[17] However, the right of veto was rarely exercised. In the five years between 1968 and 1973, the right of veto was used only 150 times in the whole of Hungarian industry,[18] which, in 1970, encompassed 5,681 industrial sites within 812 separate state enterprises, employing some 1.5 million people.[19] In the mammoth Csepel works, the union chief reported that the union had occasion to use the veto only five times between 1968 and 1974.[20]

The central problem with trade unions, and the reason for their reluctance to exercise the rights they formally possessed, was that trade union, managerial and indeed Party hierarchies were insufficiently distinct, and formed a single career structure. Workplace trade union committees tended to be dominated not by workers but by foremen and administrators – that is, by representatives from lower management – who could not be expected to act wholeheartedly in the shopfloor workers' interests. In both the Győr engineering works and the Budapest construction company studies undertaken by Héthy and Makó, the workplace trade union committee typified this trend. (At Győr the trade union committee chairman was a foreman and three out of the five members worked in administration; only two were manual workers.[21]) Lower-level management also monopolized shopfloor trade union posts in Haraszti's study of the Red Star Tractor Factory[22] and Kemény's study of motorcycle production at Csepel.[23] Management further dominated the enterprise-wide trade union committee. Of the fifteen-person enterprise trade union committee of a large road haulage and transport company, three were chief departmental heads, two were departmental heads, five were full-time trade union functionaries, one was a plant manager, another was a group leader and only three were manual workers. In another subsidiary of the enterprise, four were full-time trade union functionaries, eight were non-manual workers (including one deputy director), one was a driver, and one was a (bus) conductor.[24]

There were two further aspects to the problem of interdependence. First, the full-time trade union functionary, although in receipt of a salary (equivalent to that of a manager) from the trade union, received profit share and bonuses from the enterprise. In the enterprise studied by Andor, these amounted to 10.6 per cent of their income.[25] Thus, full-time functionaries had a considerable material interest in identifying with the company rather than the labour force. In a very real sense they were simply managerial-status enterprise employees with a particular responsibility for staff.[26] Second, trade union posts were perceived as just this by both workers and management.[27] Consequently, management, trade union, and indeed Party[28] posts effectively constituted a single managerial career structure. Before their appointment, most trade union officials would have worked as enterprise managers or administrators at some level, and many would return to management after their trade union posting. They were therefore reluctant to antagonize their former colleagues or jeopardize their future career prospects. They were unwilling, that is, to voice the structural conflicts which necessarily flowed from their position as labour representatives.[29] At a non-management level, 'the trade union and Party representative is always in a dependent relationship with his boss. It is true that he has the right to criticize and make suggestions, but all the same, his boss has countless ways of picking on him.'[30] It is difficult not to disagree with Héthy and Makó when they state that trade unions suffered from conflicting roles and that, in order to defend worker interests adequately, they required a fully independent apparatus.[31]

The constraints imposed on enterprise management from external bodies were not extensive. While, as we have already seen and will illustrate further below, political considerations continued to influence management decisions, the Party as an institution did not interfere in the minutiae of day-to-day decisions. At the same time, while trade unions had significant rights of participation in enterprise decisions, their ability to act as an independent force moulding management decisions in the interests of the workers was severely restricted.

Managerial autonomy and production decisions

This section also considers two constraints, one from above and one from below, in the forms of the planning centre, and the role of production meetings. The bureaucracy–management relationship is included as an internal constraint on management since it was almost inevitably structured around business decisions concerning access to finance and investment.

As Chapters 4 and 5 have shown, enterprise management, even under the New Economic Mechanism, enjoyed little genuine autonomy in the area of investment. The point need not be repeated here. Its impact on intra-management relations is, however, worthy of note. One consequence of the continued importance of bargaining, over plan quotas or plan regulations, with branch or functional ministries was that within enterprise management financial managers were undervalued. Laky and Szalai found not only that only a small managerial group was involved in investment decision-making, but also that technical rather than financial management is most involved. This was true for all types of enterprises and whatever the sources of investment funding.[32] As financial managers interviewed by Laky attest,

> We do not have much say over whether a development becomes part of the enterprise programme. In theory, before any investment, we should examine how much of a new product we can sell and where. But we don't do calculations like that. The technical view still dominates in the enterprise.... We generally get to know about them after the deal has been struck.[33]

Managers interviewed by Szalai make essentially the same points. Profitability calculations were made only after the event.

> decisions aren't made on the basis of profitability calculations, we decide first and then prepare all the figures that the bank asks for. That's why we don't work out any alternative plans either, although it is also because we don't have the strength to do it either.[34]

Or: 'Afterwards we never examine the profitability of the investments. Either we get the planned profit, or we don't. I've been with the enterprise for 18 years, and in 17 of those 18 we have made our planned profit.'[35] Indeed, there were penalties associated with calculating the true costs of an investment, even if the calculations were for internal use only.

> The competition now is for credit. Only an enterprise cannot calculate honestly how much an investment costs and when the break-even point is reached because then it would never get credit ... (the enterprise cannot do the calculations in secret so it has a real idea of the cost).... Because it could not be kept secret ... [and the enterpise would be guilty of] misleading the government.... If no calculation is made, the manager can say hand on heart that he only knows the same figures as the higher bodies.[36]

As the centre–enterprise relationship moved from 'plan bargaining' to 'regulation bargaining',

> the role of the economic director became to discover in the jungle of regulations the best preferences, concessions and advantages ... they were expected to ensure the optimal profit for the given year ... not more ... not

less. (Those who had the opportunity to see how each enterprise 'makes' its profit can only stare in wonder at the skill and ability to manoeuvre of the financial director.)[37]

The finance director's increased prestige did not alter enterprise power relations. When it came to major investment decisions, technical rather than economic management made the decisions, with no reference to considerations of profitability, and much bargaining with higher authorities.[38]

Investment decisions aside, management's effective control was limited to the product mix within an enterprise's permitted profile (although it could not, until 1985, produce goods or supply services which lay outside it)[39] and pricing, if the goods produced were in the free or flexible pricing categories.[40] Other than this, management had control over labour, albeit constrained by its endemic shortage. The management–labour relationship will be considered below.

Within the enterprise a further force with a potential both to constrain management decisions and to provide a focus for a separate articulation of labour interest was the production meetings, which were considered the most effective institution for representing the direct interests of workers in the workplace.[41] Empirical research, however, cast considerable doubt on their efficacy in this respect. Management interpreted the meetings as occasions for informing workers rather than accepting their suggestions and entering into dialogue with them. In a study of the steel workers in Dunaújváros, Kozák and Mod found that no managers considered production meetings as centres for debate. In reply to questions about the role of production meetings most indicated that they saw them as forums for the downward transfer of information rather than its mutual exchange. When asked what their content should be, 50 per cent did not answer at all, 20 per cent gave meaningless replies, and only 10 per cent indicated that they should consider matters which related to workers personally.[42] From the workers' side, this time questioning engineering workers at Ózd, Kozák and Mod found that roughly two-thirds of them thought that production meetings ought to consider matters other than those actually dealt with, and that, of this percentage, 40 per cent were of the opinion that they should deal more with matters concerning wages.[43]

At Győr, Héthy and Makó found that although 90 per cent of workers wanted to have a say in general enterprise affairs, no matters of serious concern to labour were discussed at production meetings.[44] 'Easy questions' were answered by management at these meetings on the spot. 'Difficult questions', such as the need to clean factory windows in order to illuminate the factory better, were replied to in writing within seven days, while 'awkward questions', such as wages and norms, were not even recorded in the minutes of the meetings.[45] In their study of a Budapest construction company, these same writers discovered that the crucial issue of paying workers wages when there was no work to perform was never discussed at production meetings,[46] and Halmos, a participant observer in another Budapest factory, noted the absence of really important issues at the Brigade meetings he attended.[47]

Andor, in his study of a haulage and transport company, painted an equally negative picture of production meetings. Focusing first on the meetings as organs of workplace democracy, his survey of management found them ignorant of the democratic rights legally invested in the institution. Only twelve of the forty-eight managers interviewed knew what the areas of competence of the production meetings were, and most thought that, for example, it was management alone, and not the production meeting, which decided who would be given the title 'excellent worker', or which drew up the form of labour competition within the enterprise. He also found that attendance at production meetings was low, and that official attendance figures in the minutes of the meetings bore little relation to reality.[48]

The above studies all related to the late 1960s and early 1970s, but Ferenc Kunszabó's study of 196 workers in the Lehel refrigerator factory in the provincial town of Jászberény in 1976 indicated that, for all the pro-working-class statements of the economic recentralizers in the Party between 1973 and 1975, production meetings did not develop as the loci of workplace democracy. As one manager interviewed by Kunszabó stated, 'When the committee sits down at the table, everything is usually already decided because we have all informed the men sufficiently and decided things amongst ourselves.' Production meetings are 'almost completely' superfluous. For every suggestion put forward via such channels, management received ten or twenty via informal channels. 'Those who have serious opinions are least likely to bring them out in front of the whole assembly.'[49] As in the case of trade union meetings, there was a problem of intimidation and the workers' fear of reprisals. Andor noted that workers tended to keep quiet at production meetings so as to avoid being given less well paid jobs by their immediate superiors,[50] and Héthy commented that managers did not like workers who criticize.[51] Problems with the effectiveness of production meetings as institutions of workplace democracy resulted in greater emphasis being placed, by the end of the 1970s, on the role of the trade union shop steward and work group meetings.[52] Although there was evidence of greater participation at these levels, there was no pretence that the collectivity should be deciding more than local workplace issues.

On the other hand, workers were oriented towards problem-solving and had their own solutions for improving productivity. Andor found, when analysing the contributions of workers to production meetings, that they predominantly concerned matters of work organization and its remuneration, and that the majority of contributions were not complaints but concrete suggestions about organizational matters.[53] Kobjakov found similarly well thought out views on wage ratios in her study of the Budapest Machine Tools Works, and Héthy and Makó, in their studies of Győr, Dunaújváros and Miskolc, found that workers had precise views on concrete matters directly affecting their work.[54] Yet, as we have seen, these views were not sought, and, if they were given expression, had little influence.

The inevitable consequence of this exclusion from the decision-making process was first disillusionment and then ignorance. Workers' opinions, as gauged by the surveys carried out by Andor, Kunszabó, Héthy and Makó and others, reflected disillusionment with production meetings. 'There's no point going to a meeting and saying this, that or the other needs doing. Nothing changes.'[55] 'They're just discussions, mainly of an informative nature.' 'At our place, industrial democracy is regulated by the director's orders.'[56] And, because production meetings and other similar forums dealt with larger issues in a one-sided manner, workers had no interest in developing more than a restricted knowledge of the enterprises in which they worked,[57] or of the collective agreement which they had signed when taking the job, despite the fact that it determined the jurisdiction of such bodies as the production meetings as well as the system of norm and wage regulation.[58] Kozák and Mod,[59] Haraszti,[60] and Kovács[61] all amply documented the extent of this ignorance. Kozák and Mod, for example, found that in Dunaújváros only 15 per cent of skilled workers, 5 per cent of semi-skilled and 5 per cent of unskilled workers knew properly the content of the collective agreement.[62] Furthermore, disillusionment and ignorance were exacerbated by the fact that the 1977 decree on industrial democracy stated that, wherever possible, production meetings should be held outside working hours.[63] As Héthy and Makó[64] and Simonyi[65] pointed out, workers were unlikely to take on this burden if they got nothing out of it. Their interests were all well defended if they remained in ignorance.

A final point of significance is that the possibility of escape from the working class by career mobility was a realistic prospect for only a very few. Comparing data from the social mobility surveys of 1962–64 and 1973, Iványi and Vass found that, while there had been some considerable mobility between levels of skill within the working class,[66] very few moved into positions which exercised control over production. Only 2.6 per cent of skilled, 0.7 per cent of semi-skilled, and 0.1 per cent of unskilled workers who changed their jobs ended up in a position of such control.[67] They concluded that career movement out of the working class had to count as the exception, while noting that the low incomes for foremen did not make such progression immediately attractive.[68]

Management pursuit of plan fulfilment and bonuses

The preceding sections have demonstrated how enterprise management in the socialist sector enjoyed autonomy in relation to both external and internal potential constraints on decision-making. But, of the two major factors of production (capital and labour), this autonomy is more extensive in the field of labour than capital. As Timár has noted: '[e]nterprises enjoy a relative autonomy in the selection, employment and dismissal of manpower'.[69] Labour policy is subject to some restriction, as was mentioned in earlier chapters. Wage levels are regulated, wage increases are controlled by taxation, and there are two types of restriction on labour mobility: measures taken to redress imbalances between state industry and other sectors, and those placing restrictions on the frequent changing of employment.[70] But these restrictions still permit management considerable flexibility with regard to the quantity of labour employed and the size of rewards paid to it.

Labour, then, is the production factor over which management has most autonomous control, and managers understandably make optimum use of this fact in achieving their plan targets. They have a material interest in so doing, since their bonuses are related to successful plan fulfilment. Managers, indeed, are considerably more interested materially in bonuses than is labour, because they receive large bonuses in respect of successful performance: 30 to 50 per cent, and in some cases even more, of basic salary.[71] Workers, on the other hand, look forward to only relatively small end-of-year profit shares, rarely as much as 10 per cent of basic salary, and dependent on factors over which they have no control.[72] Furthermore, management can only increase its basic salary by winning bonuses, while workers have the fallback of working overtime.

Under the New Economic Mechanism management plan targets consisted essentially of profit maximization, once allowance had been made for regulation bargaining and the winning of special concessions. But profits, and with them managerial bonuses, were under a tax threat arising from the forms of wage regulation which have operated since 1968. The details of these regulations are complex, and the persistence should be noted of an element of 'average wage level' regulation, in the form of the 'average wage brake', even within the forms of 'wage-bill' regulation which were introduced in the mid 1970s. The crux of all systems of enterprise wage regulation in operation until 1985 was that as soon as any permitted annual tax-free increase in the average wage for an enterprise had been exceeded, an exceptionally progressive tax – termed until modifications in the 1980s the 'wage development payment' – was imposed, which very quickly reached its highest marginal rate of some 300–600 per cent of the excessive wages. This tax impacted on management bonuses in two ways. First, the size of funds available for bonuses was reduced by payment of the tax. To be more specific, over the years since 1968, management bonuses came either from the same financial source as the 'wage development payments' or, after 1976, from a separate fund, but one whose size was itself adversely affected by the payment of the tax. From 1976, bonuses could only be awarded after all enterprise funds had been successfully established, and after the 'sharing fund' (out of which the 'wage development payments' were made) had itself been subject to progressive taxation. Second, until 1976, not only was the size of the fund out of which bonuses were paid under threat from 'wage development payments', but also the indicator on which managerial bonuses were based (total profit between 1968 and 1970, and 'sharing fund' divided by wage costs between 1971 and 1976) was adversely affected by making them. After 1976, bonuses were based on more subjective 'successful performance' and 'complex evaluation' criteria, and enterprises did have the theoretical option of not forming a 'sharing fund' at all, but failure to do so would prevent the payment of end-of-year profit shares to either lower levels of management or workers, and enterprises were reluctant to follow this course.[73]

Whatever the precise method of wage regulation, management bonuses and successful plan fulfilment itself were considerably at risk from 'wage development payments', so enterprise management used various methods of avoiding them. The most common tactic is usually termed 'labour force dilution', that is, employing reserves of cheap labour in order to keep the average wage low and so allow some flexibility in paying higher incomes to a smaller number of skilled workers at the top of the scale. Other methods included the use of students and soldiers, and straightforward falsifying of books.[74] The tendency for 'labour force dilution' was noticed immediately after the introduction of the first form of average wage control in 1957;[75] it came under particularly close scrutiny during the first few years of the New Economic Mechanism as enterprises experienced the labour problems discussed in Chapter 5; and it continued as an evergreen topic until the reforms of 1985.[76] As a manager in a Budapest construction company reveals:

'There is another worker ... who has been with us for a long time and we only keep him on because he is a cheap duffer, he improves the average wage.' Mattheisz (the site manager) explains that a bonus of 20,000 forints is a risk if the average wage is exceeded by half a percent. 'If we exceed the average wage then we cannot pick up a bonus during the year however many flats we finish. We only get a bonus at the end of the year if I've got the average wage to balance by then.'[77]

Avoidance of the 'wage development payment' by keeping within average wage limits became an important feature of enterprise labour policy, such that middle management was faced with the danger that 'If he doesn't succeed [in keeping increases in average wages within the tax-free limits], he is considered the sort of person who cannot manage.'[78]

The upshot for labour of the constellation of forces which has been labelled 'bureaucratic control' was as follows. Labour enjoyed minimal personal autonomy in the socialist sector and, despite exhibiting concern over workplace organization and enterprise efficiency, its role became that of a factor of production manipulated by management in pursuit of plan fulfilment and the bonuses that went with it.

Shortage – Labour and Industrialization

Labour in socialist industrialization is cheap and scarce

One of the paradoxes of the labour market that developed under Hungary's socialist strategy for industrialization was that labour, like many other commodities in the socialist economy, was simultaneously cheap and scarce. Chapter 3 indicated how wages in Hungary in the early years of socialist development were very low. Although living standards increased steadily in the years after 1956, wages continued to be low in relation to perceived needs. Although the continuance of poverty into the socialist period is a topic that will be considered in more detail in Chapter 7, the proximity of average wages to the poverty line is central to labour market behaviour, and should be noted here. Kemény has stated that the Central Statistical Office's minimal monthly subsistence wage was set on 1 January 1968 at 2,640 forints for a family of three, 3,320 for a family of four and 3,850 for a family of five.[79] A survey of 16,000 households undertaken in that same year found that average monthly earnings in 1967 had been 2,180 forints for men, and 1,442 forints for women.[80] On the basis of a hypothetical family income comprising the average male and female earnings (3,622 forints a month), these figures suggest that an average family at work did not earn enough to provide the minimal monthly subsistence for a family of five, although their overall income (when social benefits and other additional sources of income are included) could just provide the subsistence minimum with 3,868 forints. Families with three children are the exception rather than the rule in Hungary, the average worker family size being 3.33 in 1965 and 3.25 in 1970.[81] But even an average couple with only one child was still earning only 137 per cent of the minimum monthly subsistence level.

The fact that wages were experienced as low in real terms did not in itself mean that labour was cheap for an enterprise relative to other factors of production. Wage costs for the enterprise consisted of wages, taxes on the wage bill, compulsory social insurance and so on, and it is conceivable that these might, cumulatively, have made labour relatively expensive. This was not the case, however. Economists all agreed that 'labour was undervalued in comparison with capital',[82] and attempts to redress this undervaluation figured strongly in both the 1976 and 1985 modifications to the economic regulators.

It is also clear from Chapters 3 and 4 that labour was used extensively in the early years of socialist industrialization; and this continued to be the case, as Chapter 5 indicated, even when the focus of investment policy changed from building additional plant to making existing plant perform more successfully. The need for a switch from 'extensive' to 'intensive' industrial development was both one of the most frequently cited justifications for the inauguration of the New Economic Mechanism in 1968,[83] and one of its more conspicuous failures.[84] By the mid 1970s, the labour shortage in Hungary had become general,[85] and was being exacerbated by two factors: the employment of 'cotton wool' workers to circumvent wage control regulation (discussed above),[86] and hoarding generally. It was natural for enterprises, especially those in a near monopoly position, to hold reserve supplies of shortage items (including labour) for the moment when they were needed. Even after the introduction of the New Economic Mechanism, as we have seen in Chapter 5, production continued to be characterized by periodic bouts of 'storming' to meet important targets.[87] As Gábor has argued, in a socialist economy additional labour can be taken on until the point where, for purely physical reasons of the non-availability of resources, no additional growth is possible. The result is an unlimited demand for labour. Just as there is a necessary shortage of capital in a centrally regulated, growth-oriented, 'soft budget constrained' economy, so too is there a necessary shortage of labour; and in such conditions, hoarding labour is rational.[88]

It proved possible to keep wages low despite this chronic shortage because of average wage control and the 'wage development payment' discussed above. These measures had been considered essential to avoid inflation, to ensure a relatively egalitarian distribution of wages and, after 1968, to avoid the danger of unemployment if 'irrationally' employed labour were suddenly exposed to a profit-oriented enterprise competing for scarce labour in a market open to the pressure of world-market prices.[89] Despite its success in relation to these macro-economic goals, within enterprises average wage control necessarily placed restrictions on differentials and the scope for wage incentives both within and between grades.[90] With average wages nationally so near the poverty line, in a system where the average enterprise wage was controlled, the difference between the minimum enterprise wage and the average could not be sufficiently high to allow adequate differentiation between the average and the maximum. The scope for developing an adequate system of material incentives related to the amount of work performed was limited, especially when the established tradition demanded that a proportion of the leeway usable for differentials be devoted to reward for length of service.[91] As a consequence, workers who worked with only the average amount of effort received not very much less than those who applied themselves fully. Thus, while an individual worker's wage from the socialist sector might be low, in many cases it could be gained without great exertion.

The very success of policies designed to keep labour cheap even when it was scarce resulted in enterprises experiencing an unquenchable thirst for underutilized labour, and labour experiencing its wages as inadequate, but having only a limited opportunity for maximizing them. There was pent-up demand for access to additional sources of income.

Space for a second economy – heavy industry bias and underurbanization

A further recurrent theme of Chapters 3 to 5 was the disproportionate emphasis in economic policy on industry and heavy industry. The corollary of overinvestment in industry was underinvestment in services, the infrastructure and agriculture. And the consequence of this underinvestment was an unfulfilled demand that had to be met by other means. Priorities in socialist industrialization both created demand on the part of workers for additional sources of income, and provided huge gaps in which income-earning activity might take place. Some idea of the size of the gaps left by socialist industrialization can be gauged from two sets of figures. The first of these concerns the structure of the residual private sector. Its overall significance in the economy was tiny, producing some 1.6 per cent of national income in 1970, but it played a vital role in the neglected sectors such as services and construction outside the cities. In 1960, the private sector accounted for 67.6 per cent of services and 82.4 per cent of construction services; in 1970 the figures were 48.6 per cent and 56.2 per cent respectively.[92] And the private sector was an even more significant force in village house building. In 1970, 92 per cent of village houses were built privately, 27 per cent of them without the help of a savings bank loan. This contrasted with 28 per cent in Budapest and 34 per cent in provincial towns. Conversely, 72 per cent of privately built houses were in villages.[93]

The importance of the private sector in relation to village-based housing leads on to the second set of figures illustrating the gaps created by socialist industrialization: underurbanization. As Miklós Hegedűs has demonstrated, Hungary is 'underurbanized' – the percentage of the population dwelling in an urban setting is smaller than would be predicted from its level of industrial development.[94] Also, the infrastructural level within villages is very low, as Fodor has demonstrated with a wide variety of indicators such as the numbers of paved streets, of houses on mains drainage, or with running water, even for villages in the area immediately surrounding Budapest.[95] As a consequence, large numbers of Hungarian workers lived in villages and had to commute over large distances using inadequate means of transport. By 1970, 50 per cent of the working class, and 51 per cent of all active earners, lived in villages.[96] The extent to which villages had become the domicile of the working class, and towns that of the 'bourgeoisie', is reflected in Table 6.1.

The impact of socialist industrialization on labour, then, was the creation of both widespread demand for additional income, and a space in which it might be earned. These two forces came together in the 'second economy'.

Table 6.1 Social stratum and domicile in 1970 (% of class and domicile)

Class	Budapest	Provincial town	Villages	Together
Working class	21	29	50	100
	57	61	55	57
Cooperative peasantry	1	10	89	100
	1	6	29	17
Non-manual workers	36	35	29	100
	40	30	13	23
Petty commodity producers	16	26	58	100
	2	3	3	3
Together	100	100	100	100

Source: R. Andorka, *A Magyar Községek Társadalmának Átalakulása*, Budapest 1979, pp. 82–3.

The extent of the second economy

The 'second economy' in Hungary in the socialist era was extensive. Figures for the numbers involved in small-scale agriculture are the easiest to find, and were the ones most extensively used in the early second economy studies. In 1972, over half of the Hungarian population – 5.2 million people – lived in a household which operated some sort of small-scale agricultural plot,[97] and this despite the fact that, at that time, less than 25 per cent of the economically active population was employed full-time in agriculture. Going beyond small-scale agriculture, figures are harder to find, but those relating to village house construction were available in the 1970s. In 1975, 47,788 dwellings were built privately.[98] The official estimate for the numbers of people involved in building such dwellings was 107,000 workers,[99] yet for that same year the number of certified artisans employed in private-sector construction was only 17,600, which, when supplemented by the 7,700 private-sector employees and apprentices, makes a total of roughly twenty-five thousand. According to these official estimates then, those engaged in full-time employment in construction constituted, in 1975, only a quarter of the workforce actually involved in building houses. Since there was no unemployment in Hungary in the 1970s, the remaining 82,000 private-sector workers must also have been employed full-time elsewhere in the economy: they must have been participants in the 'second economy'. And in 1975, roughly twice as many dwellings were built privately as by the state (61,631 compared with 31,957).[100] By 1979, it was known that 42 per cent of all housing construction took place in the second economy broadly defined, and 27 per cent in its non-legalized component.[101] In the area of industrial services (vehicle repairs and repairs to electrical appliances etc.), non-legalized services created an estimated 2–3 billion forints of gross value in 1979, approximately five times greater than the production value in the legal sector of small-scale production.[102] Table 6.2 gives an indication of the size of the 'second economy' by the mid 1980s, although it should be noted that these figures cover all of the formal private sector and hence include the Small Cooperatives and Economic Work Partnerships created in 1982.

The generally accepted figure for the numbers of people who were active in some way in the 'second economy', taken from research carried out under Tamás Kolosi, was 75 per cent of families. Galasi supplemented this with the fact that 40 per cent of wage labourers in the socialist sector had an extra income amounting to a quarter of their wages, and that the incomes of the total 75 per cent of the population active in the second economy amounted to almost half of the socialist sector's wage-type outlays.[103] By the same token, net income from work

Table 6.2 Relative size of the second economy (%)

	First economy	Second economy
(1) Distribution of total active time (excluding household work and transport)*	67	33
(2) Contribution to residential construction (measured by number of new dwellings)*	44.5	55.5
(3) Contribution to repair and maintenance service**	13	87

*1984
**1983

Note: The table includes estimated figures for unrecorded activity based on extensive work by the researchers from whom Kornai draws his data. For more details, see Kornai's note to the original table. The bottom right hand 87% is made up of 14% formal private sector, 19% informal but excluding 'do-it-yourself', and 54% informal 'do-it-yourself' household activity.
Source: J. Kornai, 'The Hungarian Reform Process: Visions, Hopes and Reality', in V. Nee and D. Stark (eds), *Remaking the Economic Institutions of Socialism: China and Eastern Europe*, Stanford 1989, p. 58.

as a proportion of the population's total income fell steadily as opportunities in the 'second economy' developed, from 80 per cent in 1960 to 70.2 per cent in 1976 and 64.9 per cent in 1986.[104]

A different approach is to consider the amount of time spent on second economy activity. In 1987, on an average day, an average Hungarian spent almost four and three-quarter hours in either second economy or household work, although over 40 per cent of this was accounted for by household work.[105] The authors of the 1986/87 'time budget' study produced the following typology of second economy participants.

1. New flat building, performed by male economically active workers in the 30–40 year age group who live in villages and work typically in construction.
2. Flat repair, performed by male economically active workers in the 30–50 year age group who lived in villages and work typically in construction.
3. Traditional animal husbandry, performed by male pensioners aged over 60 who live in villages and used to work in agriculture.
4. Modern animal husbandry, performed by economically active males and pensioners aged over 50 who live in villages and used to work or currently work in agriculture.

5. Traditional crop growing, performed by pensioners of either sex in the over-60 age group who live in villages and used to work in agriculture.
6. Modern crop production, performed by male pensioners and economically active of all ages who live in villages who used to or currently work in agriculture.
7. Servicing agriculture, performed by male pensioners or economically active of all ages who live in villages and used to or currently work in agriculture or were/are independent.
8. Distribution of agricultural products, performed by male pensioners aged over 60 who live in villages and either used to work in agriculture or were independent.
9. Household repairs, performed by economically active males aged 30–50 who live in towns and typically work in construction.
10. Car repairs, performed by economically active males aged 20–40 living in towns and employed as drivers or in traditional industry.
11. Other work around the house, performed by male pensioners aged over 60 from all working backgrounds, mainly in Budapest.
12. Qualified intellectual work, performed by male economically active and pensioners of all ages in Budapest currently or formerly employed in technical white-collar jobs.
13. Unskilled white-collar work, performed by pensioners of either sex aged over 60 living in Budapest formerly employed in technical white-collar jobs.
14. Unspecified work for money, performed by male pensioners over 50 in Budapest from all employment backgrounds.
15. 'Social work' (in support of good causes), performed by both sexes from all age groups, but mainly in Budapest and mainly employed in non-technical white-collar jobs.[106]

The shortage inherent in socialist economies created a peculiar labour market in which labour was both cheap and scarce. Workers were interested in maximizing incomes: enterprises were interested in retaining labour. The sectoral bias of socialist industrialization and its accompanying underurbanization created a space in which an extensive second economy could operate which offered to workers the possibility of limited autonomy from the state and from its position of dependence in the first, socialist economy.

Second Economy – The Growth of Institutionalized Dualism

Worker-peasants in agriculture

The first manifestation of a phenomenon that was later to be brought under the umbrella term 'second economy' was the discovery of 'worker-peasants'. As early as 1956, the Central Statistical Office carried out a representative survey of commuting workers. While the term commuting workers does not cover all those who combine agriculture and industrial work, including workers who commute but have no plot, it provides a rough indicator of the phenomenon, since most commute from villages to towns, and the majority of village dwellers have some sort of agricultural plot. This study found that there were 216,000 workers who crossed into another village or town to work – that is, 25 per cent of all workers. Of these, 53 per cent journeyed less than 20 km, 26 per cent travelled 21–30 km, 10 per cent travelled 30–40 km and 5 per cent travelled over 51 km to work. A subsequent representative survey by the Central Statistical Office in 1957 (a date at which the majority of agriculture was still in private hands) approached the question of peasant workers more directly, finding that in as many as 38 per cent of farms there was one or more wage earner.[107] Between 1 January 1957 and the end of March 1958 – that is, in the first fifteen months after the relaxation of controls over land purchase following the 1956 break-up of collective farms – 37 per cent of the newly purchased land was bought by individuals who were not agricultural employees. By 1959, in Borsod county, where a peasant-worker lifestyle had a long tradition, 21.6 per cent of workers in state industry had agricultural land. Within this total, those working in the relatively new metallurgical industries were more likely to retain land than those who worked in the traditional industry of the region, mining. Only 16.5 per cent of those working in mining had agricultural land compared with 42 per cent of those working at the new Lenin metallurgical works. These 'dual-income' families tended to work in semi-skilled or unskilled rather than skilled jobs. Their industrial incomes were lower than those of their industrial worker colleagues, and the production of their farms was 30–35 per cent lower than their full-time peasant neighbours. On their plots they tended to specialize in poultry, pigs, vegetables and fruit, and were less strong on bread grains, horses and cattle.[108]

With wholesale collectivization, the combination within a household of agriculture and industrial employment became almost the norm. In 1960, 43 per cent of all cooperative farm families had at least one family member with an income from outside agriculture, the normal pattern being for the wife to join the collective and perform the requisite number of labour days in order to gain the right to a household plot. By 1966, the number of commuting workers had risen to 18.2 per cent of all earners, and between 1968 and 1970 there was a further 10.7 per cent increase, including an increase in the number of women commuters from one in ten in 1966 to one in eight by 1970.[109] By 1972, the government realized that small-scale agriculture was still a force in Hungary and a General Agricultural Compendium set about documenting its composition. It was this research which revealed the figures cited earlier, namely that roughly one half of the Hungarian population lived in a household where small-scale agricultural production was undertaken, and that slightly over half of non-agricultural manual worker households had a small-scale agricultural plot.[110] The 1970 census revealed that 40 per cent of all industrial workers, and over 50 per cent of workers in the building industry, lived in villages, while 37 per cent of the economically active village population worked in industry and the building industry.[111] In addition, there were 1,301,700 commuting workers – 26 per cent of the economically active population. Of these, 20 per cent were daily commuters and 6 per cent were weekly or bi-weekly commuters; 20 per cent of commuters journeyed to Budapest to work, 66 per cent had jobs in the same county as where they lived, 25 per cent went to neighbouring counties to work and 6 per cent went even further afield.[112] Pető and Szakács provide the figures in Table 6.3 for the increase in commuting workers between 1960 and 1970. In Table 6.4, Hanák used data from a village survey conducted by the Sociological Research

Table 6.3 Percentage of commuting workers by sex and branch of the economy in 1960 and 1970

| | Commuters as % of active earners | | | | | |
| | 1960 | | | 1970 | | |
	men	women	together	men	women	together
Industry	n.a.	n.a.	22.0	30.6	21.0	26.6
Construction	n.a.	n.a.	24.0	32.6	16.8	30.1
Agriculture	n.a.	n.a.	4.9	14.4	5.1	10.9
Transport	n.a.	n.a.	31.1	37.3	18.6	33.1
Commerce	n.a.	n.a.	12.2	20.7	12.3	15.6
Other	n.a.	n.a.	7.4	13.0	8.7	10.5
Together	n.a.	n.a.	13.4	24.6	13.4	20.0

Source: I. Pető and S. Szakács, *A Hazai Gazdaság Négy Évtizedének Története 1945–1985. Az Újjáépítés és a Tervutasításos Irányítás Időszaka 1945–1968*, Budapest 1985, pp. 678–9.

Table 6.4 Distribution of village-based heads of household by type of occupation and pattern of commuting

	Commutes daily	Commutes less often	Total commuters	Does not commute	Total
Ind. skilled	35.4	29.7	65.1	34.9	100
Ind. semi-skilled	24.0	33.3	57.3	42.7	100
Ind. unskilled	39.4	34.2	73.6	26.4	100
Workers in commercial services	16.3	17.8	34.1	65.9	100
Workers in transport & communications	35.2	25.8	61.0	39.0	100

Source: K. Hanák, 'Vázlatok a mai falusi munkásságról' *Szociológia*, 1978, no. 3, p. 373.

Institute in 1972–73 to examine the relationship between commuting and type of occupation for village dwellers.

The illegal second economy

The 'second economy' outside small-scale agriculture was universally accepted to be extensive, but has been inevitably under-researched because of its semi-legality. Everyone knew that it existed, but it was only acknowledged in qualitative, almost anecdotal terms. The most common field of activity of the illegal, moonlighting 'second economy' was in private house construction. An electrician explains:

> It's only worthwhile doing new stuff – electrical heating or an electric cooker where you need a separate circuit. It's done in a day and you can ask 1,000–2,000 forints for it. Wiring a family house, which needs two men for a Saturday and a Sunday, comes to 4,000–5,000 forints if I supply the materials.... If you really have a go at the private sector, you can earn 50,000–100,000. From spring to autumn they pass you on from person to person.[113]

János Kenedi, in his samizdat book describing his attempts to have a house built, discusses the advantages of using the illegal 'second economy'.

> The difference between a private sector operator and a moonlighter is deep and significant. The private sector entrepreneur is fully licensed, has to render invoices and has to pay tax. The moonlighter is probably just as good at the job – maybe better – but keeps no records and doesn't pay tax.... The private sector operator has to charge for purchasing and preparing materials and

supplies, the time factor involved in getting and transporting these....
However, there is an even greater potential gain from the careful selection of a
moonlighter. The real treasure is the one who brings supplies and materials
from their regular workplace. A moonlighter of good standing might allow us
to charge the most expensive items to the state enterprise – unofficially of
course ... the moonlighter doesn't have to chase items in short supply.

Problems with shortages of materials and the methods chosen to
circumvent them revealed a further aspect of the illegal 'second
economy': corruption. Shortage in the first economy led actors in the
second economy, who were dependent on goods and services from the
first economy for their second economy activity, to use illegitimate
means to get them.[114] Conversely, those in the first economy who
accepted bribes and under-the-counter payments were exploiting their
first economy position for second economy gain, although here no
expenditure of labour was required. Kemény has broken down transactions of this type into essentially two broad types: transactions by
employees to supplement income, and transactions by management to
ensure supply.[115] Galasi and Kertesi took the issue of corruption as an
economic mechanism seriously enough to provide a mathematical model
illustrating how corruption can ease blockages in the economy, but
cannot substitute for the market.[116]

Much of the activity associated with the private household construction side of the second economy took place outside the market nexus,
however. Here, the mechanism at work was one of reciprocal exchange
of labour aimed at 'balanced reciprocity'. The mechanisms of this extra-
legal, family-support side of the second economy have been examined in
fascinating detail by Sik.[117] As Table 6.5 indicates on the basis of the

Table 6.5 Persons taking part in labour exchange or market work on an average
day (%)

	Labour exchange	Market work
Construction	1.0	0.3
Agriculture	2.3	1.2
Repairs and hard manual work	1.7	1.6
Sewing and knitting	0.5	0.3
Female household work	3.5	0.3
Shopping and administration	0.6	0.2
Looking after old and sick	6.0	0.1
Total	13.7	6.1

Source: J. Farkas and A. Vajda, Időgazdálkodás és munkatevékenységek, Budapest 1989,
p. 30.

'time budget' study's generous definition of the second economy, which includes household work, the majority of time devoted to the second economy was spent in work performed on the basis of labour exchange.

Incorporating and integrating first agriculture, then industry and services

As Chapter 5 (Figure 5.2) suggested, over the 1970s the attitude towards small-scale agriculture changed from simply accepting it and legalizing it, to incorporating it and institutionalizing it into a symbiotic relationship with large-scale production. The introduction of Small Cooperatives and Economic Work Partnerships in 1982 was accompanied by mixed expectations, as we have seen, but the bulk of the evidence suggests that what was actually achieved was the incorporation and institutionalization of certain aspects of the second economy, and that this was in line with government, if not reform economist, expectations. In official publications of the time, reference to 'entrepreneurship' was conspicuous by its absence.[118] Two general points should be made in this respect. First, the majority of what was created by these new institutions was part-time work. Second, the legislative framework within which they were introduced suggests incorporation and institutionalization, rather than the creation of a dynamic autonomous private sector, as the overriding aim.

Laky saw the new small-scale sector created by the 1982 reforms as being characterized by three features. The first was a lack of capital investment. Partnerships produce 3 per cent of the nation's value-added, 4 per cent of national income, but employ less than 0.1 per cent of its fixed capital.[119] Indeed, Bakcsi and others found that even successful partnerships had minimal capital investment.[120] Laky's second characteristic was that labour input, rather than capital investment, is their most significant feature. Her third characteristic was preservation of the original workplace, and the avoidance of risk that went with it. Work in the new forms of economic organization was predominantly part-time. For example, Laky's team at the Labour Affairs Research Institute found that in 1986, 50,000 people were employed full-time in partnership compared with 400,000 part-time, and the proportion working full-time fell, if only slightly in 1986 to 13 per cent, from 14 per cent in 1985.[121] Even the enterprising Economic Work Partnerships studied by Bakcsi were wary of full-time commitment.[122]

The focus in all the regulations that accompanied the 1982 reforms, from the newly encouraged independent artisan through Economic Work Partnerships and Industrial Specialized Group to Small Cooperative and Small Enterprise, was on subcontracting to larger enterprises.

In the case of the Enterprise Economic Work Partnership the relationship of interdependence went further. Those subcontracting to their own employer added to their pension and other welfare rights even when they were working for the partnership. Benefit was based on the average income of a wage-labourer doing a similar job.[123] This directly paralleled the retention of pension rights by collective farm members when producing household plot goods for sale via the collective. In both cases, institutionalization created a symbiotic relationship between the state/cooperative employer and the private economic activity of the worker. Enterprises actually rewarded workers for participation in the second economy.

In the light of this institutional famework, it is not surprising that those who had grander expectations from the 1982 reforms were disappointed. Timár's judgement is that the Enterprise Economic Work Partnerships were little more than a new type of overtime work;[124] indeed, although it was illegal for enterprises to oblige them to sub-contract only to themselves,[125] there is evidence that, in practice, such restrictions were made.[126] But there was disappointment too for those who emphasized the incorporation of the second economy. The new Partnership and Small Cooperatives did not develop to the extent that had been expected in the area of services to the population. In these areas, moonlighting and illegal variants of the second economy remained the norm.[127] Roughly a third of household restoration, and two-thirds of household services and repairs, were still carried out by such methods in the mid 1980s.[128] Indeed, 'since 1983 an increasing number of analyses have reported on the expansion of illegal services and the increase of illegally tax-free income in the fields of car repairs and telecommunications and household appliances repair'.[129]

Workers want money and autonomy

Workers' motivations for engaging in institutionalized second economy activity were two-fold. The first was financial, the second related to personal autonomy. We have already seen the general interest workers had in increasing their incomes from activity in the second economy. Participation in the institutionalized second economy was merely an extension of the general case. The rewards were not necessarily greater than in illegal second economy activity, but there was far less hassle. Illegal moonlighting, although it yielded a reward in excess of the over-time rates in comparable industrial sectors, did not count towards social insurance.[130] Enterprise Economic Work Partnership participation counted towards social insurance, and still paid more than overtime. The ratio of basic wage rates to overtime in Hungarian industry was roughly

3:5, while that of basic wages to Enterprise Economic Work Partnership income was 3:6–8.[131]

But motives for joining these new organizations were not exclusively economic. For many there was a desire for self-fulfilment and greater personal autonomy. Kozma, for example, found that the predominant aims in setting up Work Partnerships and Small Cooperatives were first higher income (especially for those just leaving university), but second, more independent working conditions.[132] A round-table discussion in the economic weekly newspaper *Figyelő* revealed similar themes of higher income, non-hierarchical working conditions, and the ability to see the whole of the production process – non-alienated production.[133] These were also important reasons for joining the non-agricultural subsidiary enterprises of agricultural producer cooperatives in an earlier decade.[134]

Numerous studies have commented on good workplace relations within partnerships, although they disagree on whether work within them was organized on a democratic basis.[135] David Stark's work on the partnerships has opened this field to an English-speaking audience. As he indicates, it was not so much the pace or intensity of the work in the partnership that was diferent as its organization.

> In regular hours they [the managers] bring only the *detailed* blueprints that this and this is needed. But from the *master* blueprint I ... immediately see ... the obstacles, the danger spots.... In regular hours the tasks are defined almost down to the tiniest detail.[136]

> In the official hours, the worker waits until work is organized. In the VGM [Enterprise Economic Work Partnership] everybody takes part, nobody waits. No one is a supervisor or controller; everybody is an organizer.[137]

Stark was surely correct when he suggested that these alternative forms of self-organizing work group brought managerial prerogatives into question.[138]

The Dialectics of Dualism

Government intentions when extending the institutionalized dualism of the first and second economy to the industrial and service sectors were ambiguous, as we have seen. Support nevertheless continued for two reasons. First, the additional incomes institutionalized dualism allowed, while introducing a possible inflationary pressure, continued the general post-1956 policy of maintaining, if not actually improving, living standards. Second, despite numerous caveats, it increased the supply of services in many areas of the economy. To be sure, many of the more apparently entrepreneurial partnerships and Small Cooperatives turned out to be simply reincarnations, taking advantage of the reduced paperwork and financial controls in the new sector, of groups that had previously existed in a different form, such as subsidiary enterprises of agricultural producer cooperatives,[139] or the traditional forms of small industrial cooperative.[140] Worse, the new undertakings created few new jobs.[141] Nevertheless, significant new services were created. New partnerships and Small Cooperatives began to operate in a whole variety of areas – such as advertising and market research, general technical development services, washing, painting and dry-cleaning, investment organization and implementation, technological planning, machine rental, computer services and supplies, data processing, research and development[142] – which previously either had not existed or had been submerged and under-rewarded in either the first or second economy.

The advantage that enterprises derived from maintaining a system of institutionalized dualism is less obvious. There is, after all, something rather surreal in the fact that groups of workers could earn one rate for eight hours a day when they worked as employees, and then earn more than twice that during the next four hours, when they worked as a subcontracting Enterprise Economic Work Partnership, often using the same tools, often doing the same job.

But for enterprises too, the overriding motivation was self-interest. As we have already seen, in a growth-oriented 'socialist' economic system, enterprises necessarily had an unquenchable demand for labour. Good workers were a valuable commodity which enterprises had always striven to keep, by whatever possible informal manipulation of the wage mechanism and allocation of overtime opportunities.[143] The Economic Work Partnerships, especially the Enterprise Economic Work Partnership, proved to be a useful new weapon in this armoury. There have been extensive studies of 'elite' workers and their opportunities for 'informal bargaining' over wages and norms.[144] In situations where technology gave certain workers the monopoly of a central stage in the production process, many made use of systematic 'go-slows' to blackmail management into increasing wage rates, or not increasing norms, or simply not cutting overtime. Such elite workers were usually of an age when, having established a home and a family, they could adopt a longer-term perspective, and risk lower wages while they were 'going slow' in order to optimize their long-term income once the desired overtime was awarded. Workers who once maximized their income by informal bargaining of this type began to form Enterprise Economic Work Partnerships to put the relationship on a formal footing. This process, 'from informal bargaining to internal subcontracting', is well documented by Kővári and Szirácki[145] and by Stark,[146] who also showed, on the basis of his evidence from an enterprise he christened 'Minotaur', that in partnerships, it was highly skilled male workers who predominated.[147]

As a means of retaining the elite of the labour force by permitting additional earnings, the use of a subcontracting Enterprise Economic Work Partnership had one very considerable advantage over overtime: the payments were not included in average wage calculations.[148] They were costs pure and simple, not wages.[149] The danger of triggering the 'wage development payments' discussed earlier in this chapter was thus mitigated. This function of the Enterprise Economic Work Partnerships as a means for circumventing wage-control regulations can also be seen from what happened to some of the partnerships at the Duna Steel Works, which at one time had 174 partnerships within an enterprise employing over 2,000 people. When, in their second year of operation, a more flexible experimental method of wage control was introduced, so reducing the need for 'labour force dilution' and 'cotton wool workers', the focus of the Partnerships switched immediately from production to repairs and maintenance.[150]

A further material incentive in favour of institutionalized dualism was the fact that, given all the constraints already mentioned, Enterprise Economic Work Partnerships were one of the cheaper methods of obtaining additional labour. Overtime cost 30–40 per cent above normal wages, bringing in hired labour from outside cost 190–380 per cent, and employing foreign *gastarbeiter* from fraternal countries cost 350–450 per cent above normal wages. Use of Enterprise Economic Work Partnerships cost only 60–79 per cent more. If workers could not be persuaded to work overtime, it was clearly cheaper to make use of a Partnership than bring in outside labour which did not know the enterprise.[151]

So far in this chapter we have examined the position of labour in the 'first economy', considered factors in the development of the 'second economy', documented its gradual incorporation into institutionalized dualism, and examined the reasons why, despite its apparent irrationality, it was in the interests of government, management and workers alike that such dualism should continue. This chapter concludes with an account of how this dualism mapped itself on to internal divisions within the Hungarian working class.

The Hungarian industrial manual working class in the socialist era could be subdivided into four groups: 'elite', wage optimizers; wage maximizers; self-sufficient property owners; and marginalized workers. This classification is a composite derived from the works of Héthy and Makó, Kemény, and Kertesi and Sziráczki. The latter pair, publishing in the 1980s, are labour market economists while the former group, publishing through the 1970s, are sociologists. From their slightly different perspectives, they came to remarkably similar conclusions.[152]

The 'elite' workers were skilled, usually male, and over thirty-five to forty years of age. Because of their long service with a company, their knowledge of its technology and its informal channels, they had come out as winners in the firm's internal labour market. They were of central importance to the company since their skills were enterprise specific. Such workers therefore received high wages, even if this required 'labour force dilution' and the employment of 'cotton wool' workers on low wages elsewhere in the company so as to keep the average wage in balance. Traditionally they monopolized overtime. They were the prime actors in informal enterprise bargaining and were the most likely to be involved in Enterprise Economic Work Partnerships.

The 'wage maximizers' were to some extent the converse of the 'wage optimizers'. They too were workers with some skill qualifications, but were more likely to be semi-skilled or recently qualified; and, more important, they tended to be young. It was their youth which turned them into maximizers. While it is true that young unmarried workers with no family responsibilities and no home to build could get by on their normal monthly wage, this became impossible as soon as a family was started and/or the workers wanted to live in a flat or house, rather than a rented room. Money had to be got from somewhere, but, as yet, these workers did not have the informal ties of the 'elite worker', nor were they so indispensable to the company. Such workers were obliged to maximize their income in the shorter term rather than optimize it over the long term. They had to do as much overtime as possible, whatever the rate, moonlight whenever possible, eschew wage optimization strategies,[153] accept deteriorating working conditions,[154] and bribe foremen in order to obtain overtime or a well-paying job.[155] If they were piece-rate workers they had to bribe hourly-paid workers to hurry up so that their own tight norms could be met;[156] they could 'cheat the norm' or illegally fix machines so they would produce more.[157] If workers were too young and inexperienced to be highly valued on the internal labour market, they had to capitalize on the chronic labour shortage and keep on moving jobs until they had either wormed their way into an enterprise's elite, or decide to opt for the property-owning, self-sufficient approach. The most mobile sectors of the labour market were younger workers – 21–25[158] – and the less highly skilled. Kozák and Mod found that the average length of service for skilled workers was 11.5 years, for semi-skilled workers 9 years and for unskilled workers 3 years. As far as turnover is concerned, 'mobility is the younger worker's form of wage struggle'.[159] It was usually a response adopted on an individual basis, but

Héthy and Makó give an example of a group of construction workers who used group mobility and the threat of group mobility to maximize wages.[160]

The property-owning, self-sufficient stratum of the Hungarian working class has not been studied in such depth as a separate group. These were workers who for whatever reason had not found a way into the 'elite' grouping, and had opted to direct the focus of their working lives elsewhere. They needed the security of a full-time job in the socialist sector, but their lives revolved around the (legal or illegal) second economy. A large number of such workers were village-based daily commuters into Budapest; but they did not include the younger commuters who hoped one day to obtain a flat in the town. They were older workers who had built themselves a house in their village and were committed to living in it and to the commuting worker lifestyle. They almost always had a small agricultural plot, which was very likely to be run commercially and farmed intensively. The statistics on animal and small-scale plot ownership in Hungary reveal a surge in such ownership at the age of thirty, stretching on into middle age, before decreasing as people became pensioners and could not cope physically with running a small farm. In terms of skill, they were more likely to be semi-skilled or unskilled,[161] and they did less overtime than average, not only because the factory was not the main focus of their attention but also because they tended to be tied to catching a particular bus back to their village each day. It would also seem that they did not get greatly involved with enterprise affairs, even if they did not much like what was going on. A worker of this type interviewed by Földvári and Zsille, a Stakhanovite hero of the 1950s, responded to everything with a 'well, that's how things are'.[162] There came a time in certain workers' lives, it would seem, when they accepted that it was fruitless striving further to find a flat in a town and get on in the factory hierarchy, and discovered that for all the 'double disadvantagement' of commuting,[163] a good life could be made from exploiting 'second economy' opportunities in agriculture and enjoying the relatively independent lifestyle of the property-owning self-sufficient worker.

The fourth and final stratum in the modern Hungarian working class consisted of 'marginal workers'. These differed from the previous two groups to the extent that in their 'full-time' socialist sector jobs they were overwhelmingly unskilled, and that a significant proportion consisted of female workers. Because they were unskilled, no strong tie linked them to any particular enterprise, and the chronic labour shortage gave them the same ability to push up wages through constant mobility as the 'wage maximizers'. But in being mobile they had to accept losing some of the marginal benefits of longer-term employment – regular automatic pay increases, bonuses, profit share, family allowances and so on. Where such workers had an agricultural plot, it constituted an even more important element in their lives than in the case of the property-owning self-sufficient worker. This was so much the case that it was common for some workers in this category, predominantly women, to give up their full-time employment entirely at harvest time in order to concentrate on agriculture, but return to the same job again once harvest was over.[164] Such workers appeared to change jobs very often, but the pattern was a regular one of resignation from and re-employment in the same enterprise. Since women were employed disproportionately in unskilled and semi-skilled jobs, this periodic loss of income was less of a blow to the family. Such intermittent exits from socialist industry at harvest time were not related exclusively to an increased focus on the second economy and household plot. There were numerous opportunities for seasonal employment for female field workers in socialist agriculture at harvest time, and the income from such work was often greater than that from unskilled factory work.

Timár has derived five earnings-maximizing strategies from the Kertesi and Sziráczki research and elsewhere, and quantifies them as follows:

1. Undertaking to achieve extra performance in the socialist sector, partly in the form of overtime and partly with weekend work.
2. Choosing employment at an establishment or subsidiary activity (mostly industrial) or at a collective farm, rather than in a state enterprise, thus securing higher earnings.
3. Being active in the second economy, while also holding a job in the socialist sector, but limiting performance (intensity and working time) there.
4. Terminating employment in the socialist sector and undertaking legal or non-legal work in the private sector (second economy).
5. Exploiting positions in the socialist sector (monopolistic situation) to obtain non-legal but tolerated, or illegal, income.

The numbers adopting these strategies were as follows:

Strategy	Number of Persons
1	400,000–500,000
2	150,000–200,000
3	900,000–1,200,000
4	250,000–300,000
5	200,000–350,000[165]

By far the largest group (group 3) involved activity in both the first and second economies, as did group 5, if, following Gábor, we include corruption in the second economy. Large sections of the first group also included second economy activity, if we accept the change that the Enterprise Economic Work Partnerships have brought with them in substituting for overtime. The remaining two groups were wholly within one economy or the other, but it is significant that it was the smallest of all groups that was in a position to earn high full-time earnings on collective farms or similar bodies. Very few strategies for the organization of one's working life in Hungary permitted the luxury of not being active in both the first and second economies. What developed in Hungary after some thirty years of the socialist project was in many ways a deformed version of Liska's ideal. In his model, 70–80 per cent of wages would be paid to workers as a right and the remaining 20–30 per cent would depend fully on performance in the entrepreneurial socialist economy.[166] In the event, workers received 100 per cent wages in the socialist sector, but for 70 per cent of their effort; the remaining 30 per cent of their effort had been used in the second economy as labour-only entrepreneurs. This extra effort could produce more than 30 per cent of their income, but it had to be performed after hours, on top of a full working week.

Socialist Inequality: New Mechanisms within a Narrower Spread

Bureaucratic Control

This chapter continues the examination of the social consequences of bureaucratic control, shortage and secondary economy, but in the consumption and wealth-distributing dimension of social life. In this context, bureaucratic control becomes translated into two things: the imposition of non-market controls of the spread of wealth and income, and the mechanism of centralized redistribution which emerged to circulate income and resources.

The easiest way into the extensive literature on social inequalities and social stratification in postwar Hungary is via the debate that continued over a number of years between Zsuzsa Ferge and her former colleague Iván Szelényi. As with many academic debates, the ideas of the two protagonists in many ways complemented rather than contradicted one another. Both sides are necessary if a full picture is to be constructed of the inequalities that developed on the basis of Hungary's socialist industrialization. Ferge focused on the fact that social inequality was much less pronounced in Hungary (and in the 'socialist' world generally) than in the West. Szelényi focused more on the mechanism which operated within the smaller inequality spread. Whereas Ferge, more implicitly than explicitly, assumed that inequalities would disappear as economic and technical development increased the 'size of the cake', Szelényi described the operation of a new mechanism – centralized redistribution – which constantly reproduced inequality via regressive subsidization.[1] In his view, the whole system of universal benefits inspired by socialist priorities, from consumer price subsidies through rent subsidies to free education, actually benefited those who were already privileged and better off.

There was a further dimension to their disagreement, relating to the importance and significance of social benefits as against the play of market forces. While, in his earlier writings at least, Szelényi looked to an expansion of market forces to overcome the non-market inequalities of centralized redistribution,[2] Ferge always stressed the positive role played by social benefits in overcoming poverty, and criticized the Szelényi line for only looking at certain social benefits in kind, and not considering the whole effect of 'welfare distribution', noting that however unequal the system might be it was certainly less unequal than a purely market-based solution.[3]

Ferge's focus on the spread of inequalities is important for a further reason. The Szelényi case argues that the introduction of market relations would reduce inequality because centralized redistribution actually increased it. Now it is true, as we shall see, that centralized redistribution did increase inequality beyond that which would have existed if Hungary's egalitarian income distribution could have somehow existed in isolation from the distribution of other social goods. That is to say, centralized redistribution did have the effect of making overall social inequality greater than inequalities of income. But it is by no means clear that the market would have created a more equitable distribution. Once market reforms were introduced, the socialist egalitarian income distribution would necessarily itself have widened dramatically, and the new market-based overall inequalities would be unlikely to have been less than those created by centralized redistribution. To note that centralized redistribution had the effect of regressive subsidization is not to say that a market solution would necessarily be more equitable. Centralized redistribution and the inequalities associated with it are perhaps best seen as perverse corrective mechanisms which operated to ensure that socially valued groups continued to receive a disproportionately large share of the cake, even after socialist income policies had significantly reduced inequality.

The debate rotates around welfare economics writ large, and arguments concerning the relative merits and demerits of universal benefits. The Szelényi line on student grants, for example, would argue that grants disproportionately favour the middle classes, because they make most use of higher education and are in a better position to pay for it; yet grants are financed out of taxation which affects working class and middle class alike. The Ferge counter-argument is that if grants did not exist, working-class children would be even less likely to get to university in the first place, because it would be too expensive and they would be less willing to have the weight of possible loan repayments hanging round their necks. The difference between Eastern and Western Europe is simply one of scale: in the former the universal benefit principle was applied to a much wider area of social life. But the inequalities it created when centrally applied were significant. It is by no means self-evident that they can be dismissed as relatively incidental costs which can be written off in service of the greater good of social justice or civilized values.

The twin themes of increased social equality in conjunction with a new, self-reproducing mechanism of inequality – centralized redistribution – is the subject of the first section of this chapter. The section serves to reinforce the simple point that it is very difficult to overcome social disadvantage, especially if a government deliberately ignores the need for social policy. Suppression of income-based inequalities gave rise to new compensatory mechanisms and inequality continued; and in the absence of social policy to the contrary, these inequalities continued along very traditional lines. The section serves to show that the mechanisms by which 'cultural capital' is passed from one generation to another are rather more complex than market advantage. This notion is hardly novel, but there is a long-standing tradition within socialist thought (on the socialist wings of the women's and gay rights movements for example) that argues that 'real equality' is only possible once the class issue has been resolved; and this can easily lead on to the assumption that, once this is done, other problems will resolve themselves automatically.

Finally, a word of warning is necessary. Like the rest of the book, this chapter is necessarily based to a large extent on secondary sources, rendering its author entirely dependent on the categories chosen by others. Sociologists in Hungary have largely taken over Western practice when examining class or strata, and have normally assumed that the occupation of the father or male head of household is an acceptable determinant of class. This notion has been severely criticized in the West,[4] although no accepted alternative approach has yet developed.[5] This book will accept the categories used by the Hungarians in the knowledge that important gaps remain, but in the belief that quite a lot can be learned from the existing, male-biased data. Table 7.1 suggests that this is not entirely misguided. The indications are that households where husband and wife belong to different classes are relatively rare. For the sorts of statements of a high level of generality that this chapter is concerned with, the assumption that wives will be of the same class as their husbands, and thus that the husband's occupation is a good approximation for class, would appear reasonable. Andorka additionally notes, on the basis of a study of social restratification and demography in the 1960s, that many couples 'matched' their occupations after marriage, and a significant number of marriage breakdowns occurred when it was the husband in a 'mixed marriage' who was upwardly mobile.[6]

Table 7.1 The connection between husband's occupational group and wife's (%)

Husband		Wife					
		(1)	(2)	(3)	(4)	(5)	Total
Leader, intellectual	(1)	16	57	16	4	11	100
Other white collar	(2)	4	53	32	8	11	100
Worker	(3)	1	10	50	9	39	100
of which skilled	(4)	1	16	61	14	22	100
Agricultural manual	(5)	–	0	3	0	97	100

Source: R. Andorka, cited in Zs. Ferge, *Társadalmunk Rétegzödése*, Budapest 1969, p. 301.

Socialist Values – Equality Through Proletarianization

A key factor in the process of establishing a more egalitarian society was proletarianization. In Chapter 2, we saw how land reform and national-ization of the means of production, together with the 'nationalization' of much housing, effectively removed from private individuals all sources of unearned income. Between 1949 and the beginning of 1954 half a million new jobs were created, reducing the ratio of earners to depen-dants from 1.35:1 to 1.19:1.[7] The principle of 'to each according to his labour' was effectively put into practice. By the 1950s, the only source of inequality was labour, income from it and the various benefits in money and kind which accrued to particular types of employment. At the same time, social policy was downgraded to the areas of health and safety at work, and social insurance, symbolized by the abolition of the Ministry of Welfare and its replacement by a Ministry of Health in 1950.

But all forms of labour were not equal. There was a strong class bias against those who were not employed by the state. There was no pension system for any peasants, even the few in collective farms. Private peasants did not benefit from family allowances, and even those in collective farms received benefits only in 1953, and then at a lower rate and only after the third child.[8] Although open discrimination against non-proletarian elements disappeared in the 1960s, the general down-grading of social policy continued through the 1960s and 1970s. Indeed, Ferge notes that the first Party decree to deal exclusively with matters of social policy, rather than consider improvements in welfare to be an inevitable spin-off from increased economic growth, was in April 1980.[9]

In the early years, then, policy towards both women and gypsies, the most significant ethnic minority in Hungary, was structured around proletarianization. As Kulcsár put it in relation to the employment of women, 'at a certain level of industrial development the necessary supply of industrial labour is achievable only by the mass employment of women'.[10] Table 7.2 shows the incorporation of women into the Hungarian labour force. The 1986 'time budget' study develops this a little further. In 1986, 80.8 per cent of women aged between fifteen and fifty-five and not in full-time education were in work, with a further 8.1 per cent on maternity leave. Only 7.6 per cent were dependants; furthermore, 80 per cent of women thought women should work, and 77 per cent said that they would not give up work even if the opportunity arose.[11]

But, ideologically at least, there was more to the process of proletarianization than simply bringing women into the labour force. Proletarianization was intrinsic to solving the woman question. The official attitude to the woman question was very much that of nineteenth-century socialists: although the oppression of women went back further than capitalist oppression of the proletariat, the liberation of both 'could be linked in the same historical process because the oppression of women and the proletariat has both economic and social causes', which socialism would solve.[12] One of socialism's first steps therefore was to pass measures establishing equality before the law, maternity benefits and maternity leave, child benefit for the first three years for those employed in the socialist sector, equality in law for legitimate and illegitimate children, equality of access to education and jobs (except those deemed to be detrimental to female health), the principle of equal pay for equal work and so on.[13]

Similarly inflated expectations of the intrinsic merits of proletarianization characterized policy towards the gypsy minority. As Stewart

Table 7.2 Percentage of economically active women in Hungary

	As % of economically active	As % of all women
1930	26.1	22.0
1941	27.3	24.1
1949	29.2	24.9
1960	35.5	32.8
1963	36.8	32.8
1970	41.1	38.7
1981	44.9	–
1988	47.2	40.5

Source: To 1970 E. Szabady 'Kereső foglalkozás és anyaság – a nők helyzete Magyarországon', in E. Szabady (ed.), Tanulmányok a Nők Helyzetéről, Budapest 1972, p. 221; Magyar Statisztikai Zsebkönyv.

notes, 'in the Stalinist period ... the Party did not address itself to a Gypsy problem as such and assumed that, along with other oppressed groups, Gypsies would disappear in the cauldron of the People's Republic'.[14] The distinctive feature of this highly active assimilationist policy was an attempt to alter the behaviour of gypsies in the labour market. Gypsies were not seen as a 'national minority' but as a group 'excluded from capitalist society'.[15] The task, then, was to end this exclusion by making them part of society; and, in a socialist society, this meant bringing them into the labour market.

Incomes, inequality and poverty

The central socialist priority in social policy, having drawn all groups into the labour force, was to reduce income differentials. There can be little doubt that the introduction of socialist relations of production had resulted, by the 1960s, in a 'radical reduction in inequality of income distribution',[16] as can be seen from Table 7.3. Using figures broken down more finely than in this table, Ferge reported a differential in 1962 of only ten times between the top decile incomes in the highest income group and the bottom decile in the lowest income group.

This general pattern of reduced inequality remained fairly constant from the 1960s to the mid 1980s. Ferge reported that the inequality index constructed by Éltető and Frigyes which compared the top five to bottom five deciles in income spread scored 1.78 in 1960, 1.83 in 1968 and 1.84 in 1970.[17] Ferge's ten-times gap between the top decile of the highest incomes and the bottom decile of the lowest income group had dropped to eight times by 1972.[18] Flakierski's thorough study of the statistical information for the years 1962–72 reveals similar trends. While the dispersal of incomes in all income groups increased between 1966 and 1974 (with an increase in the top quintile over the bottom quintile from 3.22 in 1966 to 3.64 in 1974, and all groups having a

Table 7.3 Shares of income inequalities before the war and in 1962 (%)

	1930/31	1962
Top quintile	59	36
2nd quintile ⎫ 3rd quintile ⎬ 4th quintile ⎭	35	57
Lowest quintile	6	7

Source: Zs. Ferge, *A Society in the Making*, Harmondsworth 1979, p. 164.

pronounced upper tail, that is to say there were a few very high incomes), for the state sector as a whole,[19] there was no really significant increase in the dispersal of per capita incomes. The ratio of highest to lowest decile for per capita income moved from 5.8 in 1962, to 4.6 in 1967, to 5.0 in 1972.[20] Table 7.4 gives these figures by social strata for the years of 1967 and 1972. Flakierski concluded that the dispersion of household income per capita was 'very low by the standards of capitalist countries, both developed and underdeveloped'.[21]

Ferge provides the top to the bottom decile index figures for 1972–82. The ratio decreased again in 1977 to 4.1 times, and yet further still in 1982 to 3.8 times.[22] More recently, popular opinion stressed the similarity in spread of inequality in Hungary and Western Europe. This is not borne out by the Central Statistical Office's income statistics, although a certain degree of widening did take place in the 1980s. Éltető gives provisional income dispersal figures for 1987. The 1982 top decile to bottom decile spread of 3.8 times had grown again by 1987 to 4.6 times.[23] This slightly wider official dispersal, and increased perceived inequality, can be explained by a number of factors. Although the real value of the very lowest pensions increased between 1980 and 1984, for two-thirds of pensioners, who received more than 2,500 forints a month, the value of pensions fell. Wealthier families benefited from the maternity grant being transformed from a fixed value to a proportion of salary, and, while many of the price increases following 1978 were aimed at luxury items, the poor suffered disproportionately in periods such as 1978–80 and the beginning of 1985 when food, transport and

Table 7.4 Distribution of household income per capita by social stratum in Hungary

	Ratio of top 5 deciles to bottom 5		Ratio of top decile to bottom decile	
	1967	1972	1967	1972
Workers	1.85	1.80	4.2	4.1
Peasants	1.94	1.99	4.7	5.0
Double income	1.71	1.74	3.5	3.7
Non-manual	1.77	1.84	3.7	3.9
Self-employed	2.09	2.05	6.4	5.5
Total active	1.88	1.89	4.4	4.5
Pensioners	1.93	2.14	4.5	5.6
All households	1.92	1.96	4.6	5.0

Source: H. Flakierski, 'Economic Reform and Income Distribution in Hungary', *Cambridge Journal of Economics*, 1979, no. 3, p. 25.

household energy prices were increased by a disproportionately high amount.[24] By 1987, inequality was especially marked amongst active earners, suggesting that the increasing propensity to supplement incomes in the second economy was leading to an increase in overall inequality.[25]

An additional aspect of this reduction in overall inequality was the downgrading of 'intellectual' occupations, especially those not related to production. Ferge has shown that while the national average wage of workers in manufacturing increased by a factor of 15.4 between 1938 and 1957, the increase for engineers and technicians was only 7.8, for primary school teachers 5.9, for university professors 5.1, and for grammar school teachers 4.4. As a result, while university professors still earned 2.6 times the average workers' wage in 1957, and engineers and technicians 1.6 times, grammar school teachers earned only marginally more (1.1 times) and primary school teachers earned somewhat less (0.9 times).[26]

Greater equality did not mean the abolition of poverty, however. Ferge estimates that the percentage of the population living in conditions of social poverty between the wars varied between 55 and 75 per cent, and that in absolute terms the degree of poverty was higher then than it had been before the First World War.[27] Mass social poverty, in terms of individuals living near the subsistence level, no longer existed in Ferge's view, and, depending on the definition of poverty used, such as 'objective relative deprivation' which Bokor has taken over from the work of Peter Townsend in the UK,[28] the percentage of the poor in Hungary fell during the socialist period from 65–75 per cent of the population in 1952 to 20–40 per cent in 1960 and 10–30 per cent in 1980.[29] But, following the consistent attacks on living standards in the early 1980s, the numbers living in poverty grew again. Between 1982 and 1987 the number of those living below the subsistence minimum increased from 650,000 to almost a million,[30] and by 1987, 20.1 per cent of the population lived below the socially accepted minimum, with 9.1 per cent existing at under the notional survival minimum.

If socialism entailed proletarianization and a reduction in income inequality, it is important to see how income dispersal was structured socially. Although inequality was no longer determined by the market, it continued to be structured by a value system which prioritized certain groups.

As in many countries, poverty in socialist Hungary was closely correlated with age and family size. Table 7.5, for example, indicates how pensioners were concentrated in lower income bands than active earners. Bokor also reveals the correlation between age and poverty, reporting that the average age of the 'deprived' population she located, in a study of poverty based on a representative sample of 15,000 adults

Table 7.5 Distribution of per capita income
in families headed by active earners and pensioners (%)

Monthly income (ft)	1962		1972	
	Active	Pensioner	Active	Pensioner
Less than 600	30	45	6	22
600–800	24	25		
800–1,000	18	15	8	14
1,000–1,200	13	8	13	14
1,200–1,600	11	6	28	24
1,600–2,000	3	1	21	14
Over 2,000	1	0	24	12
Average per capita monthly income	840	689	1,643	1,083

Source: Ferge, *A Society*, p. 228.

carried out in the Party's Social Science Institute, was twenty years older than the average for the population, and that those over 60 were seven times more likely to be found in the 'deprived' group than 18–20 year olds.[31]

Family size, as was suggested in Chapter 6, has also been a major factor in determining poverty. 'The size and composition of the family, more precisely the ratio of earners to dependants, is the most important single factor in the explanation of the variance of incomes', as was revealed in the first income survey in 1959.[32] Flakierski noted that 'nearly all households with four or more children and nearly half (45 per cent) of all households with three children still have less than 1,000 forints in per capita income in a month ... on any definition they would fall below the poverty line in Hungary'.[33] Bokor confirms the importance of family size as a factor affecting 'deprivation'. Families with four or more children were ten times more likely than those with only two children to be found in her 'deprived' category. Her survey, however, suggests that the number of dependants generally, rather than number of children, was a more significant factor in 'deprivation'. For every 100 non-deprived earners there were 88 non-earners and 60 dependants. For every 100 earners in the 'deprived' category, there were 260 non-earners and 116 dependants. 'Deprived' families had twice as many dependants of working age, and fives times as many dependants over working age, as the non-deprived group; but they had only half as many children.[34] But social characteristics such as family size show class-specific patterns, as can be seen from Table 7.6. Table 7.7, adapted from

Table 7.6 Composition of households 1972 (% of household)

Head of household's occupation (econ. active only)	Ave. size of household	Regular earners	All earners	Children over 15
Managers, snr administrators, professionals	3.28	58	58	21
Skilled non-manual	3.25	58	58	22
Office workers	2.94	62	63	17
Total non-manual	3.20	58	58	21
Skilled workers	3.53	54	54	25
Semi-skilled	3.59	53	53	25
Unskilled	3.55	52	55	25
Total manual outside agriculture	3.55	53	54	25
Manual agricultural	3.56	48	60	22
All types	3.46	53	55	24

Source: Ferge, *A Society*, p. 200.

Table 7.7 Employment type of active earners and 'deprivation' (%)

	Non-deprived	Deprived
Leader	9	0
Professional	21	0
Admin. worker	7	0
Skilled worker	35	9
Semi-skilled	22	54
Unskilled	6	32
Independent	2	5
Together	102 [sic]	100

Source: A. Bokor, *Szegénység a mai Magyarországon*, Budapest 1987.

Bokor, lists the percentage of 'deprived' and non-deprived by employ-ment type, and requires no further comment.

In addition to these class-specific inequalities of income and 'depriva-tion', there is very visible gender bias. In 1967 the ratio of male to female earnings by social strata was as depicted in Table 7.8. By the time of the 1986 'time budget' study, the fact that women earned less than men was treated as a 'well-known fact', and a report based on the study focused on the concentration of women in certain professions. Two-thirds of manual female workers were found in twelve predictable professions, such as textiles, agriculture-related jobs, health and leather industries. In white-collar jobs, the concentration was in clerical and

Table 7.8 Women's earnings as a proportion of men's earnings, 1967

Leading and intellectual	75.7
Specialists	65.9
Administrative	67.3
Total intellectual	61.3
Skilled workers	71.2
Semi-skilled workers	67.6
Unskilled workers	67.0
Total non-agricultural manual	64.6
Agricultural manual	59.7
Total	66.1

Source: Ferge, 'A társadalompolitika és a nők', in Szabady, p. 50.

teaching jobs; and only 13 per cent of female white-collar workers were in leadership positions in 1986, compared with 43 per cent of white-collar men in 1984.[35] Ferge has concluded that 'the average wage for men is still about 30 per cent higher than that of women. Of this some 20 per cent might be accounted for by the fact that women still lag behind in the length of schooling, skill acquisition and access to top positions ... the remaining 10 per cent ... is ... due mainly to prejudices and tradition.'[36]

Cukor and Kertesi fill out some of the detail of how de facto inequality within de jure equality works in their study of the Hungarian labour market in 1980. They found, simply, that women did not have access to the types of jobs which resulted in higher incomes. That is to say, women were disproportionately concentrated into five occupational groups: some 75 per cent of women, and 14 per cent of men, worked in these 'female' occupations, which were characterized by the following general features. Formal qualifications were not translated into highly rewarded skills; adverse working conditions did not result in higher payments; and no jobs offered a combination of high qualifications and adverse working conditions which, in the case of male occupations, was the most successful way of maximizing earnings.[37] An important additional component of the different treatment of skills and qualifications between the sexes was the absence of career paths in the female occupations, and a much less widespread use of in-house training.[38]

Galasi and Sik conclude that labour markets are sex-specific.[39] Nagy and Sziráczki, in a labour market analysis based on 1974 data, came up with a five-segment model (similar to the segments in the working class described in Chapter 6). The fourth and fifth segments, both characterized by low salaries and relatively short length of service, were skilled female and unskilled female labour respectively.[40] Sik's study of the local labour market in Balassagyarmat found an added significant dimension, namely that while occupationally 'unstable' men moved between state sector jobs, for women, as was discussed in Chapter 6, mobility was in and out of the state labour market,[41] and, as Galasi notes, women's 'instability' in and out of the labour market is closely associated with their household roles.[42]

The earliest published source on the situation of gypsies in Hungary is Kemény's short article published in *Valóság* in 1974. He showed, on the basis of a 2 per cent sample of Hungary's population, that in a certain sense gypsies had been 'integrated' by the early 1970s, but that 'integration' had taken place at the very bottom of the social hierarchy. Gypsies were heavily concentrated in the three eastern counties of Hungary where incomes were lowest, housing was worst and educational achievement was the lowest. Gypsy families were also larger on average than Hungarian ones, having 4.52 members compared with 3.18. Some 22.5 per cent of gypsy households encompassed five or more members, compared with only 6.6 per cent of Hungarian ones. This has to be taken in conjunction with the strong correlation which we have already seen between large families and poverty. Gypsy families also had a high number of dependants. The Hungarian average of dependants per 100 earners was 82; for gypsy families it was 224.[43]

Laki, in a study of 1,047 young people, found gypsies significantly over-represented in lower income families. Only 6.4 per cent of non-gypsy families had a total family income of 40–50,000 forints annually, 26.4 per cent had 50–75,000 and a further 26.4 per cent received 75–100,000. The corresponding figures for gypsy families were 16.2, 28.3 and 19.7 respectively.[44] Other case-study research reveals similar trends. In Stewart's study, 'Gypsies are found above all in the harder and dirtier jobs. Gypsies are disproportionately represented in the Town-cleaning Department of the Council, in the Industrial Machinery and Tool Factory and in the Parquet Factory.'[45] Havas also found gypsies disproportionately concentrated in cleaning jobs, in the construction industry and in the worst paid jobs on state farms.[46] At Stewart's parquet factory the workers stood in wood dust all day with no protective breathing equipment. At the slaughterhouse, a gypsy brigade did the foulest work of disembowelling. In all these places gypsy labour constituted some 15–18 per cent of all manual labour, compared with 1.7 per cent of manual labour at the pleasantly situated lung clinic in the hills above the town. Average figures for the steel vat factory in Harangos in Stewart's study indicated that gypsies earned some 760 forints (that is, about one-fifth of the total wage) less per month than their Hungarian colleagues. They were also less well represented in Enterprise Economic

Work Partnerships. In the whole of Heves county in 1984, only eighteen gypsies had access to the significant extra earnings offered by this type of work.[47]

The pattern of inequality presented above suggests that, for all the reduction in inequality, unskilled workers, women and gypsies were not highly prioritized in the new socialist value system. This is where the mechanics of 'centralized redistribution' come in. During the socialist period, subsidies on socially valued goods were extensive, as Table 7.9 shows. The justification for these subsidies was that they allowed the poorest members of society to be able to purchase certain basic commodities, as illustrated in Table 7.10. Looked at this way, subsidies

Table 7.9 Yearly subsidy from state budget per user of a given service (forints)

	1970	1974	1974 as % 1970
One child in day nursery	13,127	17,827	136
One child in kindergarten	4,379	5,606	128
One child in primary school	2,713	4,618	170
One child in secondary school	5,878	9,140	155
One student in higher education	29,367	33,063	112
One theatre ticket	28	39	140
One cinema ticket	5	4	80
One book	2	3	150

Source: Ferge, *A Society*, p. 289.

Table 7.10 Dairy price increases and compensation
(per capita annual sums, in forints)

	Increase in annual expenditure	Annual refund	Net annual effect on income
Workers/employees			
low income	597	1,191	+594
medium	828	620	−208
high	896	311	−585
Peasants			
low income	360	926	+566
medium	489	563	+74
high	580	151	−439
Pensions	451	805	+354

Source: Ferge, *A Society*, p. 284.

had a clear redistributive effect. The counter, 'centralized redistribution' argument is presented by Ladányi. It requires that a wider view be taken of the pattern of consumption of different social groups. Consideration of the compensatory effect of subsidies on individual, 'basic' commodities is not enough. According to Ladányi's calculations, of the 183 product groups included in his study, 59 had neither subsidy nor consumption tax, 49 enjoyed the former and 66 were burdened with the latter.[48] But, when the pattern of expenditure of the different social groups in Hungary was taken into account, these subsidies and consumer taxes affected social groups rather differently. Ladányi calculated a 'real value' index of distribution made up of each social group's total expenditure, plus or minus subsidies and taxes, divided by the sum of expenditure. The results are given in Table 7.11. A redistributive effect in favour of the wealthier groups in society is clear from the table. Peasants and 'dual-income' (worker-peasant) families were net losers, and white-collar workers, especially the intelligentsia, were net gainers. Ladányi's further analysis of income level groups within each social group revealed that while the value of his 'real value' indicator decreased as incomes within each occupational group rose (evidence of some intra-group equalization effect), redistribution in absolute terms remained large. Non-manual families in the highest income group enjoyed a net redistribution almost twice as large as that enjoyed by the group with the lowest income.[49]

Table 7.11 Redistribution after total net expenditure by occupational group (per capita annual figures)

Occupation	Real value	Expenditure		Expenditure plus redistribution		Redistribution
		(ft)	(%)	(ft)	(%)	(ft)
Leaders/intelligentsia	1.048	24,084	171.1	25,232.4	172.8	1,148.4
Other white collar	1.049	21,174	150.4	22,208.0	152.1	1,034.0
Skilled and semi-skilled	1.044	16,534	117.5	17,266.8	118.2	732.8
Unskilled	1.038	14,076	100.0	14,604.9	100.0	528.9
Total white collar	1.049	21,770	154.7	22,827.4	156.3	1,057.4
Total manual workers	1.043	16,133	114.6	16,832.5	115.3	699.5
Dual income	0.981	14,035	99.8	13,789.6	94.4	−245.4
Peasants	0.989	12,694	90.2	12,560.5	86.0	−133.5

Source: J. Ladányi, 'Fogyasztói árak és szociálpolitika', *Valóság*, 1975, no. 12, p. 23.

Similar patterns of prioritization and regressive subsidization are visible beyond the arena of income distribution, in the fields of housing, education and the social services generally.

Housing

In the early years of the socialist period, the mechanism by which those whom the regime valued were provided with flats was straightforwardly political: it was an aspect of the class war. The government set out to abolish the role of the private sector and buy up property it needed at an arbitrarily imposed 20 per cent of the construction cost of a newly built dwelling. The property of all who abandoned Hungary was also taken over by the state for redistribution to the new cadres. When this proved insufficient, beginning in 1951, first pensioners and then 'class aliens' or 'declassed' elements were expelled to the countryside, a process which was facilitated after an act in 1952 nationalized all houses with more than six rooms.[50]

In the 1960s and 1970s, those who were valued by the regime retained privileged access to housing; but the mechanism at work was less overtly political. It was in studying inequalities in housing that Szelényi formulated the classic statement of the centralized redistribution case. He argued that the implementation of socialist priorities in housing had resulted in the creation of the following six housing classes:

1. Tenants of new state-owned apartments, enjoying the highest state subsidy.
2. Tenants of old state-owned flats, with comparatively little subsidy.
3. Owner-occupiers of bank-financed and cooperative apartments, enjoying considerable subsidy.
4. Builders of new family houses, with little subsidy.
5. Owners of old family houses.
6. People without houses or flats.[51]

Analysing the social backgrounds of those who occupied these categories of housing, he found that those who enjoyed higher than average income and possessed higher than average qualifications tended to be housed in housing classes 1–3. Furthermore, of those in class 6, those with high incomes were more likely to move into class 1, while those with low incomes were most likely to move into class 4. His general conclusion was that those whose housing was subsidized by the state to the greatest degree, in that it was built by the state and let at very low rents, were those earning the highest incomes.[52] This inequality in housing outcomes is illustrated in Table 7.12, while Table 7.13 clarifies the mechanism at work. Bureaucrats and intellectuals – those prioritized by the government – were most likely to be awarded housing at the government's expense.[53]

The consequence of this was that 'only 37.5 per cent of the high bureaucrats and 44.8 per cent of salaried intellectuals paid more than 20,000 forints, while about 80 per cent or more of the workers paid more than that'.[54] More generally, 'People in highly paid, highly qualified groups paid 22,000 forints less for their apartments – if they paid at all – than did people in poorly paid, poorly qualified, poorly placed groups.'[55] In a separate piece of research, Éltető and Láng reported that, in 1969, non-manual employees received rent subsidies three times greater than those received by manual workers.[56]

Zsuzsa Dániel continued the work on the hidden subsidies at work within centralized redistribution in her analysis of the 1976 household budget statistics. Using a variety of standard indicies of inequality, she found that the degree of inequality in the distribution of dwellings, especially when indicators reflecting the quality of dwelling were taken into account, was much greater than the distribution of incomes. She also duplicated the Szelényi finding that high-level officials, intellectuals and white-collar workers lived in better accommodation than others, calculating that, depending on the precise assumptions made, those living in state-owned flats received an indirect subsidy of between 14.5

Table 7.12 Who owned and who occupied housing in Pécs and Szeged in 1968

Occupational status	Number in sample	% with 1st class housing	% with other state housing	% with own bank-financed or co-op apt	% with own family house	% with housing owned by other individual
High bureaucrat	90	47.8	10.0	15.5	17.8	8.9
Intellectual	128	50.0	10.9	16.4	13.3	9.4
Technician	254	37.4	9.1	11.4	31.9	10.2
Clerical	112	46.4	4.5	6.2	28.6	14.3
Service	73	38.4	6.8	5.5	27.4	21.9
Skilled worker	473	25.3	11.6	8.0	28.2	16.9
Semi-skilled worker	271	24.4	12.2	3.7	39.9	19.8
Unskilled worker	217	23.0	10.3	1.8	48.8	16.1
Agric. worker	36	2.8	2.8	0.0	88.9	5.5
Retired intellectual	100	46.0	5.0	6.0	26.0	17.0
Retired worker	387	22.0	6.6	2.1	46.3	23.0

Source: I. Szelényi, *Urban Inequalities under State Socialism*, Oxford 1983, p. 53.

Table 7.13 How families acquired their housing

Occupational status	Number in sample	% with per capita income above 1,200 ft	% who built or bought	% awarded state housing	% exchange	% from before 1950 or by other means
High bureaucrat	89	70.8	25.8	37.1	19.1	18.0
Intellectual	126	63.5	20.6	39.7	18.3	21.5
Technician	252	46.8	33.3	28.2	15.5	23.0
Clerical	108	40.1	25.0	26.9	20.4	27.7
Service	72	30.1	29.2	20.9	23.6	26.4
Skilled worker	466	32.5	34.7	24.5	11.8	29.0
Semi-skilled	270	23.2	35.2	24.1	13.3	27.4
Unskilled worker	217	18.0	44.2	20.8	10.1	24.9
Agric. worker	36	8.6	55.5	8.4	2.8	32.3
Independent	37	16.7	35.2	10.8	13.5	40.5
Retired intellec.	98	30.3	19.3	31.7	18.4	30.6
Retired worker	381	9.6	30.7	17.9	18.4	33.0

Source: Szelényi, p. 58.

per cent and 16.8 per cent of their income, and that the subsidy was greater for those with a relatively high income than those with a low income.[57] Her conclusion was that 'the allocation of apartments or flats does not reduce but, on the contrary, increases inequality within our society'.[58]

Fóti took research into inequalities in housing provision into the 1980s by examining the 1980 census. Although the census categories did not permit the same degree of sophistication in isolating discrete social groups, the picture is clear. In terms of a complex indicator of housing quality, households where the head of household was a leader or intellectual are considerably advantaged compared with other groups, while skilled workers were best provided for amongst the manual workers, with agricultural manual labourers living in the worst conditions of all.[59]

While inequality in housing provision did not decrease following Szelényi's original work in the 1960s, the structure of the hierarchy changed.[60] A new, 'most desirable' category of suburban or commuting village villa emerged, much along Western lines. This was the most advantaged position on the seven-stage model suggested by Kolosi in 1984. These 'little castles' he saw as the dwellings of the new 'top 10,000'.[61] This process was helped not only by the rapid inflation in house prices as the housing market was partially recommodified (see below), but also by legislation which allowed the occupiers of state flats, the most heavily subsidized of all, to purchase them from the state at knock-down prices and resell them at their partially recommodified market value.[62] Although less favoured than the new 'most desirable' residences, housing estates remain relatively advantaged places to live. Fóti found that such estates were places where all groups above skilled workers were relatively more likely, and semi-skilled workers and unskilled workers were relatively less likely, to live. Szelényi's class segregation of housing estates and urban districts was also confirmed by a study by Tóth who found that not only were new housing estates relatively advantaged, but between housing estates there existed clear class-based segregation, of a type which could also be found in villages.[63]

Class-based spatial separation of this kind was also found by Csanádi and Ladányi within Budapest.[64] Significantly, however, the spatial distribution changed little over time.[65] This consistency over the forty years of socialism was also noted by Kovács.[66] The traditional urban sociology pattern of ever-changing concentric rings and 'zones of transition'[67] did not appear to hold when housing allocation was achieved, however unequally, by means of non-market principles.

The least advantaged of all on the housing market were the gypsies. They suffered both from segregation, and from concentration into zones of poor housing. Kemény reported in 1974 that two-thirds of gypsies lived on a traditional gypsy settlement, and only a quarter of them lived in an area that was neither a traditional settlement nor a new estate near the old settlement and separated from the rest of the town.[68] Laki, in his study of 1,047 young people, found that 41.8 per cent of the gypsy families lived in a dwelling with only two rooms, compared with 28.4 per cent of non-gypsy families. The figures were reversed for three-room dwellings: 33.6 per cent for gypsies, 49.9 per cent for non-gypsies.[69] Havas and Lengyel have, separately, documented the creation of new slum housing for gypsies after they were moved from their traditional isolated settlements.[70]

Education

Education is the *locus classicus* of 'cultural capital' theories. Ferge has claimed that a larger proportion of working-class children in Hungary finished secondary and higher education than in the West.[71] Nevertheless, there was, as Bokor has shown, a close corollation between lack of education and poverty. Of the two generations in her sample young enough to have been brought up under the socialist educational system, 49 per cent of the 'deprived' category aged between 31 and 40 had not finished a basic secondary education; neither had 30 per cent of those aged between 18 and 30 and 'deprived'. While the average length of schooling of those in her non-deprived group was 9.9 years, that for the deprived group was 5.5 years.[72] Éltető and Láng reported that in 1969 children of non-manual employees received over six times more higher education than workers.[73] The provision of pre-school educational facilities was similarly biased towards the middle class. In 1967, when nationally there were kindergarten places for 50 per cent of children of the appropriate age, 80 per cent of the children of managers found kindergarten places compared with only 40 per cent of the children of unskilled workers.[74]

Class bias is also reflected in educational performance, as Table 7.14

Table 7.14 Average school results (marks out of 5) in primary and secondary schools by stratum

Social group of child's father	Budapest	Other towns	Villages
		Primary school	
Intellectuals	4.2	4.3	4.5
Leaders, managers	4.1	4.2	4.2
Other white collar	3.8	3.8	3.8
Skilled workers	3.4	3.5	3.5
Semi-skilled workers	3.2	3.3	3.3
Unskilled workers	3.1	3.0	3.0
Manual agric. workers	–	3.2	3.2
Average	3.7	3.6	3.3
		Secondary school	
Intellectuals	3.6	3.7	3.7
Leaders, managers	3.5	3.4	3.6
Other white collar	3.3	3.3	3.2
Skilled workers	3.3	3.2	3.1
Semi-skilled workers	3.2	3.2	3.2
Unskilled workers	3.3	3.2	3.1
Manual agric. workers	3.5	3.3	3.1
Average	3.4	3.3	3.2
		Secondary vocational school	
Intellectuals	3.1	3.0	2.9
Leaders, managers	3.0	3.1	2.7
Other white collar	3.0	3.1	2.9
Skilled workers	3.0	3.2	3.0
Semi-skilled workers	3.1	3.2	3.0
Unskilled workers	3.0	3.3	3.1
Manual agric. workers	3.0	3.3	3.1
Average	3.0	3.2	3.0

Source: S. Ferge, 'Some Relations between Social Structure and the School System', *Sociological Review Monograph No. 17*, Keele 1972, p. 229.

indicates. Ferge's study dates from the end of the 1960s. Laki reported similar results for 1970 and 1980, as shown in Table 7.15. He also demonstrated that, amongst students who had not completed general school by the age of fourteen, there was a high percentage whose fathers fell into the semi-skilled or agricultural manual worker category, or whose mothers fell into the housewife category. Almost a quarter of such students who had not completed general school by the age of fourteen (23 per cent) were gypsies. In his survey of 1,047 young people, completed as part of the same research, Laki found further that 42.9 per cent of gypsy fathers and 50.9 per cent of gypsy mothers had received no schooling whatsoever, compared with 12.1 per cent and 11.9 per cent respectively for non-gypsy fathers and mothers.[75]

In education too, traditional sex-stereotyping continued. Women who did succeed in getting into university were more likely to be concentrated in the humanities and 'caring professions', where salaries were lower, than in engineering, as shown in Table 7.16.

Finally in the field of education, the issue of language and class is worthy of note. In the early 1970s, Pleh and Pap replicated some of the work done by Basil Berstein on 'restricted' and 'elaborated' codes within the speech of working-class and middle-class children, in the belief that these codes act as mechanisms for the reproduction of social disadvantage. They examined the language of sixty-five six-year-olds in five Budapest primary schools and found that the speech of 'advantaged' children was structurally more complex and less context-dependent than the speech of 'disadvantaged children'.[76]

Table 7.15 Average results (marks out of five) of children in the second class by social stratum (1970–80)

Social stratum of head of household	1970	1980
Leader	4.4	4.5
Intellectual	4.5	4.0
Other non-manual	4.1	4.0
Skilled worker	3.8	4.1
Semi-skilled worker	3.6	3.9
Unskilled worker	3.2	3.6
Agricultural manual worker	3.4	3.7

Source: L. Laki, *Az Alacsony Iskolázottság Újratermelődésének Társadalmi Körülményei Magyarországon,* Budapest 1988, p. 89.

Table 7.16 Percentage of women amongst those with a degree or diploma in higher education

	1949	1960	1973
Engineering	1.2	7.1	13.1
Agriculture	4.2	9.8	16.0
Economics	13.9	20.0	38.0
Medicine	17.2	33.7	40.0
Education	49.1	58.1	61.1
Law	0.6	10.4	12.1

Source: Ferge, *A Society,* p. 108.

Social Services

Health benefits in the socialist period were restricted predominantly to the employed. Employment in the state sector gave rights to sick pay, free health services, and a series of benefits, from the use of childcare facilities to the family allowance. The existence of such benefits justified low wages, and low wages, in addition to an ideological commitment to a version of female emancipation, resulted in the mass employment of women, such that in a very short time the two-earner family became the norm. But the peasantry was excluded from almost all health provision for a decade. Government propaganda of the time was enthusiastic about the fact that, whereas only 2.8 million people were insured in 1938, 4.4 million – that is, 47 per cent of the population – were by 1950. It was silent on the fact that 53 per cent of the population were not insured and were obliged to pay for their health care at prices which, at a rate of 500 forints for major surgery plus 45 forints a day in a county hospital, easily reached one and a half to two times monthly salaries. (In 1952 peasant farmers with a 2.85–8.55 hectare plot had an income of just 340 forints a month.) Hospitals were financially interested in this uninsured population because they were permitted to retain a proportion of the fees.[77]

This inequality in right of access in the early years apart, even under the universal provision from the 1960s onwards, mortality rates differed according to class, as did the propensity to suicide, as indicated in Tables 7.17 and 7.18.

Life Chances

Government policy was little more successful in creating greater equality in the area of equality of opportunity. The most complete figures for

Table 7.17 Annual mortality rates by class and stratum per 100,000 (1988)

	Men	Women
Leader	967	1,039
Intellectual	996	534
Specialist	1,210	1,146
Administrative	1,385	1,022
Direct controller of production	1,066	1,075
Worker	1,425	1,211
Direct controller of production in large-scale agriculture	976	975
Manual workers in large-scale agriculture	1,696	1,344
Independent peasants	1,458	1,310
Family member working in agriculture	1,114	332
Independent small craftsman or trader	1,337	1,259
Total	1,410	1,209

Source: A. Losonczi, *Ártó-védő Társadalom*, Budapest 1989, p. 327.

Table 7.18 Suicide rates by class and stratum per 100,000 (1988)

	Men	Women
Working class	68.36	25.14
Workers in large-scale agriculture	115.51	37.19
Intelligentsia	26.24	17.86
Middle-level administrators	35.53	25.59

Source: Losonczi, *Ártó-védő*, p. 328.

social mobility in Hungary over the majority of the socialist period are given by Andorka in a book which summarizes the findings of the two large-scale social mobility studies of 1962–64 and 1973. His overall conclusion was that whilst there was massive social restructuring in the postwar years, especially during the period of 'extensive' industrialization up to the end of the 1960s, most of the change was a direct consequence of the changes in the economic structure. Social mobility was extensive. By the end of the 1960s, some two-thirds of leaders and intellectuals came from manual worker backgrounds, and half of non-agricultural workers came from agriculture. There was also far more mobility into intellectual jobs than before the war, and the mobility of women increased. Indeed, during extensive industrialization change was so rapid that much of it took place within a given individual's career. Nevertheless, the chances of children of agricultural workers and peasants getting into leading jobs were still much lower relative to other groups, and women tended to go into jobs requiring fewer educational qualifications, although, since the 1960s, women were going more into intellectual jobs, with men still more highly concentrated in manual jobs (which were better paid).

With the end of 'extensive' industrialization, mobility within careers became much less frequent. More tellingly, a tendency became apparent for the children of intellectuals to form an increasingly large proportion of the intellectual stratum. That is to say, access to this stratum and the privileges it confers became increasingly 'closed'. In 1962–64, 54.3 per cent of men and 15.6 per cent of women born into a household where the father was leader or intellectual had a degree themselves. By 1973, the figures had increased to 60.3 per cent and 29.5 per cent respectively.[78] Conversely, Bokor found that one of the defining characteristics of her 'deprived' group was social immobility. They had not even enjoyed the structural mobility that accompanied Hungary's social and economic development.[79]

Institutional Shortage

In this section, a distinction will be made between 'shortage' and 'scarcity'. 'Scarcity' is taken to mean the fact that demand in areas such as the social services inevitably exceeds supply. 'Shortage' on the other hand is taken to mean a chronic inability to approach the level of demand, brought about, in a sense, by the fact that socialist economies have failed to develop a measure of relative scarcity in the first place. The existence of shortage was all the more telling in a society that had committed itself to socialist values and the maximum provision of services on the basis of need.

Housing

One consequence of shortage on the housing market was 'under-urbanization', which was discussed in Chapter 6. Here it is appropriate to stress the fact that village dwelling brought with it a low level of infra-structural service. Because Budapest itself received most money from the state, the communal services provided to villages generally, including those villages in the immediate vicinity of Budapest, were of a very poor quality. In 1970, while Budapest had 4.04 doctors per 1,000 of population, its surrounding villages had only 0.52; Budapest had 6.57 crèche places per 1,000, the surrounding villages had only 3.18; 87 per cent of houses in villages around Budapest had electricity, but 62.5 per cent used bottled gas for cooking, only 24.4 per cent had running water and only 4.4 per cent of houses were connected to mains sewerage.[80]

The issue of underurbanization aside, the housing situation improved quite rapidly in Budapest between 1945 and 1949 with considerable reconstruction and new building. However, industrialization and collectivization in the 1950s resulted in massive migration to the towns, especially Budapest, and the prohibition on abortions in 1951 only increased the pressure on resources. The year 1953 saw a renewed emphasis on house building, but the pressure on resources led to the building of only rudimentary flats, the most extreme example being the 'CS dwellings': one-room flats without bathroom or kitchen. The pressure on the Budapest housing market eased after 1956, when about 100,000 people left the capital, and the building of 'CS dwellings' was phased out.[81]

Some idea of absolute shortage in housing is given by the number of people living as sub-tenants in another person's house or as 'bed-tenants' (sharing a room with strangers in another person's house). In 1960, there were 173,000 sub-tenants and 47,000 bed-tenants. In 1970 both figures had increased, to 260,000 and 119,000 respectively.[82] A further indicator is simply the size and quality of the accommodation available. Some general figures are given in Table 7.19.

While it should be noted that the rooms per person in this table excluded kitchen, bathroom etc., conditions were far from generous by Western standards. As Fóti noted, large numbers of people had no space for recreation. The available housing space for the average Hungarian in 1980 was just over a third (36 per cent) that of the average Dane. In addition to this, a severe maintenance problem developed. Of

Table 7.19 Housing conditions in Hungary

	Persons per 100 rooms	1 room	3 rooms	WC	electricity
1938	257	–	–	–	–
1949	259	66	5	11	48
1960	250	61	7	18	74
1970	200	46	11	32	91
1975*	162	38	16	40	94
1980	152	27	24	–	–
1986	126	19	32	–	–
1988	122	19	33	–	–

*The first figure relates to 1975, the others to 1973

Source: Ferge, *A Society*, p. 295; P. Fóti, *Röpirat a Lakáshelyzetről*, Budapest 1988, p. 29.

the 775,000 state flats in existence when Fóti was writing (published 1988), half were due for renovation and a tenth were in need of modernization. Another source cited by Fóti found that a fifth of state flats did not meet minimum standards.[83]

Any history of shortage in housing requires that some reference be made to the measures taken to introduce market relations into housing over the 1970s and 1980s. Moves towards some sort of compromise with the private sector in the housing market began as early as 1957, although at that time this was thought to be only a temporary expedient, and the concessions were almost immediately followed by a political decree in 1958 preparing the way for the first fifteen-year plan aimed at solving the housing problem once and for all. By 1971 it was clear that this goal would not be reached, and reforms were introduced recognizing the permanent role of the private sector in housing, and beginning a trend towards a 'welfare' view of state housing in that access to state housing was gradually restricted to those who met certain welfare criteria. In 1975, this was recast as the 'large family programme',[84] and the final step in this process came in 1982, when the state implicitly recognized that housing was a commodity and rents were significantly increased.[85] The state also explicitly stated it was aiming to build about 10 per cent of new dwellings, sufficient to meet most 'social policy' objectives.[86]

In consequence, the total number of flats built in the three five-year periods 1971–75, 1976–80, 1981–85 by the state sector decreased significantly, by almost a half in the final period (148,675, 162,245, 81,483); although the total number of flats built did not vary greatly (438,138, 452,715, 369,684 respectively), and the number of flats built by the private sector also stagnated. The partial recommodification of housing, together with the extensive withdrawal of the state sector from house building, combined the worst of both systems: it retained chronic shortage in the state economy, while creating, at the same time, an anarchic and speculative market.[87] Between 1972 and 1982, house prices increased at a rate of 20 per cent a year, more than twice the rate of inflation in other goods.[88] Whereas in the mid 1970s a two-bedroom flat cost the equivalent of 5–10 years' salary for the average earner, by 1989 it cost 20–25 years' salary.[89] In 1938 a single-room house at the edge of town cost a year's salary; by 1989, a family house cost twenty years' salary.[90] Szelényi explains this worst of all worlds situation by reference to two factors: first, the state's reduction in its expenditure on housing, which, somewhat disingenuously, he states he did not expect:[91] second, the retention of too many restrictions within the recommodified sector. Housing was the only area where speculation with savings was possible, so it necessarily attracted a surfeit of funds.[92] Foti, echoing both Ferge and Szelényi, noted that commodification of the housing market could only have been successful at decreasing inequalities if it had been accompanied by a strong social policy.[93]

This crisis of 'neither one thing nor the other' resulted in a particularly bad housing situation for the young, which is perhaps a partial explanation for why FIDESZ, a party of young people, became such a significant political force. An increasing proportion of the under-thirties were obliged to live with their parents because they could not find even a sublet of their own. In the early 1980s, 55 per cent of heads of household aged twenty-nine or less began their lives as an independent household (that is to say, in the majority of cases, 'married life') in the flat of a parent or in-law. A further 11.4 per cent rented a room in somebody else's flat, and 2 per cent rented an independent flat. In Budapest, the chances of subsequently achieving independence were not high. Some 49 per cent of those aged twenty-nine or less continued to live in a flat which they either did not own or did not have independent title to; and only 5.6 per cent of these rented an entire flat privately. That is to say, with 4.6 per cent living in 'unknown circumstances', almost 40 percent were subtenants in a flat where the title was held by either parents/in-laws or other outside parties.

Education

Turning to shortage in the sphere of education, there are two important points to be made. First, on certain measures of provision of educational services, Hungary scored highly. Second, on a number of further indices, which were generally more expensive to achieve, Hungary performed markedly less well. In addition to this, Hungary's general inattention to social policy was reflected by a very traditional, Prussian educational system.

Andor has pointed out that, contrary to the propaganda claims, it was not the socialist government which solved the illiteracy problem in Hungary. The bulk of the population was literate even before the First World War, and the remainder became literate before the Second.[95] Furthermore, the government was about to introduce a system of eight years' secondary schooling on the basis of selection when the war broke out. Andor's rather more sobering verdict on education policy in socialist Hungary was to note that, after thirty-five years of socialism, some general schools were having to introduce a shift system because of insufficient classroom space, something that had been unknown between the wars.

At first glance, figures relating to Hungary's education achievement look impressive. The number of classrooms doubled between 1945 and

1977, the teaching strength trebled, the number of pupils per teacher ratio fell to 35 per cent of its 1945 level, average class size fell from 53.1 to 26.3. But the more closely the figures are considered, the less impressive they become. The bulk of the increase in school buildings over the 1945 level was accounted for by postwar reconstruction. There were 7,281 new school buildings in the five years 1945–50, but only a further 7,782 in the twenty-five years between 1950 and 1975. Furthermore, the expanding higher educational sector took over existing buildings rather than building anew, so increasing the overall pressure on buildings. Over a quarter of classrooms did not come up to the government's minimum standards, and the proportion of classes that were of a size considered 'unteachable' by teachers remained almost constant, at around 70 per cent between 1955 and 1978.

What is more, the apparent improvement in the pupil–teacher ratio could be seen as misleading for two reasons. First, there was an increase in the use of untrained teachers. Second, schools were providing more services than before, most importantly the 'throughout the day' service, whereby children were supervised in the school until their parents could collect them in the evenings. Although the number of students remained constant, this had the effect of almost doubling the load, so casting the pupil–teacher ratio in a less favourable light, although some improvement did take place. In 1948–49 the official ratio was 1:33.7 and Andor's 'corrected' figure was 1:34.2. By 1977–78, the official figure had dropped to 1:15.6, while Andor's corrected figure remained considerably higher at 1:21.7.

A further consequence of shortage and the non-availability of funds for education was the low level of teachers' salaries. This inevitably had adverse effects on the quality of teaching, as Ferge noted as early as 1971. First, the quality of teachers tended to be low because gifted people took jobs elsewhere. Second, there were large numbers of 'embittered' teachers who had a negative effect on school morale.[96]

Low teacher morale, and the general undervaluing of social policy, resulted in little attention being paid to the content of education, except in the early years when subjects such as Marxism–Leninism and Russian had to be introduced. In the mid 1970s Andor and Horváth carried out a content analysis of general school reading books, with the following findings. With the exception of teachers, women were not presented in employment, despite the fact that 43 per cent of the workforce was then female. The family was always depicted in a conventional manner, with the father at the head. Mothers did housework, fathers had 'serious' conversations with the children. Children were always 'thankful' to their parents, and the adult world was always conflict-free.[97] Such texts reinforced sterotypes and ill prepared pupils for the realities of the adult world. Ferge has pointed to two further content-related problems in education: the potentially adverse effects on the very conventional pattern of streaming children in schools,[98] and the rather conventional social values of teachers.[99]

The conventionality of content of Hungarian education was further exacerbated by the continuing importance of the political dimension in education. Political criteria still figured strongly in the selection of head teachers. Andor found that head teachers were predominantly male, middle aged, Party members (preferably with a local Party function), and politically active in the local community.[100] What is more, this continued to be the case even after 1985 when posts were openly advertised and competition was introduced to the limited extent of having a token one or two alternative candidates for the posts.[101]

Social Services

'[B]etween the two World Wars, a Hungarian townsman had one of the best health services of Europe', enjoying the highest ratio of physicians to population in Central and Eastern Europe, although 40 per cent or so lived in Budapest. Even agricultural workers and domestic servants were included in the social insurance scheme by 1938.[102] Despite this high baseline, the area in which shortage became most visible in Hungary over the years of socialism was that of health care. In this section, the focus will be on data relating to the standing of provision in the health service, rather than socio-economic factors which affected the nation's health. This latter topic has been covered extensively by Losonczi, who traces the effects of factors such as women's 'double shift' work in the second economy and the traumas of collectivization on the nation's health and on the incidence of various types of disease.[103]

The Ministry of Health was what in the UK would be termed a

Table 7.20 Social insurance incomings and outgoings (thousand million forints)

	Total in	Total out	Balance	Employer %	Employee %
1980	53.6	77.7	−24.1	67.5	24.6
1981	63.8	90.4	−26.6	66.4	25.8
1982	74.5	98.5	−24.0	67.5	24.4
1983	86.7	107.2	−20.5	67.1	23.7
1984	120.1	120.6	−0.5	72.4	19.5
1985	131.3	131.8	−0.5	70.8	19.9

Source: A. Losonczi, *A Kiszolgáltatottság Anatómiája az Egészségügyben*, Budapest 1986, p. 119.

'spending ministry', and the amounts available for health care were the result of a two-way bargaining process between the ministry and the other ministries, and the ministry and local authorities with their spending plans.[104] The bargaining position of the ministry was weakened by the fact that the security system was not self-financing, so increasing its dependence on the state budget and its status as a 'remainder department'. The basic source of funding was the wages of employees, primarily paid by enterprises; but, since wages were low, this proportion was never enough to cover actual social insurance outgoings. Table 7.20 shows this pattern of funding, the high contribution paid by the enterprise, and the fact that the move to make the scheme more self-financing in the 1980s was almost entirely at the expense of the employers' contributions. The health sector was obliged to both bargain for funds, and bargain from a position of weakness.

This had two consequences on the figures for spending on health care when compared with the developed Western nations. First, spending as a proportion of national income at 3–3.5 per cent was low (about 40–50 per cent that of Western nations), even when all the statistical problems involved comparing GNP and the traditional national material product method of calculating national production are taken into account. Second, while in Western Europe spending on health care consistently rose as a proportion of GNP, in Hungary it stagnated or fell, having reached a high point of 3.7 per cent in 1960. A third characteristic of Hungarian state budgeting, which, ultimately, was perhaps more telling than the previous two given the number of loss-making enterprises covered by the state budget, was that while spending on health remained a stagnating proportion of national income, the state budget, of which health formed a part, grew as a proportion of national income. An increasing proportion of the state budget was spent supporting loss-making enterprises. It was pressures of this kind on resources for health care that resulted in 'shortage' rather than 'scarcity', as Table 7.21 suggests.

Shortage in the health care system became particularly acute in the 1960s. In the early years of socialism, the rapid increase of social insurance paid handsome dividends. A successful battle against TB was waged, child mortality was reduced radically, expected lifespan at birth grew steadily year after year. The general indicators of the nation's health grew rapidly, as can be seen from Table 7.22. And these successes were achieved despite the fact that, as a non-productive sector of the economy, health care was not prioritized for national investment expenditure (see Table 7.23).

The Hungarian health service, then, coped adequately, without significant new investment, when it had to cover only 47 per cent of the

Table 7.21 Health and social expenditure in relation to national income and the state budget

	H & S as % national income	H & S as % state budget	Increase in H & S expenditure	Increase in real expenditure state budget
1955	2.4	n.a	n.a	n.a
1956	3.2	n.a	n.a	n.a
1968	3.3	5.3	100	100
1970	2.9	4.5	105	125
1975	3.2	4.1	167	225
1980	3.4	4.4	294	343

Source: J. Szalai, Az Egészségügy Betegségei, Budapest 1986, pp. 48 and 50.

Table 7.22 Some general health indicators

	Tuberculosis deaths per 100,000	Deaths under 1 year per 1,000 births	Life expectancy*	
			Men	Women
1920/21			100	100
1930/31			119	120
1938	100	100		
1941/2	112	102	134	135
1946	95	89		
1949/50	57	65	146	148
1954/5	26	46	159	161
1960	22	36	162	164
1965	18	30	164	167
1970	14	27	163	168
1975	9	25	163	169
1979	7	18	163	171

* 1920/21 = base. In 1920/21 life expectancy was 41 years for men and 43.1 years for women.

Source: Szalai, Az Egészségügy, pp. 56–7.

population. The weaknesses in the system only became apparent when the percentage of population insured approached 100 per cent and there was still no increase in health spending. The 1960s can be split into three periods: 1958–63, 1963–67, and the years following 1968. The first of these periods was the era of successful collectivization of agriculture, when the percentage of the population insured jumped by 25 per cent,

Table 7.23 Share of various branches' investments as a percentage of all national investments

	Industry and agriculture as % total	Communal as % total	Health as % total	Health as % communal
1950–55	59	12.5	1.3	10.3
1956–57	58	21.6	1.5	7.1
1958–63	59	13.6	1.2	9.0
1964–67	60	13.9	1.7	11.9
1968–72	56	14.2	1.3	8.4
1973–78	48	14.8	1.6	10.0
1979–81	51	16.5	2.1	12.6

Source: Szalai, *Az Egészségügy*, p. 68 (figures taken from the Central Statistical Office).

despite the fact that benefits for cooperative farm members were not so generous as those for workers. In the second of the periods, health became, organizationally, a sub-branch of the local council infrastructure with a low priority in terms of access to funds, a 'remainder' branch. In the final period, the effect of market reform on social health provision was the very opposite of decentralization. Market reform brought with it even greater centralization of enterprise funds for welfare spending, and an even greater dependence on the redistribution of those funds by the consumers of the state budget. That is to say, the degree to which health was a 'remainder' branch in the national budget actually increased. This situation of dependence was little effected by the Council Law of 1971, which was seen by many as the equivalent in local government regulation of what 1968 had been for the economy. The essence of local authority funding did not change, and the rigid hierarchical principle of the National Settlement Network conception within the new structure left many smaller villages with minimal provision of their own, and long distances to travel for additional services. Furthermore, the provision in economic regulations since 1968 for enterprises to contribute directly to social services in the area in which they operated gave central government a justification for not increasing the share of the non-productive sector in the state budget.

With full-scale collectivization in the 1960s and the introduction of an extra 25 per cent of the population to the social insurance system, the health service responded first by increasing the number of health service workers, as Table 7.24 suggests. Within hospitals, the emphasis on people rather than materials was particularly marked. The number of hospital beds increased by 32 per cent between 1960 and 1980, compared with a 95 per cent increase in the number of hospital doctors

Table 7.24 Increase in health service employees

	Number of doctors index (previous period = 100)	Health sector workers as % of economically active in first yr of 5-yr period
1955	100	
1956–59	116	
1960–64	123	1.3
1965–69	121	1.7
1970–74	115	2.0
1975–79	111	2.5
1980–81	110	2.9

Source: Szalai, *Az Egészségügy*, pp. 70–71.

(see Table 7.24). In addition, the number of hospital beds per unit of available space was maximized, and statistical practice was altered to register increases in the number of beds rather than increases in the number of hospitals. Data published in the 1970s revealed that between 1950 and 1965 the number of hospitals (including amalgamations) actually decreased by 70, while the number of beds increased by 26,000. But even using beds as the new measure, the increase in provision for 1955–79 was not substantial (see Table 7.25).

The 1960s and 1970s were also associated with the introduction of a third level in the hierarchy of health organizations between hospitals and the GP: the polyclinic. Although such bodies can be seen as sensible additions to the health service in principle, in practice, in a climate of shortage, they did not receive the necessary equipment to take significant pressure off the hospitals, and simply became an additional step in the diagnostic chain which ended up at the hospitals in any case. An additional feature of this period was the move in social policy from benefits in kind to money benefits, as Table 7.26 illustrates. Ferge interpreted this shift favourably, in that it was in the area of benefits in kind that the regressive subsidization of centralized redistribution operated most clearly. Yet, as Szalai noted, putting more money in people's pockets did not build hospitals. Spending on social benefits declined as a proportion of the state budget, and the decline was twice as large in the case of funds for benefits in kind and communal benefits. While expenses from the state budget increased two and a half times between 1970 and 1978, benefits in kind financed out of the state budget increased only 1.8 times. While social insurance expenditure was 6 per cent of national income in 1963, and almost doubled by 1979 to 11 per cent, the proportion of national income spent on health, social expendi-

Table 7.25 Increase in the number of hospital beds (previous period = 100)

	Budapest	Provinces	Nationally
1955	100	100	100
1956–59	107	112	110
1960–64	100	115	109
1965–69	100	113	109
1970–74	103	107	105
1975–79	95	102	100

Source: Szalai, Az Egészségügy, p. 73.

Table 7.26 Composition of total incomes of the population (%)

	Wages	Agricultural income	Social benefits in cash	in kind	Other*
1960	50.0	26.5	7.0	11.4	5.1
1965	51.4	23.0	8.6	12.3	4.7
1970	49.9	22.0	10.4	12.4	5.3
1973	49.5	20.3	12.5	12.8	4.9
1975	49.8	18.3	14.5	12.8	4.6

*includes income from self-employed work, interest from savings and so on

Source: Ferge, A Society, p. 190.

ture, education, culture and science hardly changed between 1963 and 1979, remaining at 8.6–8.7 per cent.

The disparity between the number of people insured and the number of hospital beds available can also be seen from Table 7.27. No new hospital was built in Budapest during the socialist period until 1979. Repairs and maintenance problems became so acute that some 3,000 hospital beds were unusable in the early 1980s. By the 1980s, because of the endemic labour shortage, and the especially low wages in the health service, there was a shortage of nurses, which was worsened by high absenteeism: 25–30 per cent of nurses would be absent on any given day.[105] The shortage of drugs had reached the level where it was often impossible to get everyday drugs such as simple pain-killers like aspirin.[106] Local doctors (GPs) spent on average only 1–1.5 minutes with their patients,[107] the average in polyclinics being 7–8 minutes. Some 75 per cent of hospitals were over sixty years old, and many of these were over a hundred. An absence of sanatoria and rehabilitation institutes meant that some 20–40 per cent of 'active' hospital beds were

Table 7.27 Changes in some basic health indicators (% change over previous period)

	Numbers insured	Number of doctors	Number of hospital beds
1938	100	100	100
1950	+57	−9	+5
1960	+93	+63	+39
1965	+15	+24	+9
1970	+10	+21	+9
1975	+5	+15	+5
1980	0	+11	+3

Source: Losonczi, A Kiszolgáltatottság, p. 39.

occupied by the chronically sick. Perhaps most disturbing of all, both the proportion of patients who died in hospital, and the proportion of patients who died within twenty-four hours of reaching hospital, actually increased between 1970 and 1981.

There were both regional and class dimensions to this deterioration in the level of health provision. The result of the new regional policy introduced in 1971 was that only 10 per cent of the money available for health service investment was spent on the 3,000 'small' villages, where some 50 per cent of the population lived. Inhabitants of Borsod-Abaúj-Zemplén had a ten times worse chance of receiving orthopedic treatment than the inhabitants of Csongrad county, and the disparity in chances of reaching a hospital appropriate for the patient's needs approached eighty times for certain illnesses. Health care figures broken down by class revealed equally worrying trends. While the mortality rates of intellectuals improved some 4 per cent over the 1970s, for workers it worsened by 18 per cent, so that, by 1980, workers experienced a mortality rate higher than that in 1970 in every category of disease. Losonczi reports national figures for men only from all classes which show a 33 per cent increase in the mortality rate between 1960 and 1980.[108] More disturbing than the overall increase, perhaps, was the disproportionate increase for those aged between 40 and 44, in the middle of their working lives, as can be seen from Table 7.28 (which uses data for 1978 rather than 1980). An additional failing of the health service which should be noted is the 'long neglect' of the problem of mental illness.[109]

The impact of the sudden increase in the numbers covered by social insurance brought about by collectivization was also reflected in the pension system, as Table 7.29 indicates. Almost inevitably, the rapid increase in the number of people covered resulted in a reduction in the level of pension provision. The figures presented in Table 7.5 suggest that, while average wages increased from 840 forints per month in 1962 to 1,643 in 1972, an increase of 196 per cent, the average size of pensions only increased from 689 to 1,083 forints per month, an increase of 57 per cent. If the years 1965 and 1975 are taken, the figures are 121 per cent and 53 per cent respectively.[110]

Sexual division of labour

A final aspect of shortage is the extent to which pressures on the family meant that the burden of servicing of the domestic economy was passed on to women. Basic data on the division of labour within Hungarian families come from the 'time-budget' studies carried out in 1965–66 and repeated some twenty years later.[111] Tables 7.30 and 7.31 clearly show the disproportionate amount of time women spent doing housework, even when they were fully employed. They also suggest, as Szalai puts it,

Table 7.28 Male mortality in 1978

Age group	% of 1960 figures
30–34	125
34–39	142
40–44	168
44–49	156
50–54	142
54–59	117

Source: Losonczi, *A Kiszolgáltatottság*, p. 225.

Table 7.29 Some characteristics of the pension system

	No. of pensioners on 1 Jan. of year (1,000s)	% pensioners within:		Total sum of pensions (thou. m. fts)
		whole population	eligible population	
1950	502	5.5	40	0.9
1960	759	7.6	40	4.4
1970	1,415	13.8	70	13.0
1980	1,775	16.9	80	26.8

Source: Ferge, *A Society*, p. 224.

Table 7.30 Time-budgets of husbands and wives at domestic activities
(1965–66)

	Husband		Wife		Both	
	(mins)	(%)	(mins)	(%)	(mins)	(%)
Intellectual workers (wife earning)						
Housework	67	27	178	73	245	100
Raising children	45	44	57	56	102	100
Intellectual workers (wife not earning)						
Housework	54	13	355	87	409	100
Raising children	19	15	105	85	124	100
Manual workers (wife earning)						
Housework	93	30	222	70	315	100
Raising children	42	37	70	63	122	100
Manual workers (wife not earning)						
Housework	88	19	386	81	474	100
Raising children	22	21	84	79	106	100

Source: J. Szalai, 'A családi munkamegosztás néhány szociológiai problémájáról', in
P. Lőcsei, *Család és Házasság a Mai Magyar Társadalomban*, Budapest 1971, pp. 186–7.

that women's tasks in the home were 'housewife tasks and not mother
tasks'. Husbands, on the other hand, contributed more to raising
children than helping round the home.[112]

A study of family relations in Békés county in south-east Hungary in
1969 confirmed this general picture. It found that even where the wife
had a job, in 55.3 per cent of cases the wife performed the majority of
work relating to the family. The figure rose to 74.9 per cent for families
where the wife had no outside job, making an average of 65.1 per
cent.[113] The Békés study also showed the traditional structure of household duties. Chores performed 'exclusively by the wife' covered
preparing breakfast (77.6 per cent), washing (71.6 per cent), cleaning
(59.9 per cent), shopping (49.6 per cent), work in the kitchen garden
(26.4 per cent), tending the animals (34.9 per cent), carrying water
(30.0 per cent) and chopping wood (11.0 per cent). The only chore
performed proportionately more only by husbands was chopping wood
(69.0 per cent), although work in the kitchen garden was performed
only by husbands 23.9 per cent of the time and in 30.0 per cent of
households 'husbands as well' performed this task.[114]

Taken together, the evidence presented in this section shows that

Table 7.31 The family division of labour in two-parent families (1986)

	Exclusively		Jointly	Other combination or outsider
	Wife	Husband		
Daily shopping	57.9	8.1	19.7	14.3
Weekly shopping	44.3	8.4	32.2	15.1
Breakfast	73.7	2.7	10.8	12.8
Cooking	82.0	0.5	7.6	9.9
Washing-up	72.9	1.1	10.2	15.8
Cleaning	59.5	1.7	18.3	20.5
Washing	80.2	0.8	6.2	12.8
Ironing	85.1	0.4	1.8	12.7
Window-washing	62.6	5.4	13.9	18.1
Preserving	62.4	0.4	9.2	28.0
Repairs, DIY	1.3	66.8	4.2	27.7
Dealing with authorities	33.6	27.3	34.4	4.7
Handling bills and money	48.2	5.6	44.0	2.2
Looking after children	22.8	0.8	73.6	2.8

Source: I. Nagy-né, 'A nők családi és munkahelyi körülményei', *Statisztikai Szemle*, 1989, no. 10, p. 869.

under Hungary's socialist economy, there was a quantitative and qualitative failure of provision in all areas of social policy, and that this went beyond the inevitable scarcity of resources relative to demand. The situation was one of absolute shortage, especially when compared against legitimately high socialist expectations.

Second Economy – Private Compensatory Provision

The third characteristic feature of Hungary's socialist economy, it has been argued, was the development of a symbiotically interconnected second economy. Chapter 6 considered its impact on the labour market and production relations. Here the focus of the discussion shifts to its effect on incomes and its role in ensuring the provision of services. The second economy provided partial and unequal compensation for the failings of the first. It constituted a market-based opportunity, from which people benefited in a necessarily unequal fashion. As with the section dealing with the second economy and Hungary's labour market, this section is necessarily much shorter than the rest. It has not been extensively researched because of the questionable legality of second economy practices.

There is no doubt that incomes from the second economy had some compensatory effect. Sziráczky, for example, showed how the propensity of lorry drivers to engage in commodity-producing activity on household plots was inversely related to their basic hourly wage. Only 18.2 per cent of those in the highest income band were active as commodity producers, while 48.4 per cent and 55.0 per cent were in the next two bands. His lowest band covers predominantly young people who were not active in agriculture to any great extent.[115]

The size of this acknowledged compensatory effect is a more complex issue. On average, the extra income amounted to only one quarter of wages. On the other hand, for certain groups extra income played an important compensatory role. Galasi found that certain skilled and semi-skilled workers earned sufficient extra income to neutralize their weak position on the labour market. He also found that the level of extra income depended upon the length and intensity of the extra working hours, and that those with high extra incomes had disproportionately high savings levels. From this, he deduced that families worked very hard for their extra income, and used it to lay the foundation for future investment. That is to say, the statistics would appear to bear out the intuitively reasonable theory that people worked in the second economy to get money to buy the big things in life, like a flat or a car, but once they had acquired such goods they lived at a less hectic pace. Crucially, Galasi found no clear relationship between labour market position and extra income. Extra income could be low or high for those in both a strong and a weak labour market position, depending on the importance of these big purchases in their family economy.[116] It would seem that the 75 per cent of the Hungarian population that participated in the second economy compensated existing structural inequality only to an extent: second economy activity did not redress the balance entirely.[117]

Bokor's study of 'deprivation' gives further information on the second economy activities of the less privileged. She found that 83 per cent of 'deprived' families had at least one member active in the second economy, compared with 72 per cent of non-deprived families. Some 76 per cent of deprived families had an agricultural plot of some kind, compared with 59 per cent of non-deprived families. Within second economy activities, the 'deprived' were more dependent on agriculture as a source of income than the non-deprived group, and they received less from it. Not only did the 'deprived' get less income from the first economy, they had to be prepared to work for less in the second, spending more time working, to earn lower incomes.[118] Bokor also found that while the non-deprived spent 32 per cent of their free time working and 30 per cent on holiday, the deprived spent 55 per cent of their free time working and only 2 per cent on holiday.[119] On the other hand, reinforcing the notion of the limited compensatory effect of second economy activity, Bokor's figures show that those in her 'threatened' position (that is, those who almost qualify as 'deprived') could thank their greater, more successful, activity in the 'second economy', especially agriculture, for keeping them outside the 'deprived' group.[120]

In housing, the compensatory aspect of the second economy can be seen in the pattern of urban and village development, that is to say in the disproportionately rapid growth in the villages surrounding Budapest which have become centres for commuting workers. At a time when, nationally, the village population was declining, the villages surrounding Budapest not only grew, they also did so more quickly than did the capital itself. While the population of Budapest increased by only 22 per cent between 1949 and 1970, that of Erd and Dunakezi roughly doubled, Erd from 16,000 to 31,000 and Dunakezi from 8,000 to 19,000. The annual growth in Budapest's population was 1.5 per cent between 1949 and 1960, in the ring of villages surrounding Budapest between the same years the annual growth was 2.3 per cent, and between 1960 and 1970 this disparity of growth rate increased.[121] As Chapter 6 demonstrated, the vast majority of house-building in villages is carried out on a private basis.

Finally in the context of private compensatory provision, the thorny issue of 'thank you money' should be discussed.[122] The first problem with 'thank you money' is the silence that surrounded it. Despite having become a universally accepted fact of life, both givers and receivers were reluctant to talk about it, and even books on medical sociology admitted that they dared not ask questions about the subject.[123] Some estimates put the total sum paid as 'thank you' at four thousand million forints, extending to 25–50 per cent of doctors, and giving those at the top an estimated 50,000–100,000 forints additional monthly income.[124] Petschnig put the value at anywhere between two and four thousand million forints. This figure was not so very high as a percentage of the population's total money income – about 1 per cent in 1981 – but it was a high proportion of the 19.7 thousand million forints spent nationally on health care. What is more, the level of the payment for standard forms of medical attention increased about three and a half times over the ten years from 1972–82, a figure which, significantly, was in line with the increase in second economy fees charged by bricklayers over the same period: the official consumer price index increased by only 50 per cent.[125]

The debate in Hungary concerning 'thank you money' did not relate to the fact that it exists, nor to its size, but to its function. Lonsonczi saw the function of the money as a means of documenting an agreement between the doctor and patient, a recognition that a form of private understanding exists between them.[126] Petschnig saw the matter in less symbolic terms. Rejecting the idea that it was actual 'thank you money' in return for services rendered, despite the fact that 65.7 per cent of people asked in a rare survey of the problem claimed this was their prime motivation for paying, she argued that it was not so much a payment for past services, as the expression of a hope for future services better performed. She rejected explanations of 'thank you money' which made reference to the low level of medical salaries for two reasons. First, because most people did not know how much the medical profession earned – indeed Petschnig found it difficult to find this out herself – and, second, there was no reduction in the practice when medical salaries were improved in the 1970s.[127] But if low medical salaries did not constitute an adequate exploration for the origins of 'thank you money', they were certainly part of the problem, and a reason why money was accepted once offered. As Petschnig noted, 'Can we moralize about whether [the doctor] has a right to put a roof over his family'?[128]

Conclusion

The conclusions that can be drawn from the diverse topics covered in this chapter are three-fold, one for each of the chapter's major sub-divisions. First, the reproduction of social disadvantage takes place in many more sophisticated ways than through market relations. Hungarian socialism achieved a considerable reduction in the overall spread of social inequality, a goal which many would agree is central to the socialist project. Nevertheless, inequalities of a kind common to all industrial societies reproduced themselves via a new mechanism which Szelényi christened 'centralized redistribution', and, given prejudices which derive from a certain reading of the Marxist classics, no consistent social policy emerged to counter them, whilst the half-hearted adoption of Szelényi's own solution of increased marketization resulted in the 'worst of all worlds' in housing allocation.

Second, the facts of waste, inefficiency and shortage in the economy, and the need to support an increasing number of unprofitable large enterprises from the central budget resources, significantly diminished the funds available for education and the social services. In education and health especially, the level of service fell far short of the high socialist objectives the regimes set themselves, and showed worrying signs of absolute decline.

Third, the institutionalized dualism, discussed in the previous chapter in connection with the production of social wealth, necessarily fed through into consumption. Absolutely basic services, which the government claimed to be providing free, could only be obtained in reality by resorting to private, under-the-counter payments.

8

Conclusion

This conclusion reviews briefly the implications of the events recounted in this book for the two big issues it raises: the future of Hungary and the future of the socialist project.

From the developments briefly discussed in Chapter 2, it is clear that the Hungarian economy experienced its golden years only when part of a larger and dynamic, yet protective empire: at the turn of the century within the Habsburg empire, and in the 1930s as an adjunct of the Third Reich. The only period when it seemed to be enjoying sustained growth as an independent nation was in the brief five years from 1925, a process brought to a sudden halt by the Depression of the 1930s. The idea of Hungary surviving without some sort of protective economic allegiance, a South Korea, or a Switzerland of Central Europe, seems implausible in this light; and it would certainly assume that the world financial system is now sufficiently sophisticated to avoid any future stock-market crash. It would also require a realistic industrial policy and a more effective use of foreign loans than was achieved in the 1920s. Some sort of integration within a larger economic structure is more likely. Hungary's declared long-term goal is to join the European Community, with membership of the European Free Trade Area as a more realistic short-term ambition. Closer cooperation with its near neighbours is also probable – indeed talks are underway with Hungary, Austria, Italy, Yugoslavia and Czechoslovakia. As Chapter 2 suggested, the Austro-Hungarian empire generated its own economic logic. It would be profoundly ironic if, some eighty years after the outbreak of World War One which destroyed them, the Empire's economic structures were resurrected. The longer the European Community takes to decide about the other prospective members currently standing in line, the more plausible such a scenario becomes. Hungary's political structure is likely to crystallize around two-and-a-half-party politics. The

225

Democratic Forum will develop into something even more similar to the German CDU, and it is more than possible that the Free Democrats will place a greater emphasis on their social democratic wing in order to increase their vote. The socialists are likely to remain a party of permanent opposition, despite their espousal of social democracy. However, it would take a number of rounds of electoral failure for the Free Democrats (the Democratic Opposition) to ally themselves electorally with the Socialist Party (the Communist establishment) in order to overcome the Christian Democratic right.

Turning to the future of socialism, the forty-five years of Hungary's postwar history suggest the unviability for relatively developed nations of not one but two models of socialist economic organization. Hungary's experience has nothing to say directly about socialism in the developing world where both socialist models might well retain some value. It is not inconceivable that a humane (but by definition not democratic) version of Eastern European socialism – such as Imre Nagy's New Course, or the golden age of the first few years of the New Economic Mechanism – might constitute acceptable models for newly industrializing economies. But for the developed world, neither the traditional Stalinist model of central planning, nor the market socialism of the New Economic Mechanism was able to produce a system of socio-economic organization that could sustain high levels of economic efficiency and thereby guarantee high levels of social welfare. Rather, they created a system in which the economy was dominated by large monopoly producers which were materially interested in maintaining the status quo, and subject to neither financial nor democratic restraints.

The Hungarian experience is a profoundly chastening one. On the one hand, as Chapter 2 suggested, once all the conjunctural factors of immediate postwar and early Cold War politics are stripped away, the most coherent strategy for extending control over Hungary's economy – and one that many who today share a belief in the socialist project would have advocated – was to pursue nationalization. That is to say, when Popular Front policies are followed through consistently, they almost inevitably result in widespread nationalization, because only the removal of private ownership gives sufficient control to allow a systematic 'breaking' of the law of value in the interest of socialist goals. This is what Hungary did, with the helping hand of the Soviet Union. The remaining chapters suggest that this additional dimension of control is both harmful and illusory. It is harmful because systematic breaking of the law of value deprives those who make economic decisions of a measure of costs and opportunity costs, and hence of a rational basis on which to exercise that control. As Chapter 3 demonstrated, all attempts to follow the prescriptions in Marx for an economy based on units of labour-time failed. They degenerated into costs-plus pricing, and the costs themselves became increasingly, and deliberately, arbitrary.

And the increased control made possible by ownership is illusory because, paradoxically, planners discovered that control was still required. A messianic streak in Marxist and much other socialist thought has suggested that once the means of production, distribution and exchange are publicly owned conflicts of interest will disappear. Control will not be necessary because, in a classless society, all will share the same interests. But as Chapters 6 and 7, together with references throughout the earlier chapters to 'plan bargaining' and 'regulation bargaining', all indicate, conflicts of interest do not automatically disappear once the means of production have been nationalized. Individual enterprises and their managers have interests very much opposed to the national interest, and the centre finds it difficult to impose its will, since enterprise managers exercise their power at the point of production.

It should also be noted that these conflicts do not disappear if they have been socialized into self-governing cooperatives. As Chapter 6 demonstrated, enterprise management was able to pursue its group interest in defending its comfortable status quo without the bother of significant pressure from below. Trade unions were weak, and despite extensive formal structures, enterprise democracy was largely ineffective. But even if economic democracy were a reality and conflicts of interest between workers and management were successfully mediated, it is not clear that the difference of interest between the enterprise and the centre would disappear. Workers as well as their management benefit from the cushion of soft budget constraints. Even if an enterprise, the bus manufacturer Ikarus for example, were run wholly democratically, it would be as much in the workers' short- to medium-term interest as it was in the managers' to produce huge runs of identical buses for the Soviet market rather than meet the changing and more demanding requirements of the West.

It could be argued that the Hungarian evidence does not show the unviability of a market socialist solution in the context of 'genuine' workers' self-management. It is certainly true that fully decentralized workers' council-run enterprises were created only in 1985. It is also true that their democracy existed in form rather than as a reality. The same could be said for collective farm democracy, although the collective farms existed as theoretically self-managed, market socialist enterprises since before the introduction of the New Economic Mechanism. But it is too easy to blame this lack of economic democracy on the absence of political democracy and the omnipresence of the Party. As Chapter 6 revealed, Party control of enterprise economic decision-making was normally indirect only. Political pluralism in the context of social ownership might well have operated against economic rationality. It could easily have resulted in enterprise claims for special status becoming an additional factor in inter-party rivalry.

The Western evidence on internal economic democracy is contradictory. There are numerous examples in history, such as 1956, of workers demanding a role for workers' councils in economic management. On the other hand, the evidence on the operation of such councils in everyday mundane decision-making suggests an ideal, a drive for personal autonomy, rather than a feasible socio-economic reality. There is also extensive evidence to suggest that there are considerable productivity gains to be won from increasing the involvement of workers in the decisions that affect their immediate working environment. Yet much of the literature on cooperatives in the West suggests that even in the most democratically conceived cooperatives strategic decisions tend to be made by a very small number of people; and that the more constraints of size require the introduction of mechanisms of representative democracy, the less committed members become to participation, and the easier it is for such mechanisms to be dominated, scarcely surprisingly, by the few that have the necessary 'expertise'.

The argument put forward in Hungary before the demise of socialism was that democracy and the interests of the national economy could better be served by replacing soft budget constraints by hard market ones. It contends that economic organizations are qualitatively different. In the market context, they are set up to pursue self-interested economic ends; but the best way of controlling enterprises with avowedly self-interested ends is not via spurious forms of internal representative democracy, but by imposing market discipline. In other words, in order to impose 'hard budget constraints', a society requires the legal mechanism of private property.

There is a sense in which private property is a fiction. As radical critiques of capitalism have long suggested, it cheats by externalizing real social costs, and by limiting liability in the case of insolvency. These costs have to be picked up by other social institutions, but the private company can conveniently forget about them. Private ownership of the means of production allows economic enterprises to behave as if these awkward social costs did not exist and pursue single-mindedly the relatively simple goal of wealth maximization. In pursuing this goal over the centuries, capitalist enterprises have developed sophisticated techniques for monitoring costs. Nationalization of the means of production, on the other hand, internalized all costs at a stroke, deprived planners of a reliable method of measuring them (within the Stalinist model at least), and prevented planners from insisting that enterprises treat them as real constraints. The Hungarian experience suggests that, absurd though it might appear, the fiction of capitalist relations which permits the externalization of costs creates more wealth and more welfare than a self-declared socialism which, by accepting the need to recognize all social costs, internalizes them. Capitalism alienates man from his inherently social species-being but, at a given level of social complexity, this con-trick is necessary social deceit in order to pursue economic growth.

If such arguments are accepted, the socialist project necessarily becomes reformist. Its primary aims are two-fold: to minimize the harmful consequences of those social costs which society deceives itself into letting economic enterprises externalize (that is to say, a strongly interventionist social policy); and to focus on the issue of creating the conditions for equality of opportunity. The 'Poverty of Theory' debate attempted to move attention away from structures and back to real individuals in concrete situations. One possible conclusion to be drawn from Hungary's postwar history is that the Althusser school was wrong about structures as well, that when capitalist economic relations are fully disembodied, all that is being described is a set of structures which make sustained growth possible. What is pernicious about capitalism, it might be argued, is not the set of economic structures based on the institutions of private ownership of the means of production, but that access to the various positions in the model is unequally distributed between real social actors. Socialism should be more concerned with the issue of opening up access to positions and roles within the economic system than with redefining ownership, more concerned with facilitating market entry and minimizing the social costs of market failure than with inter-nalizing all costs within a notional single nationwide economic enter-prise. Such policies can, and must, include the extension of the involvement of works in workplace decision-making, and support for community action groups and community planning initiatives, for any initiatives which help people break out of dependence and create institu-tions of their own break through the vicious circle of cultural dis-advantage. It can encompass all of the achievements of the GLC Economic Policy Group's 'Taste of Power', from the Greater London Enterprise Board to women's employment initiatives, to housing policy, except the illusion that those achievements had some significance as victories in guerrilla actions in a much larger campaign to establish an economy based on socially necessary production.

The only possible case for a more revolutionary political agenda would have to argue that expropriation of large businesses personally owned by private individuals or families is a necessary precondition for the good functioning of a market system based on primarily institutional rather than personal ownership, because institutional ownership makes it more possible for those who do not enjoy inherited wealth to exercise economic power. In Hungary's case, this amounts to arguing that the expropriation of the few families that dominated the economy before 1945 was a necessary prerequisite for the property reform and reprivatization that is currently underway. This case is easier to make in a late-developing country like Hungary than it is in Western Europe. But even in the Hungarian case, it both takes a sledge-hammer to crack a nut and misunderstands the dynamics of the model towards which Eastern Europe is developing. On the one hand, personal private economic power is amenable to social democratic, reformist control, as the Swedish case illustrates clearly. On the other, although Hungary currently has no vestiges of personal private economic power, new moguls will emerge whose private power, like that of Henry Ford, will then become more institutionalized over time.

Such 'reformism' is not new. It has been the common currency of mainstream politics for decades. But it is important to see how the conclusion has been reached. The criticism of socialist economics is empirical, in terms of what reformed and unreformed socialist economies have produced. It does not argue that first centralized planning and then market socialism do not work because they are theoretical nonsenses. This was said decades ago in the classic writings of von Mises, Hayek and Barone. However, their theoretical discussions lacked realism and were so overtly anti-socialist in tone that socialist sympathizers could happily accept cogent counter-arguments from Lange, on the one hand, in favour of market socialism, or classic Marxist restatements of the labour theory of value on the other. Hayek's stark choice of either individualism, the market and freedom or collectivism, planning and serfdom was massively overstated. There must be, and historically have been, many intermediate solutions. His criticism of Lange to the effect that the latter was preoccupied with efficiency in terms of static equilibrium, on the other hand, is correct, but it focused on the problem of adjustment to daily changing conditions, and not on the aspect of his focus on the static that ultimately turned out to be the downfall of both centralized and market socialism: an inability to respond quickly enough to technological change.

Rather than consider abstractions, this book has followed through four and a half decades of a socialist economy in action, and has documented how and why it did not work as intended, how it was subjected to constant revision, and why so many of those who experienced it and analysed it were willing to reject altogether the idea of an economic system based on socialist ownership. Similarly, the book's political acceptance of a 'reformist' social democratic paradigm complements Bernstein's classic 'revisionist' perspective: it does not derive from it. Bernstein accepted 'reformism' *faut de mieux*, because capitalism had proved capable of controlling its crises and socialist revolution was no longer on the political horizon. Others have accepted 'reformism' simply because, for all capitalism's failings, workers in Western welfare states with pluralist political systems have been better off than those in the socialist world. This has been true throughout the socialist period of Eastern Europe. 'Reformism' is accepted here, rather, because the revolutionary alternative of extensive public ownership of the means of production has been shown by historical experience not to work, or rather, not to be capable of internal regeneration and responsiveness to changing conditions.

Notes

Introduction

1. J. Kornai, *The Road to a Free Economy*, New York and London 1990.
2. J. Kornai, *The Economics of Shortage*, Amsterdam 1980.
3. I. Szelényi, *Urban Inequalities under State Socialism*, Oxford 1983.
4. In Gy. Konrád and I. Szelényi, 'A késleltett városfejlődés társadalmi konfliktusai', *Valóság*, 1971, no. 12, pp. 26–7, the process is described in terms of centralization followed by redistribution. In later works the process is referred to simply as redistribution.
5. Gy. Konrád and I. Szelényi, *The Intellectuals on the Road to Class Power*, New York and London 1979, p. 222.
6. Ibid., pp. 154–5.
7. J. Kornai, *Overcentralisation in Economic Administration*, Oxford 1959. The original Hungarian manuscript was submitted in 1956.
8. Konrád and Szelényi, *The Intellectuals*, e.g. pp. 234 and 252.

Chapter 1

1. J. Kornai, 'The Hungarian Reform Process: Visions, Hopes and Reality', in V. Nee and D. Stark (eds), *Remaking the Economic Institutions of Socialism: China and Eastern Europe*, Stanford 1989, pp. 86–9; W. Brus, 'Evolution of the Communist Economic System: Scope and Limits', in Nee and Stark, pp. 267–72.
2. For an account of the history of writings on property reform, see L. Lengyel, 'A tulajdonviták története és a reform', in L. Lengyel (ed.), *Tulajdonreform*, Budapest 1988, pp. 21–50.
3. T. Sárközy (ed.), *Foreign Investments in Hungary*, Budapest 1989.
4. E. Hankiss, *Társadalmi Csapdák: Diagnózisok*, Budapest 1983; *Diagnózisok 2*, Budapest 1986; *Kelet-európai alternatívák*, Budapest 1989.
5. Hankiss, *Kelet-európai*, pp. 56–8. The survey is also referenced in 'Társadalom-patológia', in *Diagnózisok 2*, pp. 99–218, when he places more emphasis on the ambivalence of the findings.
6. Hankiss, *Kelet-európai*, p. 142.
7. *Figyelő*, no. 46, 17 November 1988, pp. 1–4.
8. T. Smith, 'Inequality and Welfare', in R. Jowell et al. (eds), *British Social Attitudes: Special International Report*, Aldershot 1989, pp. 59–86.
9. Ibid., pp. 61–2.

10. Z. Ács, *Kizárt a Párt*, Budapest 1988, pp. 52–5.
11. M. Bihari, *Politikai Rendszer és Demokrácia* (second edn), Budapest 1988. The first edition was published in 1985, the second in February 1988. Between the two editions, indicative of the changing political climate, the word 'socialist' disappeared from the title.
12. More detail on political developments up to May 1989 can be found in N. Swain, 'Hungary's Socialist Project in Crisis', *New Left Review*, no. 176, July/August 1989, pp. 3–29.
13. P. Lendvai, *Hitel*, 1989, no. 5, pp. 16–17.
14. For an account of the significance of István Bibó in English, see F. Donáth, 'István Bibó and the Fundamental Issue of Hungarian Democracy', in R. Miliband and J. Savile (eds), *The Socialist Register 1981*, London 1981, pp. 221–46.
15. The Poor Support Fund (SZETA) was an independent organization formed in 1979 to help the poor. It gained legal status in the spring of 1989.
16. The Patriotic People's Front is a movement technically independent of the HSWP, whose main constitutional purpose is to organize elections. It also organizes cultural events.
17. See Chapter 2.

Chapter 2

1. I.T. Berend and Gy. Ránki, *The European Periphery and Industrialisation 1780–1914*, Cambridge 1977, pp. 107, 129, 130, 149.
2. I.T. Berend and Gy. Ránki, 'The Development of the Manufacturing Industry in Hungary 1900–1944', *Studia Historica*, no. 19, Budapest 1960, p. 162.
3. I. Pető and S. Szakács, *A Hazai Gazdaság Négy Évtizedének Története 1945–1985. Az Újjáépítés és a Tervutasításos Irányítás Időszaka 1945–1968*, Budapest 1985, p. 18.
4. Berend and Ránki, 'The Development', p. 161.
5. I.T. Berend, *Újjáépítés és a Nagytőke Elleni Harc Magyarországon 1945–1948*, Budapest 1962, pp. 23–35. He gives the example of mines in Borsod county working at 80% capacity before the former management gained access to them. See also Pető and Szakács, p. 26.
6. Pető and Szakács, p. 26; F. Donáth, *Reform és Forradalom*, Budapest 1977, pp. 46–50.
7. Hegedűs, who participated in administering the reform, suggests in his memoirs that it was too hurried, and accuses Imre Nagy and other politicians of wanting the glory of a historic reform without thinking through the consequences. See A. Hegedűs, *A Történelem és a Hatalom Igezetében*, Budapest 1988, pp. 112–18.
8. K. Benda (ed.), *Magyarország Történeti Kronológiája*, Budapest 1983, p. 1023.
9. R. Nötel, 'International Credit and Finance', in M.C. Kaser and E.A. Radice (eds), *The Economic History of Eastern Europe 1991–1975. Volume II. Interwar Policy, The War and Reconstruction*, Oxford 1986, pp. 538–9.
10. Pető and Szakács, p. 61, and Nötel, p. 539, disagree on precisely how many zeroes to these numbers. Either way, they are impossibly large.
11. Pető and Szakács, pp. 86 and 121–2.
12. Ibid., pp. 95–100.
13. J. Braunthal (*History of the International*, Vol. 3, Boulder 1980, p. 166) claims 300,000 so-called 'blue cards' (allowing those not in their place of residence to vote elsewhere) were printed, some of which might be assumed to have been genuine. Hegedűs in his memoirs admits to having voted twice and says that according to Zoltán Vas 100,000 were printed, while a document in the Party History Institute refers to 63,000. Hegedűs, p. 137.
14. I. Vida, *Koalíció és Pártharcok*, Budapest 1986, pp. 279–84.
15. P. Hall, *Governing the Economy*, Cambridge 1986, pp. 139–42; P.G. Hare, *Planning the British Economy*, London 1985, pp. 88–9 and 93.

NOTES TO PAGES 38-43

16. Pető and Szakács, p. 95. The decree announcing the nationalization was passed on 28 November 1947. It became law on 6 February 1948. S. Balogh (ed.), *Nehéz Esztendők*, Budapest 1986, pp. 197-8.
17. Pető and Szakács, p. 113.
18. Ibid., p. 99. The nationalization was ratified by the 1948:XXV tc law of 22 April 1948.
19. Balogh, *Nehéz Esztendők*, pp. 197-8.
20. W. Brus, 'Post War Reconstruction and Socio-Economic Transformation', in Kaser and Radice, p. 571.
21. Pető and Szakács, p. 22.
22. Gy. Marosán, *Az Úton Végig Kell Menni*, Budapest 1972, p. 249.
23. Pető and Szakács, p. 88.
24. *Heti Világgazdaság*, 1 April 1989, pp. 57-8.
25. Pető and Szakács, p. 102. *Heti Világgazdaság*, 15 April 1989, pp. 73-4.
26. Pető and Szakács, p. 102.
27. Ibid., p. 97.
28. Ibid., p. 98.
29. Ibid., pp. 97-8.
30. Ibid., p. 104.
31. Ibid., p. 105.
32. Ibid., p. 106.
33. Ibid., pp. 106-7; Berend, *Újjáépítés*, p. 372.
34. Pető and Szakács, pp. 109-10.
35. Ibid., p. 109.
36. Ibid., pp. 124-9.
37. Ibid., p. 113.
38. Balogh, p. 17.
39. F. Donáth, *Reform és Forradalom*, Budapest 1977, p. 36. Only five of the numerous cooperatives formed in early 1945 were still in operation by autumn of the same year.
40. Ibid., pp. 34-5.
41. This account of Nagy's changing fortune relies on Hegedűs's memoirs, Hegedűs, pp. 157-8. See also A. Nyíró (ed.), *Segédkönyv a Politikai Bizottság Tanulmánozásához*, Budapest 1989, pp. 10-12 and 298.
42. Pető and Szakács, pp. 137-8.
43. Ibid., p. 179.
44. Ibid., p. 138.
45. 14.000/1948 K sz r. Pető and Szakács, p. 179, Balogh, p. 29. For an explanation of the three types of cooperative suggested in Hungary and other East European countries at this time, see N. Spulber, *The Economics of Communist Eastern Europe*, New York and London 1957, p. 256.
46. *Magyar Közlöny*, 133/1950 (V7)MT sz r.
47. Balogh, p. 13.
48. Ibid., pp. 12-13.
49. Ibid., p. 17.
50. Ibid., p. 14.
51. Ibid., pp. 12-14; I. Tóth, *A Nemzeti Parasztpart Története 1944-48*, Budapest 1972, p. 297.
52. Balogh, p. 15.
53. Pető and Szakács, p. 110.
54. Ibid., p. 112.
55. Ibid., p. 103, Balogh, p. 23. The appropriate legislation was 1949 evi 20 sz tvr. Other minor legal milestones in nationalization were 19/1950(I.18)MT taking effect 1 February 1950 prohibiting private individuals from wholesale trade; 1950 evi 25 sz tvr published on July 1950 taking public chemists into state hands; and 1950 evi 24 sz tvr published 27 July 1950 establishing the criminal law for the defence of social property. See Balogh, pp. 197-8.

44444444444444444444
44444444444444
44444444444444444444
444444444444444444
444444444444444444
4444444444444
4444444444
44444444444

444444444444444444
44444444
4444444444444444444

56. Balogh, p. 23.
57. Ibid., p. 30.
58. Pető and Szakács, pp. 132–3.
59. Balogh, pp. 280–1.
60. Ibid., p. 158. Trade negotiations were suspended. Consulates were closed. And the USA suspended the work of the Karlsruhe committee which was considering the return to Hungary of goods taken during the war to what was now the American zone of Germany.
61. Fejtő, pp. 19–20.
62. Pethybridge, *A History of Postwar Russia*, London 1966, p. 37.
63. Cited in ibid., pp. 87–8.
64. I. Bibó, *Összegyűjtött Munkai*, vol. 4, Berne 1984, p. 1261.
65. Marosán, pp. 13–14; Schifferné Szakasíts Klára, *Fent és Lent 1945–50*, Budapest 1985, p. 9. Hegedűs recounts being flown to Zemplén county in a Soviet two-seater plane to implement the land reform, a task in which he was given considerable help by the Soviet officers in the Allied Control Commission, p. 119.
66. Pető and Szakács, p. 56.
67. Ibid., p. 54.
68. Ibid., p. 89.
69. Braunthal, p. 165.
70. Marosán, pp. 240–4.
71. Marosán was Minister of Light Industry after the fusion of the Social Democratic and Communist parties. He was arrested in August 1950 (Balogh, p. 16) and released, belatedly, in 1956. Such was the degree of his activism, that he immediately made himself available for service in a regime still dominated by Rákosi (Hegedűs, p. 245). He re-emerged in late 1989 to endorse the breakaway 'hard line' Hungarian Socialist Workers' Party.
72. The Communist Party was able to organize numerous mass demonstrations in 1946 and 1947 in favour of the left-wing bloc, or in opposition to Smallholder agrarian policies. See, for example, D. Nemes, *History of the Revolutionary Workers' Movement in Hungary*, Budapest 1972, pp. 110, 126 and 166.
73. Pető and Szakács, pp. 29–31. For the party programmes in 1945 see Vida, pp. 85–107.
74. Berend, *Újjáépítés*, pp. 171–2.
75. Ibid., p. 255.
76. Ibid., pp. 255–6.
77. I. Tóth, *A Nemzeti Parasztpárt Története 1944–48*, Budapest 1972, pp. 96–100.
78. Ibid., p. 103. Pető and Szakács, pp. 30–31.
79. Bibó, *Összegyű tött Munkái*, vol.1, Berne 1981, pp. 39–80, especially 78–9.
80. I. Bibo, 'A magyar demokrácia válsága', *Magyar Füzetek*, no. 4, p. 70. For the changing official line in the National Peasant Party, see Tóth, pp. 96–103.
81. Bibó, 'A magyar demokrácia', pp. 79–80, 99–110. F. Erdei, *Magyar Város*, Budapest 1974, pp. 209–39.
82. Bibó, 'A magyar demokrácia', pp. 99–100.
83. Pető and Szakács, pp. 29–31.
84. Balogh, pp. 226–7. The fact that such a rapid rate of growth could not be continued was not yet an issue.
85. Berend, *Újjáépítés*, pp. 195–265. Also Brus, p. 615.
86. Berend, *Újjáépítés*, pp. 195–265. Also Brus, p. 615.
87. *Heti Világgazdaság*, 15 April 1989, pp. 72–4.
88. Berend, *Újjáépítés*, p. 347.
89. Ibid., p. 347.
90. A.S. Millward, *The Reconstruction of Western Europe, 1945–51*, London 1984, pp. 120–21.
91. Hall, *Governing the Economy*.
92. Bibó, *Összegyűjtött Munkái*, vol.1, p. 1253.
93. The Peter Wright case is one of many that could be cited.

94. The most recent example in British history is perhaps the taming of Benn in the 1974–78 Labour administration, during which, on its own admission, the Confederation of British Industry threatened to take action outside the law. M. Mackintosh and H. Wainwright, *A Taste of Power*, Verso, London 1987, p. 7. *Labour Research* regularly publishes articles showing the links between right-wing organizations, UK and transnational companies, and Conservative politicians.

95. R. Murray, 'Rethinking Socialist Ownership', *New Left Review*, no. 164, p. 103. Contrast also: 'It became clear ... that employers were divided into two categories – those who knew very little about their legal responsibilities and those who thought nothing of flouting their "good employer" contracts.' Mackintosh and Wainwright, p. 284.

96. Murray, p. 96; Mackintosh and Wainwright, pp. 12, 141, 293.

97. Mackintosh and Wainwright, pp. 253–4.

98. Ibid., pp. 21, 24, 93, 243, 250.

99. D. Elson, 'Socialization of the Market', *New Left Review*, no. 172, pp. 32–42.

100. The 'B-list' was a list of officials in the national and local administrations who were considered to have been compromised under the old regime and were to be dismissed from office. Only about half of the originally targeted 100,000 staff were actually dismissed because of the shortage of replacements and pressure from the Communist Party's coalition parties. See Pető and Szakács, pp. 141–3.

101. Mackintosh and Wainwright, p. 3.

102. Ibid., p. 400.

103. Ibid., p. 433.

104. Ibid., p. 411.

105. Ibid., p. 401.

106. Ibid., p. 402.

Chapter 3

1. GLC Economic Policy Group, *Jobs for a Change*, London 1983, p. 26.

2. Ibid., p. 37.

3. M. Mackintosh and H. Wainwright, *A Taste of Power*, London 1987, p. 312; see also pp. 197–214.

4. N. Bukharin and E. Preobrazhensky, *The ABC of Communism*, Harmondsworth 1969, p. 116.

5. P. Wiles, 'Soviet Economics', in *Soviet Studies*, vol. IV (October 1952), no. 2, p. 133.

6. See J. Adam, *Economic Reforms in the Soviet Union and Eastern Europe since the 1960s*, London 1989, p. 2 and passim. This categorization follows official Hungarian practice.

7. I.T. Berend, *A Szocialista Gazdaság Fejlődése Magyarországon*, Budapest 1974, p. 87; I. Pető and S. Szakács, *A Hazai Gazdaság Négy Évtizedének Története 1945–1985. Az Újjáépítés és a Tervutasításos Irányítás Időszaka 1945–1968*, Budapest 1985, pp. 110–11.

8. J. Kornai, *Overcentralisation in Economic Administration*, Oxford 1959, pp. 75–101.

9. Berend, *A Szocialista*, pp. 87–8; B. Balassa, 'The Firm in the New Economic Mechanism in Hungary', in M. Bornstein (ed.), *Plan and Market*, Yale 1973, p. 361.

10. Kornai, *Overcentralisation*, p. 105.

11. Z. Vas, *A Hároméves Tery Befejezése-Népünk Gyözelme*, Budapest 1950, p. 5, cited in N. Spulber, *The Economics of Communist Eastern Europe*, New York and London 1957, p. 76.

12. Pető and Szakács, p. 114.

13. W. Brus, *The Market in a Socialist Economy*, London 1972, pp. 18–19.

14. E. Mandel, 'In Defence of Socialist Planning', *New Left Review*, no. 159, September–October 1986, pp. 27–8.

15. S. Bodington et al., *Developing the Socially Useful Economy*, London 1986, p. 192.

16. M. Geddes, 'The Capitalist State and the Local Economy: "Restructuring for Labour" and Beyond', *Capital and Class*, no. 35, summer 1988, pp. 85–120, especially pp. 110–11.

17. Pető and Szakács, pp. 177–8.

18. S. Balogh (ed.), *Nehéz Esztendők*, Budapest 1986, passim.

19. Gy. Vámos (ed.), *Sorshelyzetek: emlékezések az ötvenes évekre*, Budapest 1986, passim.

20. B. Szabó, *Az 'ötvenes évek': Elmélet és politika a szocialista építés első időszakában Magyarországon 1948–57*, Budapest 1986, passim.

21. Pető and Szakács, p. 162.

22. A. Heller, *The Theory of Need in Marx*, London 1974, p. 23.

23. Ibid., p. 27.

24. Ibid., p. 96.

25. Ibid., p. 121.

26. Ibid., pp. 124–5.

27. Mackintosh and Wainwright, pp. 400–401.

28. D. Elson, 'Market Socialism or Socialisation of the Market?', *New Left Review*, no. 172, p. 25.

29. K. Marx, 'Towards a Critique of Hegel's Philosophy of Right: Introduction', in D. McClellan, *Karl Marx Early Texts*, Oxford 1972, pp. 127–8; K. Marx, 'Manifesto of the Communist Party', in *Marx and Engels Selected Works in One Volume*, London 1968, pp. 44–5; Marx, 'Letter to Weydemeyer', *Selected Works*, p. 679; G. Lukács, 'Class Consciousness', in *History and Class Consciousness*, London 1971, pp. 46–82.

30. K. Marx, 'Letter to F. Bolte', *Selected Works*, p. 683, talks of the need to train the working class by agitation; V.I. Lenin, *What is to be Done?*, London 1963, chapter 2, discusses the role of the Party in moving consciousness beyond trade union consciousness; G. Lukács, 'On the Marxism of Rosa Luxemburg', in *History and Class Consciousness*, p. 42, describes the Party as the 'historical embodiment' of class consciousness, the 'incarnation of the ethics of the fighting proletariat'.

31. K. Marx, 'Letter to Weydemeyer', *Selected Works*, p. 679 and 'Critique of the Gotha Programme', p. 331, uses the phrase 'the dictatorship of the proletariat' and suggested a post-revolutionary state would be necessary, a point Lenin reinforces in *State and Revolution* (Moscow, p. 79). Some three years later, in V.I. Lenin, *'Left Wing' Communism, An Infantile Disorder*, Peking 1970, pp. 32–3, the 'dictatorship of the proletariat' and the 'dictatorship of the party of the proletariat' became synonymous.

32. F. Fehér, A. Heller, and Gy. Márkus, *Dictatorship Over Needs*, Oxford, 1983, pp. 90–1.

33. A. Nove, *The Economics of Feasible Socialism*, London 1983, p. 15.

34. J. Kis, 'A Filozófiai Intézettől a Beszélő szerkesztőségéig', *Valóság*, 1988, no. 12, p. 97.

35. Böhm-Bawerk's *Capital and Interest*, published in German in 1884, attacked from a non-Marxist perspective, and Conrad Schmidt in 1889 initiated a series of admissions from Marxist economists that all was not well. Between the publication of the second volume of *Capital* in 1885 and the third volume in 1894, numerous writers speculated on how Marx's theory of value might be rescued. See P.M. Sweezy (ed.), *Karl Marx and the Close of his System by Eugene von Böhm-Bawerk and Böhm-Bawerk's Criticism of Marx by Ruldolf Hilferding*, New York 1949 (reprinted by Orion Editions, Philadelphia, 1984), pp. vii, 6, 28.

36. The German edition of Böhm-Bawerk's work referred to above appeared in 1896.

37. R.L. Meek, *Studies in the Labour Theory of Value*, London 1956, presents an accessible account of Smith's and Ricardo's theories.

38. K. Marx, *Capital* Vol. I, London 1965, pp. 177–98.

39. K. Marx, *Economic and Philosophic Manuscripts of 1844*, London 1970, pp. 112–13.

40. Sweezy, p. xxiii.
41. Ibid.
42. K. Marx, *Capital* Vol. III, Moscow 1971, pp. 148–9, 153.
43. Ibid., p. 155.
44. Ibid., p. 155.
45. Ibid., p. 157.
46. Ibid., p. 157.
47. Sweezy, p. xxiv.
48. Meek, p. 194.
49. See Sweezy; Meek; A. Kliman and T. McGlone, 'The Transformation Non-problem and the Non-transformation Problem', *Capital and Class*, no. 35, pp. 57, 62; D. Gleicher, 'A Historical Approach to the Question of Abstract Labour, *Capital and Class*, no. 21, p. 116; J. Robinson, *An Essay on Marxian Economics*, London 1966, quoted in M. de Vroey, 'On the Obsolescence of the Marxist Theory of Value: A Critical Review', *Capital and Class*, no. 17, summer 1982, p. 34; D. Gleicher, 'Note, A Rejoinder to Eldred', *Capital and Class*, no. 24, p. 149.
50. Meek, pp. 170–76.
51. Ibid., pp. 256–60; also Brus, *Market*, pp. 13–27.
52. Brus, *Market*, p. 43. See *Ekonomicheskaya Zhizn*, no. 259, 1920.
53. Nove, *Feasible Socialism*, p. 29.
54. Meek, p. 265.
55. A. Kaufman, 'The Origin of the "Political Economy of Socialism"', *Soviet Studies*, vol. IV (January 1953), no. 3, pp. 251–2.
56. Kaufman, pp. 260–2.
57. Ibid., pp. 254–6.
58. Ibid., p. 265.
59. Ibid., pp. 261–2.
60. Ibid., pp. 263–4.
61. Meek, p. 269.
62. Kaufman, pp. 266–72.
63. Meek, p. 273.
64. Ibid., pp. 270–2.
65. J. Miller, 'A Political Economy of Socialism in the Making', *Soviet Studies*, vol. IV (April 1953), no. 4, pp. 419–20.
66. A. Nove, *The Soviet Economic System* (second edn), London 1980, pp. 341–3.
67. Ibid., p. 179.
68. X. Richet, *The Hungarian Model: Markets and Planning in a Socialist Economy*, Cambridge 1989, pp. 69–71.
69. J. Wilcsek, 'Az önköltség csökkentésének eszközei iparunkban', *Közgazdasàgi Szemle*, 1954, no. 1, pp. 37–49.
70. See for example Gy. Tauszk, 'A takarékosság kérdései a Központi Vezetőség oktoberi határozatának megvilágításában', *Közgazdasági Szemle*, 1954, no. 2, pp. 161–77.
71. Meek, pp. 281–2.
72. Ibid., p. 228.
73. The figures for the majority of this section come from Pető and Szakács, pp. 157–72.
74. Nove, *Economics of Feasible Socialism*, pp. 33–4.
75. Berend, *A Szocialista*, p. 91.
76. J. Wilcsek, 'Az önköltség csökkentésének eszközei iparunkban', *Közgazdasági Szemle*, 1954, no. 1, p. 47.
77. Elson, pp. 24–5. It is depressing that it still seems to take a woman to note that needs change with birth, death and sickness, that is to say that they change for reasons other than consumer whim; although if socialism is to accommodate fashion and style, it must accept whim-changed needs as well.
78. P. Cockshott and A. Cottrell, 'Labour Value and Socialist Economic Calculation', *Economy and Society*, vol. 18, no. 1, February 1989, pp. 71–99, argue that the size of the planning task has been exaggerated and that the time necessary to solve the full matrix of

input/output tables for a million distinct types of output might be two and a half minutes on modern super computers (pp. 96-7). To raise only technical objections to this reasoning, then a million outputs is not very many. If the Ukraine has twelve million, the UK is bound to have more. Second, if the question really were one of solving millions of simultaneous equations, then, assuming Hungary's more recent computers were 1,000 times slower, they would have achieved a result in ten days or so. Slow, but not disastrous if the job had to run only a few times a year. Third, assuming the calculation can be done in a few minutes, computer communications are much more problematic. Electronic Data Interchange and truly Open Systems are rudimentary, even in the West; and only the developed West can support their intermediate technology teletext solution. In Hungary, the telephone network supports a virtually no data transmission. But the important problems are not technical ones.

79. This section relies mostly on J. Kornai, *Overcentralisation in Economic Administration*, Oxford 1959, pp. 96-140; Berend, *A Szocialista*, pp. 90-91; and Pető and Szakács, pp. 193-5.

80. Wilcsek, p. 37.

81. Berend, *A Szocialista*, p. 90.

82. S. Balázsy, 'Javítsuk meg tervezési módszereinket', in L. Szamuley (ed.), *A Magyar Közgazdasági Gondolat Fejlősése 1954-78*, Budapest 1986, pp. 58-9.

83. P. Vas-Zoltán, *Tudomány-és Műszaki Politika Magyarországon* (2 vols), Budapest 1986, p. 514.

84. T. Liska, *Ökonosztát*, Budapest 1988, p. 77.

85. Balassa, pp. 364-5. This was not just a problem in Hungary. As Brus notes, Poland and Czechoslovakia as well 'maintained much wider economic relations with the West than did the Soviet Union, although this fact found no reflection whatsoever in institutions'. See W. Brus, '1950 to 1953: The Peak of Stalinism', in M. Kaser (ed.), *Institutional Change Within a Planned Economy*, volume III of *The Economic History of Eastern Europe 1919-1975*, Oxford 1986.

86. T. Liska and A. Máriás, 'A gazdaságosság és a nemzetközi munkamegoztás', *Közgazdasági Szemle*, 1954, no. 1, p. 79.

87. Balassa, pp. 364-5.

88. Pető and Szakács, pp. 162-5.

89. Brus, *Market*, pp. 41-61; Kaufman.

90. Berend, *A Szocialista*, p. 80, citing the Party archive 2/9-286 2925.

91. Figures taken mainly from Pető and Szakács, pp. 153-62.

92. See Vámos; and Balogh, passim.

93. K. Szakasíts Schifferné, *Holtvágányon 1950-56*, Budapest 1987, p. 92.

94. Vámos, p. 50; in H.-H. Paetzke, *Andersdenkende in Ungarn*, Frankfurt 1986, pp. 63-6, Rajk's son recounts how he was brought up with a new name. When he was finally introduced to his natural mother, he determined to call her 'mami' and continue to refer to his aunt who had raised him as 'mutti'.

95. F. Fehér, 'In the Bestiarium' in F. Feher and A. Heller (eds), *Eastern Left, Western Left*, Cambridge 1987, pp. 260-78, 271-3.

96. I.R. Sánta and P. Rényei, *A Mi Negyedszázadunk 1945-70*, Budapest 1970, p. 245.

97. Pető and Szakács, pp. 154 and 267.

98. Ibid., pp. 192-3.

99. Ibid., pp. 213-18.

100. Ibid., pp. 230-2.

101. For a fuller discussion see N. Swain, *Collective Farms Which Work?*, Cambridge 1985, pp. 25-41 and the references cited therein.

Chapter 4

1. I. Pető and S. Szakács, *A Hazai Gazdaság Négy Évtizedének Története 1945-85*.

Az Újjáépítés és a Tervutasításos Irányítás Időszaka 1945–1968, Budapest 1985, pp. 246–7.

2. Ibid., pp. 330–31.

3. L. Szamuely, *A Magyar Közgazdasági Gondolat Fejlődése 1954–78,* Budapest 1986, p. 15. Szamuely also notes that the Security Police confiscated all copies of the report in 1955. A copy of the programme was discovered by Ödön Barla Szabó in the Party archives and the most important sections published verbatim in an article in *Párttörténéti Közlemények* in 1981.

4. Gy. Péter, 'A gazdaságosság jelentőségéről és szerepéről a népgazdaság tervszerű irányításában', *Közgazdasági Szemle,* 1954, no. 3, pp. 161–77, reproduced in Szamuely.

5. F. Vali, *Rift and Revolt in Hungary,* Cambridge, Mass. 1961, p. 293.

6. Pető and Szakács, pp. 343 and 348. The Greater Budapest Workers' Council and those of the Ministry of Metallurgy and Machine Tools and the Ministry of the Chemical Industry are reproduced in I. Kemény and B. Lomax (eds), *Magyar Munkástanácsok 1956-ban,* Paris 1986, pp. 124–9; 139–50; 150–7.

7. Pető and Szakács, pp. 344–5.

8. J. Bokor, O. Gadó, P. Kurthy, T. Meitner, S. Sándorné, J. Wilcsek, 'Javaslat az ipar gazdasági irányításának új rendszere', *Közgazdasági Szemle,* 1957, no. 4, pp. 371–92. Reproduced in Szamuely, pp. 167–82. The background to the article is explained in a footnote.

9. Szamuely, p. 193.

10. Pető and Szakács, p. 352. The minutes of these committees have been preserved in the Economic Science Institute. Selections are to be found in Szamuely, pp. 193–263.

11. Pető and Szakács, pp. 353–4; Szamuely, p. 25.

12. Pető and Szakács, p. 398.

13. Szamuely, p. 26.

14. *Figyelő,* no. 33, 18 August 1988, p. 24. Interview with Béla Csikós-Nagy.

15. Swain, *Collective Farms Which Work?,* Cambridge 1985, pp. 30–41.

16. Berend, *Gazdasági Útkeresek 1956–65. A Szocialista Gazdaság Magyországi Modelljének Történetéhez,* Budapest 1983, p. 149.

17. Pető and Szakács, pp. 509–10; Berend, *Gazdasági,* p. 154.

18. Berend, *Gazdasági,* pp. 150–1.

19. Similar figures, from the same primary source, are provided in X. Richet, *The Hungarian Model: Markets and Planning in a Socialist Economy,* Cambridge 1989, p. 47.

20. Pető and Szakács, pp. 519–21.

21. Ibid., pp. 521–2.

22. Ibid., p. 526.

23. Berend, *Gazdasági,* p. 157; Pető and Szakács, pp. 527–8.

24. G. Golan, *The Czechoslovak Reform Movement,* Cambridge 1971, pp. 11–15.

25. Berend, *Gazdasági,* p. 438.

26. Pető and Szakács, p. 617.

27. Berend, *Gazdasági,* pp. 436–44.

28. Ibid., pp. 416–23.

29. Pető and Szakács, pp. 416–22.

30. T. Liska, 'Kritika és koncepció. Tézisek a gazdasági mechanizmus reformjához', *Közgazdasági Szemle,* 1963, no. 9, reproduced in Szamuely, pp. 279–302.

31. This section relies heavily on Szamuely.

32. R. Nyers, 'Visszapillantás az 1968-as reformra', *Valóság,* 1988, no. 8, p. 15.

33. Berend, *Gazdasági,* p. 144.

34. Szamuely, pp. 316–17. In the remainder of the contribution he goes on to suggest how these indirect methods could be improved.

35. Szamuely, pp. 331–40. For a more detailed discussion of agricultural reforms in this period, see Swain, *Collective Farms,* pp. 39–50.

36. R. Portes, 'Economic Reforms in Hungary', *American Economic Review: Papers and Proceedings,* vol. 60, 1970, p. 307.

37. Richet, p. 55.

38. I. Friss, 'Principal Features of the New System of Planning, Economic Control

and Management in Hungary', in I. Friss (ed.), *Reform of the Economic Mechanism in Hungary*, Budapest 1971, p. 17.

39. Nyers, 'Visszapillantás', p. 14.
40. I. Hétényi, 'National Economic Planning in the New System of Economic Control and Management', in Friss, pp. 41–66.
41. Friss, p. 15.
42. Hétényi, p. 49.
43. Friss, p. 15.
44. Hétényi, pp. 50–51.
45. Ibid., pp. 53–6.
46. Friss, pp. 18–20.
47. Hétényi, p. 54.
48. P. Marer, 'The Mechanism and Performance of Hungary's Foreign Trade 1968–79', in P.G. Hare et al., *Hungary: A Decade of Economic Reform*, London 1981, p. 168.
49. Richet, p. 74.
50. P. Hare, 'Industrial Prices in Hungary II', *Soviet Studies* XXVIII, July 1976, p. 373.
51. Marer, p. 161.
52. Friss, p. 25.
53. X. Richet, *The Hungarian Model: Markets and Planning in a Socialist Economy*, Cambridge 1989, p. 77.
54. Marer, p. 169.
55. Ibid., p. 168.
56. B. Csikós-Nagy, 'The New Hungarian Price System', in Friss, p. 270.
57. Friss, pp. 35–6.
58. J. Kornai, 'The Hungarian Reform Process: Visions, Hopes and Reality', in V. Nee and D. Stark (eds), *Remaking the Economic Institutions of Socialism: China and Eastern Europe*, Stanford 1989, p. 42.
59. Friss, pp. 36–7.
60. Ibid., pp. 37–8.
61. B. Sulyok, 'Major Financial Regulators in the New System of Economic Control and Management', in Friss, p. 179.
62. P.G. Hare, 'The Investment System in Hungary', in Hare et al., pp. 84–5.
63. Richet, pp. 122–3.
64. Sulyok, pp. 174–6 and 181.
65. Friss, pp. 253–4.
66. Sulyok, p. 180.
67. Richet, p. 137.
68. Hare, 'The Investment System', p. 98.
69. Friss, p. 27; P. Marer, 'The Mechanism and Performance of Hungary's Foreign Trade, 1968–79', in Hare et al., p. 169.
70. Friss, p. 27.
71. Marer, 'The Mechanism', p. 170.
72. Ibid., pp. 164–77.
73. Friss, p. 29.
74. Marer, 'The Mechanism', p. 162; R. Portes, 'The Strategy and Tactics of Economic Decentralisation', *Soviet Studies*, vol. XXIII, 1972, pp. 649–50; O. Gadó, *Reform of the Economic Mechanism in Hungarian Development 1968–71*, Budapest 1972, p. 296.
75. These are taken mainly from Szamuely, pp. 49–54.
76. Szamuely, p. 53.
77. Kornai, 'The Hungarian Reform', pp. 72–5 and 80.
78. T. Bauer, 'A Note on Money and the Consumer in Eastern Europe', *Soviet Studies*, vol. XXXV, July 1983, pp. 376–84.
79. Bauer, p. 381.
80. Kornai, 'The Hungarian Reform', p. 88.
81. J. Batt, *Economic Reform and Political Change in Eastern Europe*, London 1988, p. 238.

82. H.-G. Heinrich, *Hungary: Politics, Economics and Society*, London 1986, p. 66.

83. W. Brus, *The Market in a Socialist Economy*, London 1972.

84. Szamuely, p. 51.

85. W. Brus, 'Evolution of the Communist Economic System: Scope and Limits', in Nee and Stark (eds), *Remaking the Economic Institutions of Socialism: China and Eastern Europe*, Stanford 1989 pp. 267–72.

86. Brus, *Market*, see also Brus, 'Evolution of the Communist Economic System', pp. 267–9.

87. Szamuely, p. 51; reproduced in Szamuely, pp. 303–11.

88. T. Liska, *Ökonosztát*, Budapest 1988. The book is also rooted in its own time in two more trivial senses. First, a considerable portion of the book is devoted to a slanging match with Tamás Nagy and Bela Csikós-Nagy which is now of minimal interest, except that the latter probably acknowledge now that Liska was correct. Second, Liska is heavily influenced by cybernetics which enjoyed considerable vogue in Eastern Europe in the 1960s.

89. Liska, pp. 252–3 for scrutiny; passim for importance of world prices.

90. Ibid., pp. 220–21.

91. Ibid., p. 190.

92. Ibid., pp. 255–76.

93. Ibid., p. 239.

94. Ibid., pp. 231 and 240.

95. Ibid., pp. 236–7.

96. Ibid., p. 245.

97. Ibid., pp. 258–9.

98. Ibid., pp. 251–2. D. Elson, 'Market Socialism or Socialization of the Market?', *New Left Review*, no. 172, pp. 3–44, passim.

99. Elson.

100. J. Adam, *Economic Reforms in the Soviet Union and Eastern Europe since the 1960s*, London 1989, p. 58.

101. Swain, *Collective Farms*, p. 56.

102. C. Cornforth et al., *Developing Successful Workers' Cooperatives*, London 1988, p. 41.

103. Elson, pp. 30–43.

Chapter 5

1. P. Marer, 'Market Mechanism Reforms in Hungary', in P. Van Ness (ed.), *Market Reforms in Socialist Societies: Comparing China and Hungary*, Boulder and London 1989, pp. 64–5.

2. P. Galasi and Gy. Sziráczki, 'State Regulation, Enterprise Behaviour and the Labour Market in Hungary, 1968–83', in *Cambridge Journal of Economics*, 1985, no. 9, pp. 203–4.

3. R. Nyers, 'Visszapillantás az 1968-as reforma', *Valóság*, 1988, no. 8, p. 18.

4. R. Nyers, 'Gazdaság irányítás-vállalati nyereség. Beszéd a veszprémi közgazdász vándorgyűlésen', *Valóság*, 1968, no. 9, pp. 1–8, reproduced in L. Szamuely, *A Magyar Közgazdasági Gondolat Fejlődése 1954–78*, Budapest 1986, pp. 488–93.

5. B. Csikós-Nagy, 'Gazdasági mechanizmusunk fejlesztésének főbb kérdései', *Közgazdasági Szemle*, 1970, no. 4, pp. 448–58, reproduced in Szamuely, pp. 506–8.

6. I.T. Berend, 'A magyar reform sorsfordulója az 1970-es években', *Valóság*, 1988, no. 1, pp. 1–2.

7. Berend, 'A magyar reform', p. 2.

8. Szamuely, p. 486.

9. Berend, 'A magyar reform' p. 3. For the period up to 1970 Berend was able to use Party Archive sources.

10. Ibid., p. 4.

11. M. Tardos, 'A gazdasági verseny problémai', in Szamuely, pp. 547–60.

12. R. Portes, 'The Strategy and Tactics of Economic Decentralisation', *Soviet Studies*, vol. XXIII, 1972, pp. 653–4.

13. R. Portes, 'Economic Reforms in Hungary', *American Economic Review: Papers and Proceedings*, vol. 60, 1970, p. 313.

14. J. Batt, *Economic Reform and Political Change in Eastern Europe*, London 1988, p. 234.

15. Nyers, 'Visszapillantás', p. 19.

16. Batt, pp. 266–7.

17. Nyers, 'Visszapillantás', p. 16.

18. Berend, 'A magyar reform', p. 7.

19. Ibid., p. 5, cites a *Népszabadság* article of December 1973 referring to the fraternal concern of Hungary's neighbours.

20. Nyers, 'Visszapillantás', p. 22.

21. Portes, 'Stategy and tactics', p. 654.

22. P. Wiles, 'The Control of Inflation in Hungary', *Economie Appliquée*, vol. XXVII, no. 1, 1974, pp. 140–45.

23. MTA-KISZ, 'A munkaerő-vándorlás indítékai és hatásai az új mechanizmusban', *Közgazdasági Szemle*, 1971, no. 7–8, p. 805.

24. P. Bánki, 'A részesedési alap felosztásának új rendszere', *Munkaügyi Szemle*, 1969, no. 11.

25. K.A. Soós, 'Béralku és "sérelmi politika"', *Medvetánc: Magyar Gazdaság és Szociológia a 80-as években*, Budapest 1988, pp. 91–4.

26. *Figyelő*, no. 31, August 1970.

27. *Figyelő*, no. 50, December 1971.

28. *Figyelő*, no. 40, October 1971; K. Fazekas and J. Köllő, 'Fluctuations of Labour Shortage and State Intervention after 1968', in P. Galasi and Gy. Sziráczki (eds), *Labour Market and Second Economy in Hungary*, Frankfurt and New York, 1985, pp. 57–60.

29. 1048/1971 (XII.14).

30. Berend, 'A magyar reform', p. 9; *Figyelő*, no. 8, 1973; a list of the enterprises is given in E. Szalai, *Gazdasági Mechanizmus, Reformtörekvések és Nagyvállalati Érdekek*, Budapest 1989, pp. 377–80.

31. Berend, 'A magyar reform', p. 11.

32. Compare 38/1967 (X.12) Korm sz r with 34/1974 (VIII.6) MT sz r.

33. 1001/1974 (I.9) MT hat.

34. Berend, 'A magyar reform', p. 16, gives 8%.

35. 1007/1974 (III.6) MT hat.

36. N. Swain, *Collective Farms Which Work?*, Cambridge 1985, p. 199, gives precise references.

37. 1021/1974 (V.15) MT hat.

38. 1012/1974 (III.22) MT hat.

39. 6/1974 (III.22) MUM sz r.

40. Berend, 'A magyar reform', pp. 22–3.

41. *Népszabadság*, 4 April 1975.

42. O. Gadó, *The Economic Mechanism in Hungary – How it Works in 1976*, Leyden 1976, p. 18.

43. Ibid., p. 25.

44. M. Laki, *Vállalatok Megszűnése és Összevonása*, Budapest 1983, pp. 13–14.

45. Kornai, 'The Hungarian Reform Process: Visions, Hopes and Reality', in V. Nee and D. Stark (eds), *Remaking the Economic Institutions of Socialism: China and Eastern Europe*, Stanford 1989, p. 50.

46. Swain, *Collective Farms*, p. 5.

47. Cited in P.G. Hare, *Background Paper: Reform of Enterprise Regulation in Hungary – from 'Tutelage' to Market*, Edinburgh 1989.

48. P.G. Hare, 'The Economics of Shortage in Centrally Planned Economies', in C. Davies and W. Cherenza (eds), *Models of Disequilibrium and Shortage in Centrally Planned Economies*, London and New York, 1989, p. 69.

49. Ibid., pp. 74–5.
50. Kornai cited in ibid., p. 57.
51. Portes, 'Economic Reforms', p. 312.
52. T. Bauer, 'A vállalatok ellentmondásos helyzete a magyar gazdasági mechanizmusban', in Szamuely, pp. 569–77.
53. Ibid., pp. 574–7, emphasis in original.
54. Cited in Batt, p. 250.
55. T. Laky, 'Enterprises in Bargaining Position', Acta Oeconomica, vol. 22, no. 3–4, 1979, p. 232.
56. Bauer, 'A vállalatok', p. 573.
57. Laky, 'Enterprises in Bargaining', p. 232.
58. Cited in ibid., p. 237.
59. Kornai, 'The Hungarian Reform', p. 49.
60. T. Bauer, 'A bankhitel szerepe a beruházások allokációjában', Penzügyi Szemle, 1970, no. 10, p. 871.
61. M. Laki, Év Végi Hajrá az Iparban és a Külkereskedelemben, Budapest 1980, pp. 78–9.
62. Bauer, 'A vállalatok', p. 577.
63. Ibid., pp. 575–6; E. Szalai, Kiemelt Vállalat – Beruházás- Érdek, Budapest, pp. 106 and 111.
64. E. Szalai, 'Libikóka', Közgazdasági Szemle, 1989, pp. 19–27.
65. X. Richet, The Hungarian Model: Markets and Planning in a Socialist Economy, Cambridge 1989, p. 105.
66. Ibid., p. 105; see also T. Laky, 'A recentralizálás rejtett mechanizmusai', Valóság, 1980, no. 2, p. 38.
67. J. Kornai, 'Bürokratikus és piaci koordináció', in Kornai (ed.), Régi és Új Ellentmondások es Dilemmák, Budapest 1989, pp. 16–17.
68. Kornai, Régi és Új, p. 18.
69. T. Laky, Érdekviszonyok a Vállalati Döntésekben, Budapest 1982, p. 96.
70. T. Laky, 'Enterprises in Bargaining Position', p. 239.
71. A. Soós, 'A beruházások ingadozásának okai a magyar gazdaságban', in Szamuely, pp. 565–6.
72. P.G. Hare et al., Hungary: A Decade of Economic Reform, London 1981, p. 85.
73. Soós, p. 567.
74. Deak, cited in Richet, p. 140.
75. Interview with head of an enterprise development department in Laky, Érdekviszonyok, p. 254.
76. Richet, p. 133.
77. J. Kornai and A. Matits, 'Softness of Budget-constraint – An Analysis Relying on the Data of Firms', Acta Oeconomica, vol. 32, no. 3–4, 1984, pp. 223–49; J. Kornai, 'A vállalati nyereség bürokratikus újraelosztása', in Kornai, Régi és Új, pp. 92–173.
78. Kornai, Régi és Új, pp. 109–10.
79. Ibid., pp. 124–7.
80. Soós, p. 561.
81. T. Bauer, 'Investment Cycles in Planned Economies' Acta Oeconomica, vol. 21, no. 3, 1978, pp. 243–62.
82. An example of this loss of a technological lead is given in P.A. Bod, Csúcstechnikat- Hazai Módon, Budapest 1985.
83. Soós, pp. 563–4.
84. Bauer, 'Investment', pp. 246–7.
85. Soós, pp. 565–7.
86. Laki, Év Végi, pp. 18–29, 65, 73–4, 83 and 95.
87. Szalai, 'Libikóka', p. 13.
88. P. Marer, 'The Mechanism and Performance of Hungary's Foreign Trade, 1968–79', in Hare et al., Hungary: A Decade of Economic Reform, London 1981, p. 181.
89. This is based on the discussion in N. Swain, 'The Evolution of Hungary's Agricultural System since 1967', in Hare et al., pp. 244–7.

90. Gadó, pp. 18–25; 44–94.
91. 7/1976 (IV.10) MUM sz r.
92. 27/1975 (XI.15) MT sz r.
93. L. Kútvölgyi, 'Az általános jövedelemről szóló jogszabályok módosítása', *Penzügyi Szemle*, 1977, no. 2, pp. 157–9.
94. G. Komáromi (ed.), *Kisvállalkozók Jogszabály-Gyűjteménye*, Budapest 1985, pp. 11–14.
95. T. Sárközy, 'A gazdasági alkotmányosság lehetőségéról és szükségességéről Magyarországon', *Valóság*, 1986, no. 2. p. 9.
96. Changes in the economic regulators from 1978 to 1984 are presented in the following issues of *Figyelő*: no. 49, 7/12/77; 50, 14/12/77; 51, 21/12/77; 45, 7/11/79; 46, 14/11/79; 49, 5/12/79; 50, 12/12/79; 6, 6/2/80; 12, 19/3/80; 41, 8/10/80; 45, 5/11/80; 50, 10/12/80; 45, 11/11/81; 49, 9/12/81; 50, 16/12/ 81; 51, 23/12/81; 48, 2/12/82; 49, 9/12/82; 50, 16/12/82; 45, 10/11/83; 48, 1/12/83; 3/1/84.
97. M. Timár, *Szürke Pénzügyek*, Budapest 1989, pp. 145–7.
98. *Figyelő*, no. 14, 5/4/84, p. 17.
99. Fazekas and Kőllő, p. 61.
100. *Figyelő*, no. 44, 1/11/84, pp. 1 and 6.
101. Szalai, 'Libikóka', p. 15.
102. Kis, pp. 103–5.
103. J.-C. Asselain, *Planning and Profits in Socialist Economies*, London 1984, pp. 223–5.
104. Richet, p. 156.
105. I.T. Berend, *Magyar Gazdasági Reform Útja*, Budapest 1988, p. 400.
106. *Figyelő*, no. 45, 7/11/79, p. 5.
107. P.G. Hare, 'The Beginnings of Institutional Reform', *Soviet Studies*, vol. XXXV, no. 3, July 1983, pp. 317 and 320; *Figyelő*, no. 50, 10/12/80, p. 4.
108. Hare, 'The Beginnings', p. 324.
109. Berend, *Magyar Gazdasági Reform Útja*, p. 403.
110. Marer, 'Market Mechanism', p. 59.
111. Hare, 'The Beginnings', p. 320.
112. Ibid., p. 321; *Figyelő*, no. 50, 10/12/80. p. 4.
113. Hare, 'The Beginnings', p. 322; Bölönyi, p. 247.
114. E. Szalai, 'A reformfolyamat újszakasz és a nagyvállalatok', *Valóság*, 1982, p. 32.
115. Szalai, 'Libikóka, pp. 15–21.
116. Ibid., p. 22; Berend, *Magyar Gazdasági Reform Utja*, p. 381.
117. Berend, *Magyar Gazdasági Reform Útja*, pp. 382–4.
118. L. Lengyel, 'A tulajdonviták története és a reform', in Lengyel (ed.), *Tulajdonreform*, Budapest 1988, pp. 24–9. Csillag's account includes a fourth variant, where the state retained the Property Supervision Ministry which retained the right to intervene in enterprise affairs. This view is associated with Tamás Sárközy. See I. Csillag, 'Az új "vállalat" szervezet alapvonásai', *Valóság*, 1983, no. 7, pp. 45–59.
119. Lengyel, pp. 28–30 and 45.
120. Z. Ács, *Kizárt a Párt*, Budapest 1988, p. 22.
121. Cited in Berend, *Magyar Gazdasági Reform Útja*, p. 384.
122. Ibid., p. 388.
123. I. Gábor, in *Figyelő*, no. 46, 12/11/80, pp. 1 and 4.
124. 48/1981 (X.27) MT sz r and 25–30/1981 (IX.14–15) MT sz r.
125. Komáromi, pp. 9–10; 15–23; 32–40.
126. T. Laky, 'Half-hearted Organisational Decentralization: The Small State Enterprise', *Acta Oeconomĭca*, vol. 39, no. 3–4, 1988, pp. 247–90.
127. T. Laky, 'Small Enterprises in Hungary – Myth and Reality', *Acta Oeconomica*, vol. 32, no. 1–2, 1984, pp. 39–63.
128. Ibid.; N. Swain 'Small Co-operatives and Economic Work Partnerships in the Computing Industries: Exceptions that prove the Rule', in C.M. Hann (ed.), *Market Economy and Civil Society in Hungary*, London 1990, pp. 85–109.
129. I.R. Gábor, 'Második gazdaság: a magyar tapasztalatok általanosítható tünő

tanulságai', *Valóság*, 1985, p. 21.
130. T. Laky, 'Az új gazdálkodási formák és az illegális (második) gazdaság', in A. Böhm (ed.), *Munka, Gazdaság, Társadalom*, Budapest 1985, p. 87.
131. A.V. Chayanov, *The Theory of Peasant Economy*, Illinois 1966 (Manchester 1987).
132. P. Juhász, 'Agrárpiac, kisüzem, nagyüzem', in T. Miklós (ed.), *Medvetánc: Magyar Gazdaság és Szociológia a 80-as Években*, Budapest 1988, p. 49.
133. These types are discussed more fully in Swain, 'Small Co-operatives', pp. 85–109.
134. Galasi and Sziráczki, 'State regulation', pp. 216–17.
135. Szalai, 'Libikóka', pp. 23–7.
136. E. Szalai, 'Reformtörekvések és nagyvállalati érdekek a 80-as években', in L. Lengyel (ed.), *Tulajdonreform*, pp. 80–81.
137. L. Lengyel, 'Végkifejlet IV', *Figyelő*, no. 1, 5/1/89, p. 24.
138. *Figyelő*, no. 51, 23/12/81, p. 3.
139. Kornai. 'The Hungarian Reform', p. 66.
140. T. Kun, *A Társasági Törvény*, Budapest 1988, pp. 46–7.
141. Ibid., p. 53;
142. Marer, 'Market Mechanism', p. 60; *Figyelő*, no. 34, 23/9/84, pp. 1 and 6.
143. See e.g. *Figyelő*, no. 3, 19/1/84, pp. 1 and 4; no. 35, 30/8/84, p. 7; 1/11/84, p. 3.
144. 1986 evi 11. sz tvr; 1044/1986 (VII.16) MT hat; 26–28 (VII.16) MT sz r; 19–20 (VII.16)PM sz r.
145. 28/1986 (VII.16) MT sz r.
146. Á Balassa, *Figyelő*, no. 51–52, 22/12/83.
147. *Figyelő*, no. 17, 26/4/84, p. 3.
148. *Figyelő*, no. 20, 17/5/84, p. 3.
149. Szalai, 'Libikóka', p. 28; *Magyar Mezőgazdaság*, no. 7, 13/2/85, p. 5.
150. E. Várhegyi, 'Monetáris politika és gyakorlat 1987–88-ban', in I. Csillag (ed.), *Jelentések az Alagútból II*, Budapest 1988, p. 16.
151. B. Balassa, 'The "New Growth Path" in Hungary', in J.C. Brada and I. Doboczi (eds), *The Hungarian Economy in the 1980s: Reforming the System and Adjusting to External Shocks*, Greewich, Connecticut, 1988, p. 26.
152. Sárközy, pp. 11–13.
153. *Figyelő*, no. 45, 8/11/84, pp. 11–12; 46, 15/11/84, p. 3; *Magyar Mezőgazdaság*, no. 47, 21/11/84, p. 21; 48, 28/11/84, pp. 20–21.
154. *Figyelő*, no. 45, 8/11/84, pp. 13–14.
155. 1/1985(I.10)MT sz; 17/1986(V.16)MT sz r; 62/1986(XII.17)MT sz r.
156. Swain, 'Small Cooperatives', p. 87.
157. T. Laky, *Újtipusú Kisvállalkozások 1987*, Budapest 1988, p. 153.
158. Szalai, 'Libikóka', p. 29.
159. Szalai, *Tulajdonreform*, p. 87.
160. Szalai, 'Libikóka', p. 28.
161. N. Swain, 'Hungarian Agriculture in the Early 1980s, Retrenchment followed by Reform', *Soviet Studies*, vol. XXXIX, no. 1, January 1987, p. 34.
162. Swain, *Collective Farms*, chapters 5 and 6; C. Cornforth et al., *Developing Successful Workers' Cooperatives*, London 1988, chapter 7.
163. *Figyelő*, no. 50, 15/12/89, p. 3. The comment is by András Hegedűs.
164. Kornai, 'The Hungarian Reform', p. 36.
165. M.Z. Petschnig, 'A lakossági jövedelmeink és a lakossági megtakarításoknak az alakulása a nyolcvanas évek második felében', in Csillag, p. 87.
166. Paetzke, pp. 174–82.
167. Heinrich, p. 67.
168. Ács, p. 25.
169. E. Várhegyi, 'Monetáris politika és gyakorlat 1987–88', in I. Csillag (ed.) *Jelentések az Alagútból II*, Budapest 1988, p. 13.
170. E. Szalai, 'Libikóka', p. 30; 'Válság és nagyvállalati érdekervényesítés', in Csillag, pp. 47–8.

171. Ibid., p. 48.
172. Ibid., p. 51.
173. Szalai, 'Libikóka', p. 31.; 'Válság', p. 48.
174. Marer, 'Market Mechanism', p. 66.
175. *Figyelő*, no. 26, 4/6/87, p. 1.
176. *The New Banking System in Hungary, 1987 and Supplementary Information on the New Banking System in Hungary.* Budapest 1986.
177. Szalai, 'Libikóka', p. 33; 'Válság', pp. 51-2.
178. L. Lengyel, 'Adalékok a Fordulat és Reform történetéhez', Fordulat és Reform, *Medvetánc*, 1987, no. 2 sz melléklete, p. 149.
179. Marer, 'Market Mechanism, p. 66.
180. Szalai, 'Libikóka', p. 35.
181. L. Lengyel, 'Végkifejlet IV', *Figyelő*, no. 1, 5/1/89, p. 24.
182. Várhegyi, p. 24.
183. Szalai, 'Válság', pp. 75-81.
184. *Figyelő*, no. 49, 8/12/88, p. 4.
185. *Figyelő*, no. 44, 3/11/88, p. 5.
186. Szalai, 'Válság', p. 51.
187. *Figyelő*, no. 41, 13/10/88, p. 7.
188. *Figyelő*, no. 16, 16/4/87, p. 1.
189. *Figyelő*, no. 11, 12/3/87, p. 3.
190. *Figyelő*, no. 21, 26/5/88, p. 11.
191. *Figyelő*, no. 37, 15/9/88, p. 10.
192. *Figyelő*, no. 48, 1/2/88, p. 8.
193. *Turnabout and Reform* as modified by Patriotic People's Front Social Policy Council comments, 31 Jan 1987, pp. 4-7.

Chapter 6

1. F. Merényi and F. Simon, *A Gazdaság Pártirányítása*, Budapest 1979, p. 47.
2. Ibid., p. 51.
3. L. Lantos, 'A gazdasági vezetők beszámoltatása', *Pártélet*, no. 5, 1976, p. 19.
4. Merényi and Simon, pp. 54-5.
5. Gy. Juhász, *Iparvállalatok Munkájának Pártellenőrzése*, Budapest 1974, p. 56.
6. Lantos, p. 19.
7. L. Héthy and Cs. Makó, *Vezetés, Vezetőkiválasztás, Ösztönzés*, Budapest 1979, pp. 30-31.
8. Juhász, p. 48.
9. Merényi and Simon, pp. 71-5 and 87.
10. Juhász, pp. 49-57.
11. L. Gál, 'The Veto and Its Use', *Hungarian Trade Union News*, December 1975, pp. 8-9.
12. *A Munka Törvénykönyve és Végrehajtási Rendelete*, Budapest 1973, pp. 19-21, and 281-6.
13. Ibid., p. 184.
14. Ibid.
15. 28/1975 (XI.15) MT sz r; 37/1975 (XI.15) PM sz r.
16. L. Héthy and A. Simonyi, 'Munkásrészvétel a döntésekben és a munkafeltételek', in L. Héthy (ed.), *A Munkásság Helyzete az Üzemben*, Budapest, 1984, pp. 127-8.
17. Ibid., p. 128.
18. Gy. Czippan, 'Vétójog', *Magyarország*, no. 36, 1973, p. 45.
19. *Statisztikai Évkönyv*, 1978, p. 141.
20. K. Macsári, 'A szakszervezetek szervezeti önállóságáról és pártirányításáról, a szakszervezetek jogok gyakorlásáról', *Társadalmi Szemle*, 1974, p. 47.
21. L. Héthy and Cs. Makó, *Munkásmagatartások és a Gazdasági Szervezet*,

Budapest 1972, p. 177; 'Labour Turnover and the Economic Organisation', *Sociological Review*, 1975, no. 2, pp. 267–85; *Munkások, Érdekek, Érdekegyeztetés*, Budapest 1978, p. 252.
22. M. Haraszti, *A Worker in a Worker's State*, Harmondsworth 1977, p. 91.
23. I. Kemény, 'La chaine dans une usine hongroise', *Actes de la Recherche en Sciences Sociales*, no. 24, 1978, p. 71.
24. M. Andor, *Az Üzemi Demokrácia Feltételei és Érvényesülése egy Szállitasi Vállalatnál*, Budapest 1979, p. 44.
25. Ibid., p. 45.
26. Héthy and Makó, *Munkásmagatartások*, p. 179.
27. L. Héthy, *Az Üzemi Demokrácia és a Munkások*, Budapest 1980, p. 91.
28. Héthy and Makó, *Munkásmagatartások*, p. 177; *Vezetés*, pp. 30–31.
29. Andor, *Üzemi Demokrácia*, p. 46. For further discussion, see Haraszti, *A Worker*, p. 33; Héthy, *Üzemi Demokrácia*, p. 91. Héthy and Makó, *Munkásmagatartások*, p. 177; A. Hegedűs and M. Márkus, *Ember, Munka, Közösség*, 1966, p. 94.
30. I. Lunczer, 'Hogyan látják a munkások az üzemi demokráciát', *Társadalmi Szemle*, 1974, p. 77.
31. Héthy and Makó, *Munkásmagatartások*, p. 178.
32. T. Laky, *Érdekviszonyok a Vállalati Döntésekben*, Budapest 1982, p. 100.
33. Ibid., p. 146.
34. E. Szalai, *Kiemelt Vallalatok*, Budapest 1976, p. 129.
35. Ibid., p. 134.
36. Laky, *Érdekviszonyok*, p. 148.
37. Ibid., p. 239.
38. Ibid., p. 240.
39. B. Balassa, 'The Firm in the New Economic Mechanism in Hungary', in M. Bronstein (ed.), *Plan and Market*, New Haven, Conn., pp. 347–72.
40. See discussion in Chapter 5 and P.G. Hare, 'Industrial Prices in Hungary – Part I', *Soviet Studies*, vol. XXVIII, no. 2, pp. 189–206.
41. Héthy, p. 128.
42. Gy. Kozák and A. Mód-né, *A Munkások Rétegződése, Munkája Ismeretei és az Üzemi Demokrácia a Duna Vasmű Két Gyárrészlegen*, Budapest 1974, pp. 89–90.
43. Gy. Kozák and A. Mód-né, 'Az Ózdi Kohászati üzemek munkásai és az üzemi demokrácia', *Valóság*, 1975, no. 2, p. 63.
44. Héthy and Makó, *Munkámagatartások*, p. 146.
45. L. Héthy and Cs. Makó, *A Teljesítményelv Érvéyesítése és az Üzemi Érdek-és Hatalmi Viszonyok*, Budapest 1970, pp. 115–16.
46. Héthy and Makó, *Munkások, Érdekek, Érdekegyeztetés*, p. 260.
47. F. Halmos, *Illő Alázattal*, Budapest 1978, pp. 50–51.
48. Andor, *Üzemi Demokrácia*, pp. 6, 25 and 30.
49. F. Kunszabó, *Jászföld*, Budapest 1980, p. 264.
50. Andor, *Üzemi Demokrácia*, p. 24.
51. Héthy, p. 96.
52. Héthy and Simonyi, pp. 128–30.
53. Andor, *Üzemi Demokrácia*, pp. 10–18.
54. Héthy, pp. 181–8.
55. Andor, *Üzemi Demokrácia*, p. 20.
56. Lunczer, pp. 74 and 77.
57. Héthy, p. 179.
58. 53/1953 (XI.28) MT szr 7§.
59. Kozák and Mód-né, *A Munkások*, and 'Az Ózdi'.
60. Haraszti, p. 95.
61. F. Kovács, *A Munkásosztály Politikai-ideológiai Műveltségéről és Aktivitásáról*, Budapest 1976, p. 230.
62. Kozák and Mód-né, *A Munkások*, p. 86.
63. 1081/1977 (V.7) MT SZOT hat.
64. Héthy and Makó, *Munkások, Érdekek, Érdekegyeztetés*, p. 328; L. Héthy,

"Bérvita" az építkezésen', *Valóság*, 1979, no. 1, pp. 76-88.
   65. A. Simonyi, 'Az üzemi demokrácia a munkások oldaláról nézve', *Társadalmi Szemle*, 1976, no. 7, pp. 56-65; 'Munkásrészvétel üzemi bérezési döntésekben', *Társadalmi Szemle*, 1977, no. 10, pp. 99-101.
   66. L. Iványi and D. Vass, 'Munkás-előmenetel és tanulás' in Héthy and Simonyi, pp. 111-14.
   67. Iványi and Vass, p. 117. On the following page they give a table showing that the vast majority of such mobility is within the firm.
   68. Ibid., p. 125.
   69. J. Timár, 'Strategies and Realities for Employees and Management', in Galasi and Sziráczki (eds), *Labour Market and Second Economy in Hungary*, Frankfurt and New York 1985, p. 251.
   70. Swain, *Collective Farms Which Work?*, Cambridge 1985, p. 199.
   71. Andor, *Üzemi Demokrácia*, p. 39; *Figyelő*, 1979, no. 47, p. 5, 1982, no. 48, p. 4.
   72. Andor, *Üzemi Demokrácia*, p. 39; A. Hegedűs and M. Márkus, p. 108; Héthy, '"Bérvita"', p. 28.
   73. For a detailed discussion see N. Swain, 'Collectivisation and the Development of Socialist Wage Labour in Hungarian Agriculture 1946-77', University of Cambridge PhD, 1981, pp. 49-64. Marrese (1981) gives a brief summary of all systems of wage regulation in Hungary since 1950.
   74. L. Héthy and Cs. Makó, *Vezetés, Vezetőkiválasztás, Ösztönzés*, Budapest 1979, p. 45.
   75. A. Hegedűs, *A Munkabérezés Rendszere Iparunkban*, Budapest 1960.
   76. Balázsy, 1978, refers to it as an 'evergreen' problem. Laky 1980 refers to it as the 'classic' problem.
   77. Héthy and Makó, *Munkások, Érdekek*, p. 231.
   78. Héthy and Makó, *Vezetés*, p. 159.
   79. I. Kemény, 'Poverty in Hungary', *Social Science Information*, vol. 18, no. 2, pp. 248-9.
   80. Central Statistical Office, *Statisztikai Időszaki Közlemények*, no. 214, p. 25.
   81. Central Statistical Office, *Háztartásstatisztika*, 1975, p. 10.
   82. G. Révész, 'Az előmunka helyesítő gépesítés korlátairól', *Közgazdasági Szemle*, 1972, no. 2, p. 157.
   83. See for example L. Fehér, *Agrár-és Szövetkezeti Politikánk 1965-69*, Budapest 1970, pp. 283-4; J. Kádár, *For a Socialist Hungary*, Budapest 1974, p. 269; R. Nyers, *Népgazdaságunk a Szocializmus Építésének Útján*, Budapest 1973, pp. 35-39.
   84. I. Buda, 'Wage Regulation and Manpower Management', in Gado, p. 91.
   85. I.R. Gábor, 'Munkaerőhiány a mai socialista gazdaságban', *Közgazdasági Szemle*, 1979, no. 2, pp. 171-87; J. Timár, 'Foglalkoztatáspolitikánkról és a munkaerőgazdálkodásunkról', *Közgazdasági Szemle*, 1977, no. 2, p. 129.
   86. See also F. Nemes, *Érdekeltség - Magatartások - Tartalékok*, Budapest 1976, pp. 128-9.
   87. M. Laki, *Év Végi Hajrá az Iparban és a Külkereskedelemben*, Budapest 1980.
   88. Gábor, 'Munkaerőhiány'.
   89. Buda, pp. 91 and 98.
   90. Héthy and Makó, *Munkásmagatartások*, pp. 50-51; 'Labour Turnover'.
   91. Andor, *Üzemi Demokrácia*, p. 37.
   92. Central Statistical Office, *Magánkisipari Adattár*, 1971, p. 9.
   93. R. Andorka, *A Magyar Községek Társadalmak Átalakulása*, Budapest 1979, p. 142.
   94. M. Hegedűs, 'Some Factors Influencing Urban Development in Hungary', *Acta Oeconomica*, vol. 12, no. 2, 1974, pp. 171-89.
   95. L. Fodor, *Falvak a Nagyváros Árnyékában*, Budapest 1973.
   96. Andorka, *A Magyar Községek*, p. 83.
   97. R. Andorka and I. Harcsa, *A Községi Népesség Társadalomstatisztikai Leírása*, Budapest 1973, p. 97.

98. Central Statistical Office, *Epítőipari Adatok*, p. 343.
99. Ibid.
100. Central Statistical Office, *Statisztikai Évkönyv 1975.*
101. Gábor, 'Munkaerőhiány, p. 173.
102. Ibid., p. 177.
103. P. Galasi, 'Extra Income and Labour Market Position' in Galasi and Sziráczki, pp. 295-6; I. Kovách, 'A társadalom rétegződése és a mezőgazdasági kistermelés', in A. Böhm (ed.), *Munka, Gazdaság, Társadalom*, Budapest 1985, p. 123.
104. *Figyelő*, no. 28, 14/7/88, p. 1.
105. J. Farkas and A. Vajda, *Időgazdálkodás és Munkatevékonységek. Az 1986/87 évi időmerleg felvétel adatai*, Budapest 1989, p. 27.
106. Ibid., p. 25.
107. *Társadalmi Szemle*, no. 1, 1959, p. 27.
108. M. Kovács, 'A kétlakiság Borsod-Abaúj-Zemplén megyében', *Statisztikai Szemle*, 1960, no. 8-9, pp. 883-7; *Társdalmi Szemle*, 1959, p. 31.
109. J. Rétiné, 'Az ingázók számának, összetételének változása és az ingavándorforgalom főbb irányainak alakulása', *Munkaügyi Szemle*, 1976, no. 3, pp. 24-5.
110. R. Andorka and I. Harcsa, *A Községi Népesség Társadalom-statisztikai Leírása*, Budapest 1972, p. 98.
111. P. Galasi, 'A községekben élő ipari-építőipari munkások mint a munkaerő sajátos csoportja', *Közgazdasági Szemle*, 1976, no. 3, p. 293.
112. Andorka and Harcsa, p. 91.
113. L. Héthy, '"Bérvita" az építkezésen', *Valóság*, 1978, no. 1, pp. 83-4.
114. I.R. Gábor, 'Második gazdaság: a magyar tapasztalatok általánosítható tünő tanulságai', *Valóság*, 1985, p. 30.
115. I. Kemény, 'The Unregistered Economy in Hungary', *Soviet Studies*, vol. XXXIV, no. 3, 1982, pp. 349-66.
116. P. Galasi and G. Kertesi, 'Patkányversény a korrupciós piacon', *Közgazdasági Szemle*, 1988, no. 7-8, pp. 900-20.
117. E. Sik, *Az 'Örök' Kaláka*, and A. Kelen, *A Társadalmi Munka Szociológiája*, Budapest 1988.
118. I. Markó, *A Kisgazdaságok Hazánkban*, Budapest 1986, pp. 9-15.
119. T. Laky, *Újtipusú Kisvállalkozások 1987*, Budapest 1988, p. 164.
120. I. Bakcsi, A vállalattal együtt vállalkozó vállalati gazdasági munkaközösségek, Labour Affairs Institute, Budapest 1987, p. 19.
121. Laky, *Újtipusú*, pp. 162-3.
122. Bakcsi, pp. 28-9.
123. 30/1981 (IX.14) MT sz r 10§.
124. Timár, p. 257.
125. *Figyelő*, no. 24, 14/6/84, p. 19.
126. Laky, 'Mitószok és valóság', p. 8.
127. *Figyelő*, no. 26, 28/6/84, pp. 1 and 6.
128. *Figyelő*, no. 26, 28/6/84, p. 6.
129. T. Laky, 'Half-hearted Organisational Decentralisation: The Small State Enterprise', *Acta Oeconomica*, vol. 39, no. 3-4, 1988, p. 263.
130. Héthy and Makó, *Munkások, Érdekek*, pp. 197-8.
131. D. Stark, 'The Micropolitics of the Firm and the Macropolitics of Reform: New Forms of Bargaining in Hungarian Enterprises', in P. Evans et al., *States vs Markets in the World System*, Beverly Hills 1985, p. 22.
132. Personal communication based on research in Labour Affairs Research Institute.
133. *Figyelő*, no. 14, 7/4/83, pp. 1 and 5.
134. K. Rupp, *Egy Termelőszövetkezet Melléküzemeinek Gazdalákodása*, Economic Science Institute, Budapest 1973.
135. A. Mód-né, 'Hétköznapok munkásszemmel – üzemi krónikák tükrében', *Valóság*, 1988, no. 2, pp. 99-108; I. Javor, 'Egy vállalati gazdasági munkaközösség alkalmazkodása a feltételrendszerhez, *Valóság*, 1984, no. 8, pp. 63-8; L. Neumann, 'A

munkaszervezeti megújúlás lehetőségei a vállalati gazdasági munkaközösségekben', *Medvetánc*, 1985, no. 4, 1986, no. 1.

136. D. Stark, 'Coexisting Organisational Forms in Hungary's Emerging Mixed Economy', in V. Nee and D. Stark (eds), *Remaking the Economic Institutions of Socialism: China and Eastern Europe*, Stanford 1989, p. 151.

137. Ibid., p. 152.

138. D. Stark, 'Rethinking Internal Labour Markets: New Insights from a Comparative Perspective', *American Sociological Review*, 1986, p. 28.

139. Laky, 'Mitózok', pp. 11-12.

140. T. Laky, *Small Organisations in the Hungarian Economy: An Experiment in New Forms*, World Congress of Sociology, New Delhi 1986; *Figyelő*, no. 14, 7/4/83, pp. 1 and 5.

141. Laky, 'Mitózok', p. 16.

142. Laky, *Újtipusú*, p. 69.

143. G. Kertesi and Gy. Sziráczki, 'Munkasmagatartások a munkaerőpiacon', *Valóság*, 1983, no. 7, p. 21.

144. Halmos; Haraszti; I. Kemény, 'La chaine dans une usine hongroise', *Actes de la Recherche en Sciences Sociales*, no. 24, pp. 62-77; Héthy and Makó, *Teljesítményelv*; *Munkásmagatartások*; Laki; A. Simonyi, 'A központból a perifériára', *Valóság*, 1978, no. 1, pp. 89-98.

145. Gy Kővári and Gy. Sziráczki, 'Old and New Forms of Wage Bargaining on the Shop Floor', in Galasi and Sziráczki, pp. 264-92.

146. Stark, 'Rethinking'.

147. Stark, 'Coexisting', p. 155.

148. *Figyelő*, no. 18, 3/5/84, p. 4; no. 26, 28/6/84, pp. 1 and 6.

149. Timár, p. 258.

150. *Figyelő*, no. 15, 12/4/84, p. 6.

151. Timár, p. 258.

152. I. Kemény, *Ouvriers Hongrois 1956-1985*, Paris 1985, pp. 134-57; G. Kertesi and Gy Sziráczki, 'Worker Behaviour in the Labour Market', in Galasi and Sziráczki, pp. 216-45.

153. Héthy and Makó, *Teljesítményelv*, ch. 3; Hegedűs and Márkus, p. 226.

154. Haraszti.

155. M. Andor, 'Konfliktus vagy harmónia a munkaszervezetben', *Látóhatár*, 1974, no. 4, p. 170; Héthy and Makó, *Munkások*, p. 188; Haraszti, pp. 23 and 49; T. Földvári and Z. Zsille, 'Hát maguk nem tudták ezt', *Mozgó Világ*, 1978, no. 2.

156. Andor, 'Konfliktus'.

157. Haraszti, pp. 53 and 151.

158. Hegedűs and Márkus, p. 240.

159. Magyar Tudományos Akadémia, KISZ, p. 812.

160. Héthy and Makó, 'Labour Turnover and the Economic Organisation', *Sociological Review*, 1975, no. 2, pp. 267-85; L. Héthy, *Az Üzemi Demokrácia és a Munkások*, Budapest 1980.

161. I. Kemény, *A Csepel Vas-és Femművek Munkásai*, Budapest 1970; Kozák and Módné.

162. Földvári and Zsille.

163. Gy. Konrád and I Szelényi, 'Social Conflicts of Under-Urbanisation', in A. Brown et al., *Urban and Social Economics in Market and Planned Economies*, vol. 1, New York 1974, pp. 206-26.

164. Kertesi and Sziráczki, 'Munkasmagatartások', p. 35.

165. Timár, p. 253.

166. T. Liska, *Ökonosztát*, Budapest 1988, pp. 220-24.

Chapter 7

1. I. Selényi, 'Social Inequalities in State Socialist Redistributive Societies', *Inter-*

national Journal of Comparative Sociology, vol. XIX, 1–2 (1979), pp. 63–87; 'Inequalities and Social Policy under State Socialism', *International Journal of Urban and Regional Research*, vol. 6, 1982, pp. 121–7.

2. In R. Manchin and I. Szelényi, 'Szocialpolitika az allamszocializmusban', in T. Miklós (ed.), *Medvetánc: Magyar Gazdaság és Szociológia az 80-as Években*, Budapest 1988, pp. 150–99, a more complex line is argued, which will emerge when we consider the specific issue of housing, namely that the market both reduced inequality, but introduced its own inequalities in such a fashion that the inequalities of the market and of redistribution reinforced each other. They go on to distinguish between 'economic distribution' and 'welfare distribution', seeing a need for the latter but not for the former, pp. 187–92.

3. Zs. Ferge, 'Zsortolódó megjegyzések Szelényi Iván és Manchin Róbert tanulmányához', in Miklós, pp. 200–15, especially p. 211. She also implicitly develops the distinction between 'welfare' and 'economic' redistribution, noting on the basis of OECD figures that Hungary spends 30% of GDP on economic redistribution compared with the Western norm of 6–17% (p. 207).

4. M. Mann and R. Compton (eds), *Gender and Stratification*, Cambridge 1986.

5. Mann, 'A Crisis in Stratification Theory', in Mann and Compton, pp. 40–56.

6. R. Andorka, *A Magyar Községek Társadalmak Átalakulása*, Budapest 1979, p. 301. The study was by A. Klinger and E. Szabady of the Demographic Research Group of the Central Statistical Office.

7. Zs. Ferge, *Fejezetek a Magyar Szegénypolitika Történetéből*, Budapest 1986, p. 52.

8. Ibid., pp. 158–60.

9. Ibid., p. 169.

10. K. Kulcsár, 'A család helye és funkciója a modern társadalomban', in P. Lőcsei, *Család és Házasság a Mai Magyar Társadalomban*, Budapest 1971, p. 22.

11. I. Nagy-né, 'A nők családi és munkahelyi körülményei', *Statisztikai Szemle*, 1989, no. 10, pp. 875 and 882.

12. H. Vass, 'A munkásmozgalom és a nőkérdés', in E. Szabady (ed.), *Tanulmányok a nők helyzetéről*, Budapest 1972, p. 7.

13. Ibid., p. 32.

14. M. Stewart, 'Gypsies, Work and Civil Society', in C.M. Hann (ed.), *Second Economy and Civil Society in Hungary*, London 1990, pp. 140–62.

15. Ibid.

16. Zs. Ferge, *A Society in the Making*, Harmondsworth 1979, p. 164.

17. Ibid., p. 174.

18. Ibid., p. 203.

19. H. Flakierski, 'Economic Reform and Income Distribution in Hungary', *Cambridge Journal of Economics*, 1979, no. 3, pp. 15–32, esp. pp. 19–20.

20. Ibid., p. 23.

21. Ibid., p. 26. Ferge publishes similar figures taken from the same Central Statistical Office sources, *A Society*, p. 191.

22. Ferge, *Fejezetek*, p. 57.

23. Ö. Éltető, 'Növekvő jövedelmi különbségek', *Figyelő*, no. 14, 2/4/88, p. 9.

24. Ferge, *Fejezetek*, pp. 177–9.

25. Éltető, p. 9.

26. Ferge, *A Society*, p. 172.

27. Ferge, *Fejezetek*, p. 42.

28. A. Bokor, *Szegénység a mai Magyarországon*, Budapest 1987, p. 27.

29. Ferge, *Fejezetek*, pp. 58–64. See also Bokor, p. 45.

30. T. Kolosi, 'Tendenciák a társadalmi szerkezet alakulásában a nyolcvanas években', in S. Kurtán et al. (eds), *Magyarország Politikai Évkönyv 1988*, Budapest 1989, p. 130.

31. Bokor, pp. 47–8.

32. Ferge, *A Society*, p. 211.

33. Flakierski, p. 29.

34. Bokor, pp. 49–53.

35. Nagy-né, pp. 876–82.
36. Ferge, *A Society*, p. 184.
37. E. Cukor and G. Kertesi, 'Difference in Pay and Modes of Earning', in P. Galasi and Gy. Sziráczki (eds), *Labour Market and Second Economy in Hungary*, Frankfurt and New York, 1985, pp. 70–120, especially p. 96.
38. Ibid., pp. 98–102.
39. P. Galasi and E. Sik, 'Vállaltközi kapcsolatok a helyi munkaerőpiacon', in Galasi, pp. 122–33.
40. A Nagy and Gy. Sziráczki, 'Munkaerőpiaci szegmentáció Magyarországon a hetvenes évek közepén', in Galasi, p. 55.
41. E. Sik, 'A helyi munkaerőpiac körülhatárolása és jellemzése', in Galasi, p. 105.
42. P. Galasi, 'Összefoglalás és következetések', in Galasi, p. 169.
43. I. Kemény, 'A magyarországi cigány lakósság', *Valóság*, 1974, no. 1, pp. 63–72.
44. L. Laki, *Az Alacsony Iskolazottság Újratermelődésének Társadalmi Körülményei Magyarországon*, Budapest 1988, p. 174.
45. Stewart, p. 146.
46. G. Havas, 'Foglalkozásváltási strategiák különböző cigány közösségekben' in M. Andor (ed.), *Cigányvizsgálatok*, Budapest 1982, pp. 181–202.
47. Stewart.
48. J. Ladányi, 'Fogyasztói árak és szociálpolitika', *Valóság*, 1975, no. 12, p. 20.
49. Ibid., p. 24.
50. J. Hegedűs and I. Tosics, 'Housing Classes and Housing Policy: Some Changes in the Budapest Housing Market', *International Journal of Urban and Regional Research*, vol. 7, 1983, pp. 467–93.
51. I. Szelényi, *Urban Inequalities under State Socialism*, Oxford 1982, p. 51.
52. I. Szelényi, 'Housing System and Social Structure', *Sociological Review Monograph*, pp. 281–2.
53. Szelényi, *Urban*, p. 58.
54. Ibid., p. 59.
55. Ibid., p. 60.
56. Reported in Flakierski, p. 29.
57. Zs. Dániel, 'The Effect of Housing Allocation on Social Inequality in Hungary', *Journal of Comparative Economics*, 9 Dec. 1985, pp. 391–409.
58. Ibid., p. 408.
59. P. Foti, *Röpirat a Lakáshelyzetről*, Budapest 1988, pp. 50–51.
60. Szelényi summarizes his findings on zoning on pp. 141–3 of *Urban Inequalities*.
61. Fóti, pp. 95–6; 119.
62. Manchin and Szelényi, p. 177. They also confirm the trend of a relative fall in status of the state built housing estates (pp. 168–9).
63. Fóti, pp. 77, 91–2 and 94.
64. G. Csanádi and J. Ladányi, 'Társadalmi csoportok terbeni elkülönülésének különböző léptékekben történő vizsgálata Budapesten', *Szociológia*, 1988, no. 1, pp. 1–16.
65. Ibid., p. 9.
66. Z. Kovács, 'Rich and Poor in the Budapest Housing Market', in C.M. Hann, pp. 110–24.
67. Kemény, 'A magyarországi', p. 66.
68. Ibid., p. 72.
69. Laki, p. 151.
70. G. Havas, 'A Baranya megyei teknővajó cigányok' and G. Lengyel, 'Települési és társadalmi különbségek egy falusi cigány közösségben', in M. Andor (ed.), *Cigányvizsgálatok*, Budapest 1982, pp. 61–140 and pp. 141–59 respectively.
71. Ferge, *A Society*, p. 153.
72. Bokor, pp. 75 and 80.
73. Reported in Flakierski, p. 29.
74. Ferge, *A Society*, p. 255.
75. Laki, pp. 112–29.
76. Cs. Pleh and M. Papp, 'Social Class Differences in the Speech of 6-year-old

Hungarian Children', *Sociology*, 1974, pp. 267–75.

77. J. Szalai, *Az Egészségügy Betegségei*, Budapest 1986, pp. 25–66.

78. R. Andorka, *Társadalmi Mobilitás Változásai Magyarországon*, Budapest 1982, pp. 237–8 and 250–8.

79. Bokor, pp. 222; 248–9.

80. L. Fodor, *Falvak a Nagyváros Árnyékában*, Budapest 1973, p. 72.

81. Hegedűs and Tosics, pp. 469–79.

82. I. Pető and S. Szakács, *A Hazai Gazdaság Négy Évtizedének Története 1945–1985. Az Újjáépítés és a Tervutasitásos Irányítás Időszaka 1945–1968*, Budapest 1985, p. 704.

83. Fóti, pp. 55, 151 and 159.

84. Hegedűs and Tosics, pp. 480–89.

85. Fóti, p. 42.

86. Kovács, p. 115.

87. I. Szelényi, 'Housing Policy in the Emergent Socialist Mixed Economy of Eastern Europe', *Housing Studies*, 1989, vol. 4, no. 3, p. 173.

88. Manchin and Szelényi, p. 176.

89. Szelényi, 'Housing Policy', p. 173.

90. Fóti, p. 132.

91. Szelényi, 'Housing Policy', pp. 167–76.

92. Ibid., p. 174.

93. Fóti, p. 45.

94. Ibid., pp. 103–6 and 194.

95. The following comes from M. Andor, 'Dolgozat az iskoláról', in Gy. Csoma (ed.), *Oktatási Rendszerünkről*, Budapest 1982, pp. 61–118.

96. Zs. Ferge, 'A pedagógusok önértékelésére ható tényezők', in Zs. Ferge (ed.), *Társadalompolitikai Tanulmányok*, Budapest 1980, pp. 211–29, especially p. 25.

97. M. Andor and A. Horváth, 'Társdalomkép az általános iskolai olvasókönyvekben', *Szociológia*, 1974, no. 4, pp. 562–76.

98. Ferge, *A Society*, p. 151.

99. Ferge, 'A pedagógusok képe az iskola társadalmi szerepéről', in Ferge, pp. 179–209.

100. Andor, 'Dolgozat,' pp. 108–115.

101. M. Andor, 'Az iskolaigazgatók kiválasztása', in J. Szalai et al. (eds), *Arat a Magyar*, Budapest 1988.

102. M. Kaser, *Health Care in the Soviet Union and Eastern Europe*, London 1976, pp. 166–7.

103. Losonczi, *Ártó-Védő Társadalom*, Budapest 1989.

104. The following is taken from Szalai, *Az Egészségügy*.

105. A. Losonczi, *A Kiszolgáltatottság Anatómiája az Egészségügyben*, Budapest 1986, pp. 41, 85, 98 and 233.

106. Ibid., p. 191. She actually refers to Algopyrin, which is the standard painkiller in Hungary.

107. This and the following comes from Szalai, *Az Egészségügy*, pp. 144–90.

108. Losonczi, *A Kisszologáltatottság*, p. 224.

109. Ferge, *A Society*, p. 292.

110. Ibid., pp. 227–8.

111. J. Szalai, 'A családi munkamegosztás néhány szociológiai problémájáról', in Lőcsei, p. 176; Nagy-né.

112. Szalai, 'A családi', pp. 187–8.

113. J.H. Sas, *Életmód és Család. Emberi Viszonyok a Családban*, Budapest 1976, p. 113.

114. Ibid., p. 99.

115. Gy. Sziráczki, 'Egy belső munkaerőpiac kialakulása és működése', in Galasi, p. 223.

116. P. Galasi, 'Extra Income and Labour Market Position' in Galasi and Sziráczki (eds), *Labour Market and Second Economy in Hungary*, Frankfurt and New York, 1985, pp. 300–11.

117. Kovách, p. 132.
118. Bokor, pp. 101–3.
119. Ibid., p. 178.
120. Ibid., p. 104.
121. Fodor, p. 14.
122. Ferge, *A Society*, pp. 270 and 293; Kaser, pp. 181–2.
123. M. Petschnig, 'Az orvosi hálapénzről – nem etikai alapon', *Valóság*, 1983, no. 11, pp. 47–55.
124. Losonczi, pp. 123 and 233–4.
125. Petschnig, p. 51.
126. Losonczi, p. 128.
127. Petschnig, pp. 49 and 52.
128. Ibid., p. 54.

Index